ENGLISH CHAMBER MUSIC

Da Capo Press Music Reprint Series

GENERAL EDITOR

FREDERICK FREEDMAN

VASSAR COLLEGE

ENGLISH
Chamber Music

The History of a Great Art

ERNST H. MEYER

𝄞 DA CAPO PRESS • NEW YORK • 1971

A Da Capo Press Reprint Edition

This Da Capo Press edition of
English Chamber Music
is an unabridged republication of the
first edition published in London in 1946.

Library of Congress Catalog Card Number 71-127281

SBN 306-70037-9

Published by Da Capo Press
A Division of Plenum Publishing Corporation
227 West 17th Street, New York, N.Y. 10011

Manufactured in the United States of America

*For Distribution and Sale Only in the
United States of America*

ENGLISH CHAMBER MUSIC

ENGLISH
Chamber Music

The History of a Great Art

From the Middle Ages to Purcell

ERNST H. MEYER

LONDON

LAWRENCE & WISHART

1946

MADE AND PRINTED IN GREAT BRITAIN
AT THE CHAPEL RIVER PRESS
ANDOVER, HANTS
·8.46

CONTENTS

CHAPTER   PAGE

      INTRODUCTION   1

   I   THE MEDIEVAL BACKGROUND   12

  II   ON THE THRESHOLD OF MODERN TIMES   ..   63

 III   THE EMANCIPATION FROM THE CHURCH   ..   78

 IV   CHURCH MOTET AND DANCE TUNE, THE PARENTS

        OF ENGLISH CHAMBER MUSIC   97

  V   THE AGE OF PLENTY   125

 VI   THE CRISIS 173

VII   LAST RISE—ECLIPSE   204

VIII   AFTERMATH   247

MUSICAL EXAMPLES IN TEXT

(Unless stated, examples are instrumental)

c=complete example ; ꞯ=quotation (incomplete)

No.		DATE	PAGE	
1 :	Orlando Gibbons, fantasia for three viols	circa 1615	3–7	c
2 :	Summer is icumen in, vocal	end of 13th ct.	23	ꞯ
3 :	French three-part round, vocal	13th ct.	24	c
4 :	English dance tune	Ditto	39	ꞯ
5 :	Sequence " Prosa de Sancto Dionysio," vocal	Medieval	40	ꞯ
6 :	Antiphon " Statuit," vocal	Gregorian	42	ꞯ
7 :	Hymn to St. Magnus, vocal	13th ct.	45	ꞯ
8 :	English dance tune	13th ct.	48	c
9 :	English motet with two presumably instrumental parts, partly vocal ..	circa 1375	57f	ꞯ
10 :	Ritornello to English chanson	15th ct.	58	c
11 :	Ditto	Ditto	59	c
12 :	Christmas carol, vocal (no words) ..	circa 1460	60	c
13 :	English dance tune	circa 1425	60	ꞯ
14 :	Hugh Aston, from motet " Adoramus," vocal	early 16th ct.	67	ꞯ
15 :	Henry VIII, dance tune for three instruments	early 16th ct.	68	c
16 :	Blow thy horn, hunter (folksong), vocal..	16th ct.	69	ꞯ
17 :	From My Lady Carey's Dump	early 16th ct.	70	ꞯ
18 (a–c) :	John Taverner, from motet " Et exultavit," vocal	Ditto	80	ꞯ
Without number :	Fragments from Taverner's Tedeum, vocal	Ditto	81f	ꞯ
19 :	The " In Nomine " cantus firmus ..	middle of 16th ct.	83	c
Without number :	Fragments from In Nomine by Tye	Ditto	87f	ꞯ
20 :	R. Parsons, from In Nomine a 5	middle of 16th ct.	89	ꞯ
21 :	R. White, from motet Ad te levavi, vocal	Ditto	92	ꞯ
22 :	R. Parsons, Galliard a 5	Ditto	98	c
23 :	A. Holborne, The Night Watch a 5 (melody only)	1599	99	c
24 :	Ditto, from Galliard a 5	1599	99	ꞯ
Without number :	Fragments from Morley's duos	1595	104	ꞯ
25 :	E. Blanke, from fantasia a 5	before 1578	105	ꞯ
26 :	W. Byrd, from In Nomine a 5	late 16th ct.	105	ꞯ
Without number (in footnote) :	Mich. Guy, long section from fant. a 3	Ditto	107	ꞯ
27 :	Thomas Morley, from duo	1597	108	ꞯ
28 :	Ditto, from duo, " Il Torello "	1595	108	ꞯ
29 :	Ditto, from duo III	1597	109	ꞯ
30 :	A. Holborne, from " Moretta " a 5 ..	1599	110	ꞯ
31 :	Ditto, from " Patiencia " a 5	1599	111	ꞯ
32 :	Ditto, from pavan a 5 (melody only) ..	1599	111	c
33 :	" The leaves be greene " (" Browning "), vocal	middle of 16th ct.	112	c

No.		DATE	PAGE	
34 (a–b) : J. Dowland, from pavan a 5 ("Lachrimae")	.. .. ..	1605	122f	Q
Without number : A. Holborne, from pavan a 5 ("The Funerals")	.. ..	1599	123	Q
35 : Ditto, from galliard a 5 ("The Sighes")		1599	124	Q
36 : G. Gabrieli, from Christmas Motet, vocal		1615	129	Q
37 : Th. Lupo, fantasia a 3	.. ..	circa 1605	144–147	c
38 (a–e) : Th. Ravenscroft, from fantasia a 5 ..		early 17th ct.	149f	Q
39 : A. Ferrabosco, jun., from fantasia 1 a 4 ..		Ditto	151	Q
40 (a–c) : Ditto, from fantasia 17 a 4 ..		Ditto	152f	Q
41 : Ditto, from fantasia 3 a 4..	.. ..	Ditto	153	Q
42 and 43 (a–c) : O. Gibbons, from fantasias a 3 and 4	.. .. ..	circa 1615	154	Q
Without number : A. Ferrabosco, jun., and Th. Lupo, from fantasias	.. ..	early 17th. ct.	157	Q
44 (a–c) : W. Byrd, from fantasia a 6	..	1611	156f	
45 (a–d) : O. Gibbons, from fantasia 7 a 3 ..		1610	158f	Q
46 : A. Ferrabosco, jun., from fantasia 3 a 4		early 17th ct.	160	Q
47 (a–b) : W. White, from fantasias a 5 and 6		Ditto	160	Q
48 : A. Ferrabosco, jun., from fantasia 13 a 4		Ditto	160	Q
49 and 50 : O. Gibbons, from fantasias a 3 ..		Ditto	161f	Q
51a : Th. Preston, from In Nomine a 4		circa 1575	162	Q
51b : J. Ward, from fantasia a 4	..	circa 1615	162	Q
52 : Ditto, from fantasia a 5 ..	.. ..	Ditto	163	Q
53–55 : O. Gibbons, from fantasias a 3	..	early 17th. ct.	163f	Q
56 : L. Grosso da Viadana, from Concerti ecclesiastici, vocal		1615	165	Q
57 : Th. Lupo, from fantasia a 6 (chest of viols)		early 17th ct	166	Q
58 : W. Cranford, from fantasia a 6 ..		circa 1615	168	Q
59 : R. Deering, from fantasia a 5 ..	..	circa 1620	169	Q
60 : Th. Ravenscroft, from fantasia a 5	..	Ditto	170	Q
61 : Th. Tomkins, from fantasia a 6 ..	..	circa 1625	170	Q
62 : Ditto, from fantasia a 3	.. ..	Ditto	170	Q
63 (a–f) : Th. Ford, from fantasia ("ayr") a 4		circa 1635	177f	Q
64 : W. Lawes, almand from "Royal Consort"		circa 1640	181f	c
65–68 : Ditto, from various fantasias a 5 and 6		circa 1635	183ff	Q
69 : J. Hilton, from fantasia a 3	.. ..	circa 1640	196	Q
70 (a–e) : Five tunes from "The English Dancing Master"	.. .. ..	1650	197f	c
71 : J. Jenkins, from fantasia a 5	..	circa 1635	220	Q
72 : Ditto, from Sonata for two bass viols ..		circa 1655	222	Q
73 : Ditto, from aria for violin, bass viol, Bc. (melody only) ..	.. ..	circa 1660	223	c
74 : Ditto, from fantasia a 3 ..	.. ..	circa 1665	223	Q
75 : Ch. Coleman, from fantasia a 5 ..	..	circa 1660	225	Q
76 (a–b) : J. Hingeston, from fantasias in suites		circa 1665	225f	Q
77 : Chr. Simpson, from fantasia "Spring "..		circa 1665	226f	Q
78 : M. Locke, air for two instruments	..	1654	232f	c
79 : Ditto, hornpype (melody only) ..		circa 1670	234	c
80 (a–c), 81, 81a and 82 : Ditto, from fantasias a 3 and 4	.. ..	1654–1660	234f	Q
83 : Ditto, Curtain Tune a 4 from "The Tempest"	.. ..	1672	236–239	c

MUSICAL EXAMPLES IN APPENDIX

No.		DATE	PAGE
I.	Alfonso Ferrabosco, jun., fantasia for four stringed instruments	circa 1610	257
II.	Giovanni Coperario (John Cooper), fantasia for four stringed instruments	1610	262
III.	William Lawes, fantasia for six stringed instruments	circa 1635	265
IV.	Ditto, fantasia for two violins, bass viol (cello) and harp (or any keyboard instrument) ..	circa 1640	271
V.	Michael East, fancy for four stringed instruments	1638	278
VI.	John Jenkins, fantasia for four stringed instruments	circa 1645	280
VII.	Ditto, fantasia for two violins and bass viol (cello)	circa 1665	288
VIII.	Christopher Gibbons, fantasia for two trebles (violins) and bass viol (cello)	circa 1670	294
IX.	Henry Purcell, fantasia " upon one note " for five stringed instruments	1681	297

xi

PREFACE

THIS book has its origin in events which date back to my student days in Berlin in the late 'twenties when I was doing some research on the early instrumental music of various European countries. I soon became fascinated by the wealth of material slumbering on the shelves of the ancient French, Dutch and German monasteries and music schools and I remember my excitement as I found more and more scores which were often anonymous and in some cases not even listed.

It was the well-ordered catalogues of the British Museum and the Oxford Christ Church libraries which first drew my attention to early English chamber music. According to these catalogues there still survived a considerable body of " fantasias " and other forms of music for stringed instruments composed in 16th and 17th century England, of whose existence continental musicians and musicologists seemed to have little knowledge. My curiosity was aroused and finally I succeeded in securing one or two of the few English publications of such music. It was chiefly these scores (I believe it was the 3-part fantasias by Orlando Gibbons) which induced me to apply for an academic scholarship to enable me to study the whole period more closely. This scholarship was granted in 1931 by the Notgemeinschaft der Deutschen Wissenschaft.

Events in Germany prevented me from writing at once a full account of all this music—the same events that were to lead me later on to settle in this country, this time for a much longer stay. However, the plan for such a book was in my mind all the time.

When I did set to work on it, I found myself faced with these very puzzling problems : What was the reason for the appearance of so extensive and significant a period of art ? and why was its music unknown on the continent ? Why was it not the pride and boast of at least the English people ?

It was first the reading of the works of some English historians, especially those of Tawney and Trevelyan, which made the facts

xiii

of the history of music appear to me in a new light, and it was my study of the works of F. Engels and K. Marx which finally led me to venture the attempt to represent a period of musical history as a natural part of a general social development.

It has not been an easy task to complete this book. The main part of the actual writing was done in London in 1940 and 1941 when libraries were closed and difficulties of other kinds existed in abundance. The book might never have been finished in the circumstances prevailing during these years, had it not been for the advice and assistance of a number of colleagues and friends. I am deeply indebted to the Incorporated Society of Authors who made a grant from their Crompton Bequest Fund towards the publication costs of this book—an act of generosity by which I feel both honoured and encouraged.

My heartfelt gratitude is also due to my friend Russell Ferguson. He not only corrected and improved the English of the book which I had to write in a language not native to me, but moreover took part in the conception of important sections of the text. My sincere thanks also go out to Gerald Hayes, Dona Torr, Professor R. H. Tawney, Arnold Goldsbrough, Diana Poulton, Professor Wormington, Storm Jameson, Benjamin Frankel, C. B. Oldman, F. D. Klingender, Dr. H. S. Middleton and many other friends too numerous to thank individually, but whose help has been invaluable.

ERNST H. MEYER

ENGLISH CHAMBER MUSIC

INTRODUCTION

CHAMBER music, the most intimate and elaborate of all musical forms, is also one of the youngest of the arts. While painting, sculpture, architecture and literature look back on a development of thousands of years, while music itself, taken as a whole, has accompanied mankind throughout the ages, chamber music in its present form is not more than four centuries old.

Not that a combination of several individual players co-operating was impossible before the 16th century. On the contrary, there is plenty of proof that at all times both inside and outside Europe more or less informal gatherings of small numbers of musicians took place. But the essential feature of that particular practice which we are accustomed to define as ' chamber music ' (and in this book only *instrumental group music* will be discussed), that particular relationship between the few players who take part in the execution of the music, the attitude of the players and listeners towards their art, is entirely new ; it is, in England, a creation of the age of Henry VIII and Elizabeth.

The essential attitude of the chamber musician is a kind of inwardness, a devotion to music for what it says to the player rather than for any effect on the audience, a devotion to the free, pure and self-sufficient creation of a seemingly abstract beauty. It is this attitude on the part of composers and players which sets chamber music in such striking contrast to all medieval music. Neither the spirit of religious devotion as in the choral masterpieces of the middle ages, nor the stirring movement of medieval dance tunes, nor the pageantry and splendour of ceremonial Court music will be found in the new domestic chamber music of Reformation and post-Reformation times. A performance of chamber music seems to originate solely in the desire of the musicians to seek diversion and enjoyment, through their own playing. They use chamber music as a means of expressing what is working within them, and of satisfying and solving what seems unsatisfiable and insoluble by any other means of expression.

I

It is true that the ' chamber music attitude ' of the 16th and 17th centuries is in many respects different from that of our own age. In particular there are varying degrees of distinction between the kind of entirely ' free ' chamber music just characterised, and certain small-scale musical activities at the courts of the 16th and 17th centuries which were to some extent functional. But to a high degree this element of privacy and detachment from any visible purpose is already found in very early examples of 16th century chamber music. It is essentially music to be played without audience or, at most, to a very small one.

Among all the musical centres of Europe in the 16th and 17th centuries Britain was first and foremost in the realm of chamber music. In this field the supremacy of this country was undisputed. For decades English instrumental music influenced all kinds of instrumental art in other nations, and after 1600 many English musicians, especially string players, were engaged by foreign courts and chapels, just as, before, Netherlands composers and, later, Italian bel-cantists swept Europe.

Chamber music occupies an important place in the development of a national culture in post-Reformation England. Indeed the part it played in English cultural life was for a considerable time of a significance that was only equalled by the poetry of the same age.

Here is a passage from Fletcher :

> Orpheus with his Lute made Trees
> And the Mountaine tops that freeze
> Bow themselves when he did sing.
> To his Musicke, Plants and Flowers
> Ever sprung ; as Sunne and Showers,
> There had made a lasting Spring.
> Everything that heard him play,
> Even the Billowes of the Sea,
> Hung their heads, and then lay by.
> In sweet Musicke is such Art,
> Killing care, and griefe of heart,
> Fall asleape, or hearing die.

And here is an example of the very sort of music Fletcher must have had in mind—a fantasia by his great contemporary Orlando Gibbons :

Example 1 : Fantasia for three viols by Orlando Gibbons.[1]

ORLANDO.GIBBONS
FANTASIA A 3

Disc. Viol

Bass Viol

Double Bass Viol

[1] From Dublin, Marsh Library, MS. Z.2, 1, 13.

GIBBONS (2)

GIBBONS (3)

GIBBONS (4)

GIBBONS (5)

Now Fletcher's poem and the poetry of his age are loved wherever the English language is spoken. There are also individual enthusiastic admirers of early English madrigals and quite a number of choral societies which perform to a certain extent such sonnets in the musical settings of 17th century musicians. But this fantasia by Gibbons, together with the rest of the instrumental music of his age, is still far too little appreciated, especially by the public at large, in spite of the fact that attention has recently been focussed on the instrumental productivity of this period by a number of scholars as well as practical musicians.

Why is this? Is it because the music is inferior?

It is certainly conceivable that there might have been an age which produced at the same time great poetry and poor music, but the 16th and 17th centuries in England were not such an age. For Fletcher's passage can be matched in music a hundred times. The poets of that day and age were themselves great lovers of instrumental music and have left their testimony to the great emotional power and beauty of the chamber music of their time.

Perhaps the music was good then, but is not good now? This might be a possible explanation, if it were true. The music *is* good now. Gibbons's Fancy, a representative example, is a beautiful piece of work, highly wrought and deeply felt. But for some reason it is regarded as music of the past.

Bach's music was also once regarded as music of the past, until certain discerning musicians became aware of the wonderful qualities to which generations before them had been insensitive, and initiated a revival of Bach which has since become one of the most interesting musical phenomena of recent times.

Of late the popularity of John Donne and other 17th century poets has borne witness that the poetry of the period is peculiarly meet for today. It is my belief, based on careful study, that the chamber music of that great age is also particularly suitable for the present time, for reasons which in due course will appear in this study.

But it is not quite so easy to bring to life the music of the past as it is to revive the poetry of a bygone age. The difference between poetry and music has many aspects, but that which most concerns us now is this: whereas we are accustomed to read literature and drama in the context of history, recognising that a poet or a dramatist speaks out of his time and period, our study of music is not yet conducted in the same way. Even some highly cultured musicians mistakenly assume that the old music yields up its secrets at a casual hearing.

If we take old music as it is, straight from the century-old dust of the libraries, if we listen to it as too many people listen to a Mozart Symphony, that is to say, without considering the life and spirit of the time and the circumstances in which it was produced, then we run the risk of finding all such music dull and lifeless, completely remote from our normal musical experience.

The style and meaning of the music of a period cannot be thoroughly understood if it is to be detached from its living background. If we are to understand the distinctive structure, style and character of the music of any period wè must first ask, what kind of people composed and performed it and for what sort of audience ? Who commissioned the music and especially, why and for what purpose was it produced ? Was it to furnish pleasant distraction from everyday life, or to instil religious devotion, or to rouse enthusiasm ?

*   *   *   *   *

This is the first discussion *in extenso* of the great age of English chamber music, but it certainly does not claim to be the first work which has drawn attention to the period. Great tribute is due to the work of a few musicologists and practitioners who in the face of utter indifference and even violent opposition or ridicule spent their lives revealing some of the uncounted treasures of early English instrumental art.

First and most important of all is Arnold Dolmetsch, who not only unearthed much of this music but also searched for and found ways of presenting it to enthusiastic if small audiences. With admirable patience and scientific exactitude he rebuilt the old instruments on which this music had once been performed, and successfully evolved a proper technique and style in the playing of them. The annual performances of his consorts of viols and recorders in London and Haslemere will always be remembered by musicians and musicologists, amateur and professional. Now, after the master's death, it is manifest that his work marked the turning point in the battle for the recognition of ancient music in England.[1]

A whole school of eager and understanding scholars and students gathered round Dolmetsch and his famliy. Outstanding among them is Gerald R. Hayes : he was the first to collect and produce systematically all the historical matter that had so far been neglected ; this was done in his classic work, *Musical Instruments and their Music*.[2] This book is at the same time an introduction to the nature of early instruments and a general survey of the music written for them. It contains valuable material concerning the production of this music. *King's Music* by the same author[3] is most important in its scholarly exposition

---

[1] A treatise by A. Dolmetsch on *The Interpretation of the Music of the 17th and 18th Centuries* appeared in 1915. Several gramophone records of old music played by the Dolmetsch family were published by the Columbia Graphophone Co.
[2] London, 1930.   [3] London, 1941.

of the development of the Chapel Royal and in its method of research : it not only states the facts but also shows them in their historical relationship. Hayes' *Lute's Apology* is a treasury of information, especially on the technique of the lutes, citterns, guitars and other plucked instruments.[1]

A pupil of Dolmetsch, Robert Donington, has made a detailed study of the music for viols, which is as yet unpublished.[2]

In any account of work on the subject of early English instruments and their music, F. W. Galpin's *Old English Instruments of Music* must be particularly noted.[3] There are further E. H. Hunt's brief but fine studies on music for the recorders,[4] and among the works of older writers, H. St. George's *The Bow, its History, Manufacture and Use*,[5] H. C. de Lafontaine's *The King's Musick ; a Transcript of Records* (1460–1700),[6] and E. Van der Straeten's *The Romance of the Fiddle*,[7] and *History of the Violoncello*.[8]

Grove's and Scholes's Dictionaries contain welcome material upon our subject,[9] as do also J. Pulver's Dictionaries of old music,[10] and editions by E. H. Fellowes, Sir R. Terry and other scholars of old music—alas, they are not numerous.[11]

In general works on the history of music, references to early English chamber music are mostly few and short, with the exception of Eric Blom's *Music in England*,[12] G. Reese's *Music in the Middle Ages*,[13] and P. H. Láng's *Music in Western Civilisation*,[14]

---

[1] London, 1941 (the plates of this book were, alas, destroyed during the bombing of London, but an early reissue is to be hoped for).

[2] Donington also wrote a pamphlet, *The Work and Ideas of Arnold Dolmetsch*, Haslemere, 1932.

[3] London, 1910.

[4] *The Recorder or English Flute*, London, 1936. Cf. also Hunt's *Recorder News-Letters*, 1940 ff. Far less scholarly, Christopher Welch on the same subject, London, 1911.

[5] London, 1895.   [6] London, 1909.

[7] London, 1911.   [8] London, 1915.

[9] Grove, latest edition, 1940 ; Scholes's *Oxford Companion to Music*, 1939.

[10] Chiefly the *Biographical Dictionary of Old English Music*, 1927.

[11] Fantasia for 6 instruments by W. Byrd, 8 Elizabethan Dance Tunes, 9 Fantasias a 3 and 1 a 4 by O. Gibbons, Pavan and Galliard a 6 by Gibbons, 1 Fantasia a 6 by Tomkins, all ed. E. H. Fellowes (Stainer & Bell) ; 2 In Nomines by Parsons and Parsley, ed. Sir R. R. Terry (London, 1923) ; Sonatas by W. Young, ed. by G. Whittaker (Oxford University Press) ; instrumental works by Purcell, ed. P. Warlock (London, 1923) ; 6 Fantasias by Locke, ed. P. Warlock (1932, *ibid.* a suite for 3 stringed instruments) ; Incidental Music to *The Tempest* by Locke, ed. G. Whittaker, London, 1936, and small publications of works by Morley and others. In Hayes' *King's Music* there are some publications of works by Henry VIII, Ferrabosco, W. Lawes and others.

[12] Penguin Books, 1942, pp. 34–70.

[13] London, 1941.   [14] London, 1942.

though some of the instrumental works of a few individual composers such as Byrd, Gibbons and Purcell have been treated with greater care and understanding by their respective biographers.[1]

So we see that the greatness of early English chamber music has been recognised by certain individual scholars, and some good specimens have been published and played. Yet this outstanding period remains generally unknown to the English musical public. For though it is good that some pieces of old music should be played and published, it is not enough. A successful revival of old music entails chiefly a revival of the active musician and music lover ; but to be loved, music must be understood. It is in order to promote an understanding of a neglected part of England's heritage that this book is written. The subject has led me to investigate certain aspects of the inter-relationship between music and social habits which to some might appear to lie outside the scope of musicology. I have not hesitated to follow where the subject has led me, believing such inquiries to be essential to the true appraisal of a really great period of music and to its worthy celebration in present-day musical practice.

[1] E. H. Fellowes, *Byrd*, 1936. F. Howes, *Byrd*, 1928 ; E. H. Fellowes, *Gibbons*, 1925 ; J. A. Westrup, *Purcell*, 1937, p. 222 ff.

CHAPTER I

THE MEDIEVAL BACKGROUND

THE age in which chamber music reached maturity may be characterised as a decisive stage in the fight between an old and a new principle of social structure, the fight between social, economic and cultural conservatism, represented by the feudal order of the middle ages,[1] and the rising middle classes who demanded greater individual freedom in every sphere of life.

In the sphere of religion which played so vital a part in the development of music in the middle ages, this struggle appears as the antagonism between Catholicism and all the religious movements that led up to Protestantism.

Far from being merely a religious creed, medieval Catholicism strove to be the spiritual authority that would direct and inspire the entire social life of the ' community of the faithful.' The political and social aspirations of the Church had first been formulated in St. Augustine's *De Civitate Dei*—and in this ' State of God ' it was the mission of the *papal hierarchy* to determine and control mankind's temporal organisation, so as to guide man through the fallacies of earthly life to his celestial salvation.

The Catholic Church of the middle ages was the strongest bulwark of the static order of society. It stood and fell with the principle of absolute authority and the divinely ordained unchangeability of things. Being itself built on the fixed system of landownership the Church struggled to keep down such tendencies as those which were being spread by the rising secular forces of the later middle ages, especially by the merchants. The world outlook of medieval Catholicism was static—as static as the social order based on self-sufficient agrarian economy and rights in land, as static as the universe of which the secular order of things is taken to be but a dim reflection. " Credo ut intellegam " wrote Anselm—*the belief* prevails, the immutability of things is accepted. And the Church had to foster as the ideal attitude of popular religious opinion towards the external world of social institutions and economic relations, a creed which would " stand on one side in ascetic aloofness and regard them as in

[1] In the use of the term ' feudal ' we shall follow as closely as possible the definition given by H. Pirenne in his *History of Europe*, 1917 ; English edition (Allen & Unwin, 1939), pp. 146–160.

their very nature the sphere of unrighteousness—from which men *may* escape—from which, if they consider their souls, they *will* escape—but which they can conquer only by flight."[1]

Music played an essential part in this " creation of mentalities." The musical expression of this Catholic attitude of mind, the reiterated assertion of the unchallenged stability of Church and the worldly order of things, came to be choral polyphony.

Choral polyphony, the music of the later medieval Christian Church, is an important part of the foundation of the music of Europe, and is especially relevant to chamber music. As such we must give it some consideration.

Vocal music in general, carrying the message of the ritual, and increasing its effect and intensity both by musical and acoustic means, has been used in every kind of service almost as long as religious cults have existed. When a text is expounded by a musical choir the power of its religious message is intensified. The Christian Church has made use of this power ever since its beginnings in the catacombs of Rome and North Africa. In this practice the suggestive and emotional possibilities of music were made entirely subservient to the purpose of the biblical texts. The Gregorian Chant, that great collection of melodies used in the Catholic service, was codified, fixed and authorised in a deliberate official recognition of the power which music can be made to wield.

From the 10th century onwards the effect of the choral interpretation of the gospel was further broadened and deepened by the introduction of polyphony, i.e. the co-operation of all parts of the choir in the building of a contrapuntal whole. The crowning period of choral polyphony was the time of the so-called Netherlandish Schools which flourished during the 15th and 16th centuries. Throughout this period the polyphony of Church music was continuously elaborated, until towards the middle of the 16th century the holy melodies of the Gregorian choral, through the medium of which the liturgical message was announced, were finally produced by all the three, four, five or six voice-groups of the choir, each of them moving along independent contrapuntal lines, and all being of equal musical importance. The effect of this intense and highly ' organised ' music was hypnotic.

This music, calm, majestic, and magnificently uniform, echoing

[1] R. H. Tawney, *Religion and the Rise of Capitalism*, 1926, p. 16.

through the twilight of the Gothic cathedrals in a neutral and unbroken flow, never failed to consolidate in the minds of the listeners a firm belief in the immutability of world, Church and established society—such indeed was its purpose. The fact that the Latin language was used in the music of the service essentially contributed to the impersonal and magic effect of the singing.

It will be easy to understand why the official art, especially of the earlier part of the middle ages, was vocal religious music, and why, indeed, no musical practice could ever hope for any official encouragement unless it were devoted to religion. St. Augustine, in his *Confessiones* (about A.D. 400) says that he " inclined . . . to allow the old usage of singing in the church ; that so by the delight taken in by his ears, the weaker minds be roused up into some feeling of devotion."

Hence the primacy of vocal music throughout the middle ages. The position of instrumental music is contrary and complementary.

As everywhere on the continent, the use of musical instruments declined in England with the eclipse of the Roman Empire. In ancient times musical instruments had occupied an all-important place in social life, in philosophy and even in politics. Non-Christian communities always believed in the magic power of instruments. But Christian culture shrank from activities so devilish and heathenish as the artificial working-up of profane emotions by aulos and cithara, especially when after A.D. 100 instrumental music began to play a prominent part in the debaucheries of the degenerate Roman aristocracy.

> Not the singing itself belongs to the puerile stage, but the singing accompanied by instruments which have no souls, and by dancing and stamping. Therefore instrumental accompaniment in the churches has been abolished and only the pure singing has been kept.[1]

St. Clement of Alexandria, one of the oldest patristic writers, says :—" Only one instrument do we use, viz., the word of peace wherewith we honor God, no longer the old psaltery, trumpet, drum and flute." St. Chrysostom (d. 407) is just as uncompromising :

---

[1] *Quæstiones et Responsiones ad Orthodoxos* (A.D. 370). F. W. Galpin mentions that occasionally lyras and cytharas had been used in the very earliest stages of the Christian Church, accompanying religious worship. Such cases were, however, isolated and confined to certain places. See F. W. Galpin, *Old English Instruments of Music*, London, 1910, p. 273.

David formerly sang in psalms, also we sing today with him ; he had a lyre with lifeless strings, the Church has a lyre with living strings. 'Our tongues are the strings of the lyre, with a different tone indeed, but with a more accordant piety.[1]

That was the attitude of the young Christian Church towards musical instruments and their music, and the suspicions surrounding instrumental music were never completely allayed throughout the middle ages. It may be that in the times of Celtic Christianity before the Synod of Whitby (664) the Church in Britain exercised somewhat greater tolerance towards the ancient practice of instrumental music (as the stories of Caedmon and his harp seem to indicate), for the pre-Roman Church in England contained quite a number of relics from the times of tribal paganism. But it seems most probable that after the establishment of Roman Catholic rule the Church behaved more and more unkindly towards the ' soulless ' musical instruments in this country just as it did everywhere else.

In all the cultures subsequently conquered by Christianity where instrumental music still played an important part in the official life of the community, the full power of the " ecclesia militans " was mobilised to subdue it. In England the old instrumental art of the Bards and Celts which up to the 7th century was considered as something divine and supernaturally powerful, was pushed back during the process of cultural unification under the rule of Christianity.[2] The Church had to establish its universal sway by breaking down tribal gods, tribal separateness, and many tribal customs.

It must be stressed that during the first centuries of Christianity the stand of the Church against profane instrumental music had its progressive aspects inasmuch as it was directed against the decaying system of the Roman slave-empire and against tribal pagan influences. After all, the Church had brought a new moral standard to the masses, it had given economic security to

[1] See E. Dickinson, *Music in the History of the Western Church*, London, 1902, p. 54 ff.

[2] As early as in the 4th century the art of harp playing among the Celtic Bards was recognised as an important part of their cultural activities. See Ammianus Marcellinus, L. XV, chapter IX: " . . . the Bards of the Celts celebrated the actions of illustrious men in heroic poems which they sang to the sweet sounds of the lyre." For more details on harps in early medieval England see Galpin, Chap. I ; also Burney's *History of Music*, II, p. 352 ff.

its subjects, it had created a literate class and a new standard of art and learning which developed enormously with the further consolidation of the clerical organisation. In fact, during the early middle ages it was the great civilising force that prevented Europe from relapsing into barbarism. The austerity prescribed by all the patristic writers was part of the spiritual armour of the young movement. St. Augustine pleaded that it was better even to plough on the Lord's day than to desecrate it with dancing and riot.[1] In the 9th century it was decreed that bishops and abbots must not possess birds of prey, dogs or jugglers (minstrels).[2] Prohibitions of minstrels, worded in the strongest possible terms, were decreed at various councils,[3] such as Cavaillon (650), Tours (813), Glasgow (747), and in particular Mainz (847 and 852).[4] This policy stands out despite the appearance of some very ancient British instruments such as the rotta[5] in 8th and 9th century pictures in early psalters or in carvings in churches.[6] For it was even more the player of an instrument than the instrument itself which incurred the disfavour of the Church.

So the heralds of Christianity waged a holy war against those people who still continued the forbidden practice. No value was attached to any instrumental activity. To say the least, it was considered useless ; just empty " playing." One must remember that from the early middle ages a musical instrument was " played," " gespielt," " joué," etc., in nearly all the European languages, while in pre-Christian languages the respective terms were mostly " blown," " plucked," " struck " or " sounded." Basically the English development differed in no way from that on the Continent. When King Alfred disguised himself as a harpist to get into the camp of the Danes before the battle of Edington (878) he did so in order to conceal his Christian state from his enemies. His harp showed him to be a heathen, for it was an instrument of pagan culture which the Christian Church

[1] *De Decem Chordis*, serm. ix, para. 3. See G. G. Coulton, *The Medieval Village* Cambridge, 1925, p. 93.

[2] Boretius, *Capitularia Regum Francorum*, 1883, I, 64.

[3] See P. H. Láng, *Music in Western Civilization*, 1942, p. 83.

[4] See Boretius, *Capitularia*, and E. K. Chambers, *The Medieval Stage*, 1903, p. 38 ff.

[5] Rotta is the triangular or U-shaped harp of the early middle ages, often identical with the chrotta (crwth, crowder, cruit or chorus), the rectangular harp, which was at first plucked, later often bowed.

[6] Galpin, pp. 4, 5, and *passim*.

did not tolerate.[1] Alcuin (Albinus Flaccus of York, 735–804), friend and teacher of Charlemagne, warned a friend in a letter which he wrote in 791 that he apparently did not realise that " by inviting jugglers and dancers to his house he admitted a mass of unclean spirits."[2] At the end of the 11th century John Cotton, well-known English theoretician, in his treatise *Joannis Cottonis Musica* speaks very contemptuously about wind instruments in particular. In his opinion these instruments sound " indiscretely " (which means dissonantly), " like the laughter or the groaning of men, the barking of dogs or the roaring of lions." Only the well-tempered movement of voices can be called music—this Cotton felt obliged to use as an argument against those " idiots who are stupid enough to call *any* sound music."[3]

It was stated as an exceptional and daring venture that St. Aldhelm, Bishop of Sherborne (about 640–709), should have deemed it necessary to attract people to the church by playing a harp—only then, having played the pagan instrument, did he succeed in gathering around him an audience sufficiently large to enable him to deliver his sermon.[4] And Bishop Dunstan (10th century) had the uncomfortable experience of being called a sorcerer for having constructed an Æolic harp which sounded when placed against a crevice in a wall.[5] Only for a short time immediately after the Norman invasion do we find some court ' jongleurs ' brought over by the conquering noblemen such as Berdic, William's minstrel—while the remainder of the English-

---

[1] E. H. Poole, in his essay on *Music in the Early Drama*, mentions a similar incident of the year 457 which occurred in York during the wars between Saxons and Britons ; there is also the story of Baldulph, given in Chappell's *Old English Popular Music*, 1893, p. 6.

[2] Quoted by A. Schering, *Handbuch der Musikgeschichte*, 1923, p. 97.

[3] See M. Gerbert, *Scriptores ecclesiastici de musica*, II, p. 234 : " Artificiale vero instrumentum est, quod non per naturam sed per artificium ad reddendum sonitum adaptatur. Naturalis autem sonus alius est discretus, alius indiscretus ; discretus est, qui alias habet consonantias ; indiscretus est, in quo nulla discerni potest consonantia, ut in risu vel gemitu hominum, et latratu canum, aut rugitu leonum. Simili modo discretum et indiscretum sonum in artificiali perpendere potes. Fistula namque illa, qua decipiuntur aviculæ, vel etiam illa pergameno superducta, unde pueri ludere solent, indiscretum reddunt sonitum. At vero in sambuca, in fidibus, in cymbalis, atque in organis consonantiarum bene et distincte discernitur diversitas. Illum ergo sonum, quem indiscretum esse diximus, musica nequaquam recipit : solus autem dumtaxat discretus, qui etiam proprie phthongus vocatur, ad musicam pertinet ; est enim musica nihil aliud quam vocum congrua motio. Hæc autem contra idiotas præcipue diximus, quo illorum compesceremus errorem, qui quemlibet sonum esse musicum stulte autumant."

[4] Galpin, p. 17.   [5] Ibid., p. 72.

speaking minstrelsy were now driven into hiding by the Normans and forthwith rambled up and down the country as enemies of the authorities.

*   *   *   *   *

On the other hand, however, we can at least say—with all due caution—that on balance the persecution of instrumental music by the Church in England was progressively, if slightly, relaxed during the 12th and 13th centuries. As we reach the 12th century we can begin to speak of something like a reluctant (and certainly temporary) toleration of certain instruments by the Church.

The fact is that popular musical activities outside the Church were decidedly on the increase in the 12th century.

Instrumental music was the cheerful accompaniment of the growth of the new burgher classes. The nobility, too, especially the continental knights at the time of the crusades, had contributed substantially to the consolidation of secular music in general and instrumental music in particular. Much as the Church disliked this development, it could not ignore it.

For many centuries it had kept down instrumental activity. Whilst trying to utilise painting, literature, pageantry, and many pagan festivals and customs (such as Yule) by gently diverting them into Christian channels, instrumental music it either vituperated or brutally persecuted. Not only did it appear valueless to the Church, for the simple reason that the music of the vielles, pipes and shalms seemed to contain hardly any elements worth mentioning which could be transformed and thus utilised for Church purposes—it was positively harmful to the souls of the people. Instrumental music introduced an element of secular pleasure ; it disturbed the atmosphere of devotion, the unity of the service. It distracted the churchgoers from their sacred duties. Altogether the listening to and particularly the playing of musical instruments had an activising effect on human beings as individuals—an influence small in appearance but dangerous in its possible consequences. If St. Gerome preached that " a Christian maiden ought not even to know what a lyre or a flute is, or what it is used for,"[1] he must have had his reasons.[2]

[1] Dickinson, p. 55.

[2] Antagonism to instrumental music in the Christian service reappears as a feature of several later movements. Here is the opinion on the matter as expressed

But instrumental music became more and more powerful, and by 1150 it had become a deeply-rooted 'evil.' And now the Church was repeatedly compelled to come to terms with instrumental music, in an effort to absorb what it could not destroy.

The Church had to give in and try to make use of musical instruments (or at least of some of them) by taking the pagan stigma from them and incorporating them in its own inventory of recognised service furniture. This indeed the Church authorities did by having angels and saints pictured praising the Lord no longer merely by singing, but by playing harps and dulcimers ; sometimes indeed they actually had them played in the monasteries and cathedrals. In such a way the Church no doubt hoped to attract the villagers back to the service and to close a dangerous gulf between itself and the people at large.

The 12th century was a time when the Church in England could afford this temporary relaxation. For then the position of the Church was still relatively secure. From the times of the Norman invasion approximately till the 13th century, feudalism in England existed in its most complete form (and the Church was " implicated to the hilt in its economic fabric, especially on the side of agriculture and land tenure.")[1] Feudal landowning and villeinage, which formed the secular basis of the power of the Church, were then most stabilised and worked well, while spiritually and intellectually the Church was certainly the dominant influence.

So the ' ecclesia triumphans ' for a time made it its policy to compromise with the allurements of popular entertainment. In fact, quite a number of strange happenings occurred in 12th and early 13th century churches in the way of pageantry and music, especially on the Continent. In this country there are several instances of people choosing the churches or churchyards of all places for singing vulgar songs and love carols and performing quick step dances (Giraldus Cambrensis, in his *Gemma ecclesiastica,*

[1] Tawney, p. 56.

by Dr. Kippis, well-known dissenter of the end of the 18th century : " The use of instrumental music in Christian worship has no foundation in the New Testament, which is the standard of our faith and practice. If once we depart from this standard there will be no end to innovations. An opening will be laid to the introduction of one superstition after another, till the simplicity and purity of the Gospel service are wholly lost. *Every thing, therefore, which tends to divert men from a rational inward devotion to external pomp and ceremony ought to be discouraged as much as possible.*" From *A Tractate against Instrumental Music in Churches,* by Dr. Samuel Green, Controversial Tracts, 5.

has a whole chapter against dancing and singing in churches). Among the first instruments that played a certain part in the service we name the organ—it was the only instrument which hardly ever incurred the disfavour of the Church. This great instrument was very early adopted for use in the service. Its majestic and somewhat otherworldly (if in its young days somewhat harsh) sound made it particularly apt for this function.[1] Baudri of Bourgeuil (1046–1130) expressed his admiration for the organ at Worcester Church with great eloquence :—

" The organ, whence harmonious voices run,
Is joy that gives our lives their ordering.
Driven on varying ways, we draw to one :
As one we chant the praises of our King.
The power of unity in different voices
Is that which spreads our energies, yet controls.
The driven air along each reed rejoices :
So God combines with flesh our struggling souls,
To blend our lives in mystic symphony.
His breath of power, unifying, blows
And many lives within one life are furled,
The secret glory that sustains the world.
Thus from concordant hearts the music flows.
Great Prior, here's the song you asked of me."[2]

Under the favour of the Church organ music was able to develop freely.[3]

[1] As early as the 8th century an illumination in the Utrecht Psalter shows two monks playing the organ. Dunstan, in the 10th century, is said to have made an organ with brass pipes. At the same time a gigantic organ at Winchester Cathedral is mentioned. There are numerous illustrations showing organs being used in the service in the 11th and 12th centuries. See also H. Davey, *History of English Music*, 2nd ed. (1921), p. 9 ff., and F. W. Galpin, *Old English Instruments of Music*, 1910, picture plates.

[2] From Jack Lindsay, *Medieval Latin Poets*, 1934, p. 112.

[3] We possess a highly important document which is generally considered as the earliest specimen of organ music ; it is of the 14th century and not immediately connected with the service itself. It consists of two parchment leaves which are annexed to a register of Robertsbridge Abbey ; now Brit. Museum, MS. Add. 28550 (see also Wooldridge, *Early English Harmony*, pp. 42–45). These contain several purely instrumental movements, partly intavolaturas of vocal pieces, among others from the French Roman de Fauvel (beginning of 14th century; see J. Wolf's *Geschichte der Mensuralnotation*, I, p. 357 ff.). Two of the pieces are solo preæambula for organ, possibly intended for use before service started. These pieces must be considered as typical of the style of organ music of the time. They are 2-part pieces which expand into 3-part harmony towards the cadences. All are influenced by the continental ' ars nova ' with its greater rhythmic decision, although they are, on the whole, kept in the stricter style of the earlier middle ages.

Moreover after 1100 some soft-toned stringed instruments make their appearance in sacred surroundings more and more frequently, chiefly the organistrum,[1] the psaltry[2] and the dulcimer.[3] Even trumpets and other brass instruments are sometimes pictured in Church mss. where the biblical context justifies it[4]; and such examples are on the increase during the 12th and 13th centuries.

Around 1300 a theoretician tells us of string, wind and keyboard instruments which reinforce the sound of the voices " to the greater praise of the holiest divine glory."[5] Just about the same time Bishop de Swinfield of Hereford is reported to have allowed some minstrels to play to him in one of his pastoral rounds. After listening for a while, he ordered that each of them should be given the sum of " a penny a piece."[6] We even come across such 13th century stories as that of Benedictus of Abingdon who turned out two itinerant priests in disappointment that they were not minstrels to entertain him.[7]

There is a beautiful continental example of this temporary

[1] The hurdy-gurdy, also called symphony ; a predecessor of the violin with an internal circular bow turned round by way of an external handle.

[2] Psalterium ; a flat hollow box with a stringboard ; the strings are played with a plectrum or the fingers.

[3] Like the psaltry, but the strings are played with hammers.

[4] King David is sometimes shown with his musicians ; there are also pictures of the trombones of Jericho, of Saul's instrumental ensemble, etc. It must be stressed, however, that the appearance of pictures of an instrument in certain sacred surroundings does not necessarily prove that it had in fact been used in the service.

[5] The treatise of this anonymous writer is called De Sinemenis and is affixed to that of the 13th century English 'Anonymus 4' in Coussemaker's Scriptores. The passage in question runs : " Quæ quidem supradicta ad sanctissimam gloriam divinam multiplicandam cum quibusdam aliis, prout in cordis, in flatu, in cimbalis bene sonantibus." (Coussemaker, I, p. 365).

[6] Jusserand, English Wayfaring Life in the Middle Ages (14th century), London, 1920, p. 202. A penny at the time would equal about 3½ shillings in present currency (1944) : see G. G. Coulton, The Meaning of Medieval Moneys, Hist. Ass. Leaflet No. 95, 1934.

[7] Anthony à Wood, Hist. Antiq. Oxon., Vol. I, p. 67.

The general appearance of the pieces is of such completeness and security of style as to suggest that they were results of a long tradition. There is one more indication of what early English organ music might have been like ; it is contained in the Treatise from Bury St. Edmunds written by an English 13th century writer, generally known as " Anonymus 4 " in Coussemaker's Scriptores. He talks about " bordunos organorum " which suggests an instrumental bordune tone, a sustained note kept in the bass in a similar way as in the music of our Scotch pipers, while other voices play or sing melodic counterpoint. See Charles E. H. de Coussemaker, Scriptores de musica medii ævi, 1864–76, I, p. 327 ; also Marius Schneider, Geschichte der Mehrstimmigkeit, II, 1935, p. 19 ff. and p. 43 ff.

change of policy on the part of the Church in a situation similar
to the English. It is contained in a late 13th-century treatise
by Johannes de Grocheo. Talking about Stantipes and Ductia,
Grocheo describes the object of these dance-cantilenas which
were either instrumental or vocal as purely moral. These tunes
which originally derived from popular practice he represents as
intended to distract the minds of young ladies and gentlemen
from wicked thoughts and lead them, by their great degree of
difficulty, away from " that passion which is called love " to
assiduous study and other praiseworthy activities.[1]

The modification of the attitude of the Church towards musical
instruments after 1150 roughly coincides with the first appearance
of vernacular poetry in England after the Norman Conquest.
Although the old Anglo-Saxon heroic tradition and alliterative
verse lived on in new transformations, the development in the
Middle English period proceeds towards the greater freedom in
narrative, lyrical and romantic poetry which was to culminate
in the 14th century with Chaucer.

One is tempted to consider these two facts, the rise of lyrical
poetry and the greater tolerance shown by the Church towards
instruments, together, as two aspects of one and the same development : the growing consolidation and independence of cultural
activities outside the Church. So the second half of the 12th
century appears as a time dividing the middle ages into two main
periods, the later centuries being characterised by the growing
emancipation of the secular burgher and middle classes from
clerical tutelage.

But at the same time the developments in poetry show quite
clearly that it would be wrong to see the art of the later middle
ages in a straight-line oppositional development of ' Church
versus middle classes.' The latter were always intensely religious,
and in general there was a continuous and strong interplay
of the cultural elements of both forces, as well as vivid interaction
of the art of the court, serfs, the educated individuals at universities and monasteries, and the wandering scholars.

Just as " the first popular songs of the modern world were the

---

[1] " Stantipes . . . facit animos iuvenum et puellarum propter sui difficultatem
circa hanc stare et eos a cogitatione prava devertit . . ." " Ductia vero est
cantilena levis et velox in ascensu et descensu, quæ in choris a iuvenibus et puellis
decantatur. . . . Hæc enim ducit corda puellarum et iuvenum et a vanitate
removet et contra passionem, quæ dicitur amor . . . valere dicitur." See J.
Wolf's article in Sammelbände der Internationalen Musikgesellschaft, I, p. 93 f.

hymns of St. Ambrose and the oldest fashion of popular tunes is derived from the Church,"[1] so in the later middle ages many songs sung by the people were produced by musically highly skilled monks. A striking example is the famous "Summer Canon" (about 1280) :[2]

Example 2 : The Summer Canon.

This piece was for a long time considered a typical ' popular ' song, typical of both the simplicity of the musical thinking of the ordinary country folk and of elements of style peculiar exclusively to the English. Neither opinion can be completely refuted, but it is important to see that there are in pieces like the "Summer Canon" elements of the style of the music of the highly educated classes (as well as of foreign countries, which in this case is not the point to be discussed). It has been called " a learned composer's adaptation of a reverie or chant of welcome to the spring,"[3] and those who look more closely will find how true this is, for there are many evidences of a truly ingenious mind contained in the score. Its musical form is closely related to the contemporary French isorhythmic secular ' minstrels ' motet, which is certainly based on a highly difficult and even refined pattern.[4] Moreover the original copy of the song has a Latin text as well as an English one (Latin had long ceased to be the language of the common people in England). At the same time there certainly are popular influences and sources clearly discernible in this piece ; one of them is the popular French rondeau as exemplified in the following melody :[5]

[1] W. P. Ker, *Medieval English Literature*, 1912, p. 76.

[2] Dr. M. Bukofzer (*Sumer is icumen in, a revision ;* University of California Publications in Music, 1944) believes that this famous *rota* cannot possibly have been written before 1280. See also E. J. Dent in *The Music Review*, vol. VI, No. 2 (May 1945), pp. 107–109.

[3] E. K. Chambers and F. Sidgwick, *Early English Lyrics*, 1907.

[4] See H. Besseler, *Musik des Mittelalters und der Renaissance*, Potsdam, 1934, p. 170 ff.

[5] From Joh. Wolf, *Geschichte der Musik*, I, 1930, p. 62, the second and third voices come in in the second and third bars.

Example 3: 13th century 3-part round (Northern French).

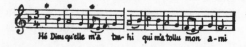

Hé Dieu qu'elle m'a tra- hi qui m'a tollu mon a - mi

The trend of French influences in 13th century English poetry and music thus shows just this interaction of social forces. These influences came from popular *as well* as " polite " circles and they affected the fashionable and courtly efforts of good society over here *as well as* popular activities in country and town (for instance such festivals as celebrate the coming of May with dances and games).

Such considerations are important if we want to see the development of spiritual life outside the Church in its proper perspective. However, it will not be denied that behind this changing interplay of social forces and influences there·*are* these two antagonistic factors, Church and burgherdom, as guiding spirits of the development. One of the manifestations of this hostility was the suspicious attitude of the Church towards many expressions of secular gaiety—it will presently be shown that this struggle was to become violently obvious in our own field of instrumental music, and even during the era of compromise between 1150 and 1300 we cannot say that the Church was exactly kindly disposed towards it.

In the words of B. L. Manning, it " sanctioned what it was obliged—after many protests—to tolerate."[1] And even during this period the critics of instrumental music were active enough : e.g. Nigellus, præcentor in the Church of Canterbury and favourite of Bishop William de Longchamps.[2] In *Aldhelmi Ænigmata* there is a very rude poem directed against various instruments,[3] also a cruel satire on a trumpet.[4] A picture of

---

[1] *The People's Faith in the Time of Wyclif*, 1919, p. 124.

[2] In his " Speculum Stultorum " (The Mirror of Fools), *Rerum Britannicarum medii ævi scriptores, Satirical Poets and Epigrammatists* (12th century), Vol. I, 1872 (ed. Thomas Wright).

[3] Ibid., Vol. II, 1872, p. 540. Here is the poem and ·a rough translation :

De barbito sive organo	*On the lute, or perhaps the organ*
Quamvis ære cavo salpinctis classica clangant Et citharæ crepitant, strepituque tubæ modulentur; Centenos tamen eructant mea viscera cantus, Meque strepente stupent mox musica corda fibrarum.	Though the battle signals of the trumpet bellow out through the hollow brass, And the harps clatter, and the trombones move noisily up and down ; Yet my bowels belch up chants by the hundred, And when I start all those soulful musical gutstrings are dumbed as I blurt on.

[4] *De Salpinge, ibid.*, II, 556.

about 1200 shows a recorder blown by a bear,[1] and on a capital of the crypt at Canterbury Cathedral we see a shalm[2] played by a really abhorrent goat (a donkey next to it holds a cornet).[3]

The popular notion of Satanas with his fiddle or pipe, viewed in this historical context, appears in a new light : it was the Church that gave him the fiddle or pipe, not to dignify him, we may be sure, but to degrade the instrument.

> A Winnock Bunker in the East—
> There sat Auld Nick in Shape o' Beast ;
> A Towzy Tyke, Black, Grim, and Large—
> To gie them Music was his Charge.
> He screwed the Pipes, and gart them skirl
> Till Roof and Rafters a' did dirl.[4]

It would be interesting to find out to what degree musical instruments in the middle ages played their part in witchcraft. It has been said that many ordinary men who felt that Church and state were leagued against them turned for consolation to the old enemy of Christian mythology, the Devil. The French historian Michelet declares that " the medieval peasant would have burst but for his hope in Beelzebub." Witchcraft must have been widespread and dangerous in its uncontrollable fierceness, and musical instruments have been connected with magic beliefs as long as music has existed, from the fertility charms of the ancient bullroarer to the ' hautboys' for the witches' cave in Shakespeare's *Macbeth*.[5] Even such a distinguished writer as Alanus Anglicus (12th century)[6] emphasises the *magic* powers of music. There is the story of the Sacrilegious Carollers (1303) : thirteen persons of both sexes (the chief being the priest's daughter) danced in a churchyard and instrumental musicians accompanying the ceremony are shown in a picture illustrating the incident.[7] We know from the end of the middle ages that instrumental music was an integral part of witchcraft ceremonies. In the 15th and 16th centuries " trumps " or " Jew's

[1] Galpin, p. 137.

[2] Early predecessor of the oboe family.

[3] For pictures see Galpin, pp. 80, 140, 159, 170, and 190.

[4] *Tam o' Shanter*, by Robert Burns.

[5] See also Chaucer, *House of Fame*, I, 169, on jugglers and witchcraft.

[6] Alani Anglici Anticlaudianus ; see *Rerum Britannicarum medii ævi scriptores*, Satirical Poets and Epigrammatists, Vol. 2, 1872, pp. 323 ff.

[7] Margaret A. Murray, *The God of the Witches*, p. 113 and plate XIV.

harps " (jaw's harps) were played at such celebrations.[1] Jonet Lucas at Aberdeen was accused that " thou and they was under the conduct of thy master the Devil, dancing in a ring, and playing melodiously upon one instrument."[2] Occasionally one person held the position of " piper to the Devil," and indeed pipes (as accompaniment of the dances) or sometimes citterns seem to have been the most frequent instruments on such occasions.

In view of the often anticlerical use of many instruments of music some churchmen extended their hatred of such instruments to every kind of instrumental practice. A vivid example of this radical attitude is contained in a sermon by Ethelred Abbot of Rivaulx, Yorkshire (end of the 12th century), who did not even approve of the use of organs : " To what purpose, I pray you, is that terrible blowing of Belloes, expressing rather the crakes of Thunder, than the sweetness of a voyce ? " But when the attempt was made to introduce instruments apart from the organ into the churches Ethelred boiled over with rage : " The common people standing by, trembling and astonished, admire the sounds of the Organ, the noyse of the Cymballs and Musicall Instruments, the Harmony of the Pipes and Cornets."[3] When it actually happened that honours were granted to minstrels or other secular musicians there were protests from the high Church officials such as John of Salisbury who, in the 12th century, thundered against the " fools of this age who pour out rewards to minstrels and monsters of that sort."[4]

*   *   *   *   *

After the brief interlude of the 12th and part of the 13th century the attitude of the Church towards instruments underwent a new change. It is perhaps too early to pass a final opinion on the exact nature of this change, since the evidence at our disposal is scanty and somewhat contradictory. But as far as can be ascertained, it seems that the Church authorities had more or less generally accepted the organ in the service. There are also a number of examples of certain stringed instruments and some privileged musicians having been tolerated. But in general the Church authorities resumed their denunciation of instrumental playing. In the struggle for and against these " devil's tools "

[1] M. A. Murray, *Witchcraft in Western Europe*, 1921, p. 55.
[2] *God of the Witches*, p. 67.
[3] Translated by Prynne ; see Davey, p. 16.
[4] Chappell, *Old English Popular Music*, 1893, I, p. 5.

their antagonists had won the day and their hatred became most violent whenever it was directed against the *itinerant* musicians (who formed the vast majority of minstrels in later medieval England).

The reason for this stiffening of the opposition to musical instruments is not far to seek.

In its early days the *ecclesia militans* had to proscribe as unholy anything that recalled the sins of its Roman and pagan opponents. From the middle of the 13th century onwards the Church once more (and even more passionately) attacked instrumental music, but now it was on the defence against the new and progressive middle classes which began to challenge the very basis of its existence. About 1300 the old medieval order was definitely on the decline. The old domainal and manorial system which formed the economic foundation of Church and nobility, had given stability, but now it " checked progress and denied freedom."[1] With the increasing demand of the popular masses for greater social, national and economic independence the Church progressively lost its moral and intellectual leadership—especially when from the 14th century onwards the prophets of new spiritual and social freedom appeared within its own ranks.[2] The Church, however, " refused every concession, effected no reform and called in brute force to repress heresy."[3]

The development of its attitude towards music reflects the change which was going on in the wider field of Church policy. The minstrel's art of instrumental playing, grudgingly tolerated for a transitory period, had become too powerful. The unorthodox element in the long run must not be allowed to invade the medieval church in the form of recorders, shalms and

[1] G. M. Trevelyan, *History of England*, 1934, p. 237.
[2] Here is one of the stories that illustrate the somewhat changed attitude of many ordinary people to Church music which was becoming a more and more isolated and intellectual affair : " Jacobus de Vetriato tellis how that ther was a preste that trowid he was a passand gude synger, not-with-standyng he was not so. So on a day there was a gentyl-womman that satt behynd hym and hard hym syng, and sho began to wepe ; and he, trowyng that sho wepid for swettnes of his voyse, began to syng lowder than he did tofor ; and ay the hyer sho hard hym sung, the faster wepud sho. Than this preste askid hur whi sho wepud so as sho did, and sho answerd hym agayn and sayd : ' Sur, I am a pure gentill-womman, and the laste day I had no calfe bud¹ one, and the wulfe come and had it away fro me and evur when that I here you syng, onone I remembre me how that my calfe and ye cried (a)like.' And when the preste hard this, onone he thoght shame, and remembred hym that that thing (th)at he thought was grete lovyng unto God, was unto Him grete shame and velany ; and fro thens furth he sang nevur so lowde." (From Coulton, *Social Life in Britain*, 1919, p. 266).
[3] G. M. Trevelyan, *History of England*, 1934, p. 245.

fiddles. And many minstrels really must have become quite a menace if we are to believe such witnesses as the Abbot of Rivaulx.

The fight against the minstrels and their instruments was not, on the whole, as violent in England as on the Continent. There these " joculatores," " mimi," " ministeriales " or " histriones " were often outlawed " while alive " or at least prevented by law from entering towns. Minstrels were often excluded from the mass. To mention only one of many examples, the " Sachsenspiegel," a German juridical code of the 13th century, contains a law according to which a minstrel was only allowed to hit the *shadow* of anyone who might have done him wrong.[1] The famous Bull of Pope John XXII, decreed from Avignon (1322) against the " secularisation " of service music, is an illustration of the same policy ;[2] yet to quite a high degree the later medieval English Church too did its best to discourage the minstrelsy and, as a matter of fact, all kinds of secular activities. There, were repeated attempts to stop dancing[3] and from 1337 onwards to prohibit even games as apparently harmless as ball-play,[4] wrestling, the stone-throwing sport, etc., where many fellows " vainly glory in their bodily strength and exercise themselves in such like things."[5]

The Council of Oxford, following the rule of the Lateran Council, decided that members of the clergy " must not listen to actors, jigglers and minstrels."[6]

The Statutes of St. Paul's of the year 1450 direct the beadles " to keep off and throw out the minstrels who make their noises, void of devotion, openly before the altar of the Virgin and the Cross."[7] Scottish minstrels were handled even more roughly. In 1449 the King, obviously on the instigation of the very discredited Scottish Church, asked the minstrels to live decently

---

[1] Johannes Wolf, *Geschichte der Musik*, Berlin, 1930, I, p. 35. H. Riemann, *Geschichte der Musiktheorie*, Leipzig, 1898, p. 210, says that instruments were generally out of the church by the advent of the 13th century. But on the basis of our evidence the date should be put slightly later, as far as England is concerned.

[2] See E. Dickinson, *Music in the History of the Western Church*, 1902, p. 146.

[3] G. G. Coulton, *The Medieval Village*, Cambridge, 1925, pp. 559–600.

[4] Ibid., p. 93 (Law of 1382).

[5] Ibid., p. 561 (Decree of 1401).

[6] E. K. Chambers, *The Mediæval Stage*, 1903, p. 39.

[7] " . . . quod menestrallos coram altaribus Virginis et Crucis indevote strepitantes arceant et ejiciant," Statutes, i, 5, 4, cf. W. S. Simpson, *Register of St. Paul's*, 1873, p. 72.

or to leave the country ; any minstrels found forthwith should have their ears cut off and, if caught again, be hanged.[1]

Musical theorists often followed the lead of the authorities. Simon Tunstede, writer about 1350, refers contemptuously to minstrels whose music had nothing to do with art.[2] In a treatise called *De Origine et Effectu Musicæ*, written by an English monk about 1400, it is asserted that " Roundellas, Ballads, Carollas and Springas " (that is to say, the secular songs and dances which were often played by instruments) are " fantastic and frivolous ", and that " no good musical writer has ever thought it worth to explain their texture."[3]

Many musical instruments disappeared from the churches during the 14th century, especially the small ones that could be carried about and thus smelt of " wayfaring."

Robert Manning, in 1303, still mentions some of them in a poem about the life of Bishop Groteste (1253) :

> Yn Harpe and Taborn and Symphan gle
> Worschippe God yn Trumpes and Sautre ;
> In Cordes, yn Orgones and Bellis ringyng,
> Yn all these worschippe the hevenes Kinge.[4]

---

[1] " Gif there be onie that makis them fuiles (jesters), and ar bairdes or uthers sik like runnaris about, and gif onie sik be fundin, that they be put in the king's waird, or in his irons (stocks) for their trespasses, als lang as they haue any gudes of their awin to liue upon—that their eares be nailed to the trone (pillory) or till ane uther tree, and their eare cutted off, and banished the cuntrie—and gift thereafter they be funden againe, that they be hanged." See W. Dauney, *Ancient Scottish Melodies*, Edinburgh, 1838, p. 72. More decrees against histriones (especially during the second half of the 13th to the end of the 14th century) are quoted by Helen Waddell, *The Wandering Scholars*, 1932, pp. 261 and 265 ff. Orders dealing with Welsh minstrels are contained in Brit. Mus. MS. Add. 15003 and Ms. Add. 15038 ; they contain a statute attributed to Griffith ap Cynan (1055–1137) relating to minstrelsy, and the ancient order of Deheubarth, " Llyma Drefn ar wyr wrth Gerdd Dafawd " (before Griffith).

[2] Coussemaker, *Scriptores IV*, p. 295 f.

[3] See Hawkins, *General History of the Science and Practice of Music*, I, 246.— A 15th century monk complains that most singers sing " naughty " songs for " empty renown " ; he warns his colleagues " for God's sake " not to do so, so that they may be led " to the everlasting fatherland " :

> Cantatores sunt plerique
> Quorum artes sunt inique.
> Vanam querunt gloriam.
> Libens cane non inane
> Propter deum ut in evum
> Ducaris in patriam.

This verse occurs in a poem composed in motet style contained in the " Old Hall " MS. which is assumed to have been completed between 1438 and 1444. The Old Hall MS. (large collection of motets mostly liturgic) was edited by Rev. A. Ramsbotham and Dom Anselm Hughes, 1933–35.

[4] Galpin, p. 56.

But in 1397 Bartholomæus de Glanville triumphantly announces,:
" And nowe holy chyrche useth only this instrument of musyk
(the organ), in proses, sequences, and ympnes : and forsakyth
for men's use of minstralsye all other instrumentes of musyk."[1]
Here we have proof that the whole question of instrumental music
was not a side-issue, but that the Church considered it of great
importance, and that it had a well-considered policy towards it.
And if the Church in the 14th and 15th centuries was no longer
strong enough to suppress such instrumental music as was produced outside its immediate jurisdiction, at least it kept it out of
its service as far as possible.

There were exceptions to the rule. But they only confirm the
vigour of the rising forces of secular music that defied the strictures
of the Church ; the minstrels were not ecclesiastical but *secular*
musicians.

These exceptions, one of which has already been mentioned,[2]
are found chiefly in the popular mystery plays. These, however,
were not organised by the Church but by craft guilds through
private theatre companies and they are but another indication
that in some measure an interaction of the cultural activities of
the various social forces was taking place all the time. These
plays formed a connecting link between the Church and the
secular world. There is often great freedom and popular
originality in the mystery plays. They were sometimes enormous
in scope, size, duration and expense. The people developed
them further and further away from the Church pattern of
religious practice. They express ideas of a religion with which
the people were at home and which they freely developed in
their own comic imagination. There were comic episodes in the
middle of these performances, there were shepherds' dances and
other secular scenes. It is quite true that there were many con-
demnations of clergy who took part in them.[3]   Such condemna-
tions express the anxiety of the Church to prevent these plays
(and with them clerical control of the people's religious belief)
from getting out of hand. But just as often these plays enjoyed
a certain amount of patronage or at least the connivance of the
Church. It must be remembered that the craft guilds of the
towns which organised these plays in many cases helped both to

---

[1] *De proprietatibus rerum*, 1397.   See Hawkins, p. 268.
[2] See above, p. 21.
[3] See Coulton, *The Medieval Village*, Vol. II (Appendices).

build and to endow the churches outside which they were con-
ducting the plays.

Minstrels were often asked to perform in such plays. In the
account books of the companies there are mentioned minstrels as
pipers, harpists, lutists, drummers, and flutists. Much of this
music must have been purely instrumental ; altogether instruments appear to have been used in these plays because of the
great appeal they had for the popular masses, for whom the
mystery plays were intended as propaganda so-to-speak " in their
own language." In the " Assumption of the Virgin," shown in
Coventry about and after 1400, a remark is found : " Here the
angel descends while citherns play." In " Origo Mundi," of
Cornwall, of the same period, the minstrels are asked " in the
name of the Father to pipe immediately."[1]

There is further the question of the slow " tenores " (cantus
firmi) in the motets in the already mentioned Old Hall Manuscript.[2] This collection contains pieces mostly liturgic which were
used in the Royal Chapel, presumably during Henry VI's reign.
Some of these complicated vocal scores contain biblical cantus
firmi with extremely long notes which seem to be unfit for vocal
performance ; these may, indeed, have been intended for organs,
but it is just possible (though perhaps unlikely) that they were
played by some soft wind or string instruments of long sustaining
power.[3]

As far as can be seen there are few definite instances of instrumental music (harps and dulcimers only) having been used within
14th- and 15th-century churches.[4] In the account books of
certain priories, such as Thetford, Maxstoke, and Durham, we
find occasional evidence of the use of instruments in churches.
Few though the instances of monks practising gitterns or listening

---

[1] H. E. Poole gives more examples from " Creation and Fall and Death of Abel "
(Chester, 14th and 15th centuries).

[2] See above, p. 29, footnote ([3]).

[3] As a typical example we mention Th. Damett's Salvatoris mater pia, No. 107,
p. 89b, 90a.

[4] Early in the 15th century a train of pilgrims were allowed to have bagpipes
with them to cheer them up on their journey ; see Galpin, p. 176. A number of
instruments once again appear as ornaments in churches (again almost exclusively
lutes, crowds and psaltries). Burney mentions that in the annual account-roll of
the Augustine priory of Bicester (Oxfordshire) for the year 1431, an entry is made
of a fee expended for a harpist ; see History of Music, II, 428. In the Maxstoke
Priory account books there are two items of rewards given to minstrels (" cuidam
citharistæ, 6d.") and a sum to " Duobus citharistis de Coventry." Further
examples given in E. K. Chambers, The Mediæval Stage, 1903, pp. 243-245.

to minstrels' vielles in the 14th and 15th centuries may be, we may, I think, be sure that they represent a spiritual revolt within the Church. The anomalous fact that, though the Church did not want instruments, in some churches they were heard all the same, illustrates a breach within the clerical organisation itself. In fact, the Church was seething with controversy, with an uneasy, sinister expectancy of approaching climax.

Although there were these belated compromises on the part of the Church the general trend of its policy towards instrumental music stands out—a policy which was the musical counterpart of the ecclesiastical obscurantism of the opponents of the Lollards and the jailers of Bishop Pecock. And this policy was fraught with danger.

Rejected and despised, the outlawed musicians turned against their persecutors and criticised the established order. During the 14th century, especially during its latter half, instrumental minstrels and other itinerant musicians sometimes became a real menace to the authority of Church and State.[1] Now the true nature of medieval instrumental music as part of the struggle of the lower classes for individual freedom and secular gaiety begins to be obvious. While the authorities " showed indulgence to the armed retainers of the great, they feared the rounds made by those glee men with no other arms than their vielle or tabor, but sowing sometimes strange, disquieting doctrines under colour of songs. These were more than liberal, and went at times so far as to recommend social or political revolt."[2] They sang of the heavy taxes imposed on the peasantry by monasteries and manors alike ; they sang of the vice of the monks and the infamy of many distinguished rogues.

A minstrel (reign of Edward II) sings about the lot of husband-men of his time :

> Ich herde men upo mold make much mon,
> Hon he beth—tened of here tilyynge,
> Gode yeres and corn bothe beth a-gon,
> Ne kepeth here no sawe ne no song syng.
> Now we mote worche, nis there non other won,
> Mai ich no lengore lyve with my lesinge ;

---

[1] See the treatise of Thomas de Cobham (Bishop of Salisbury) (1303) against the ministrelsy ; cf. E. K. Chambers, *The Mediæval Stage*, I, pp. 60 f. and II, pp. 262–3.

[2] Jusserand, pp. 211–212.

Yet ther is a bitterore bid to the bon,
For ever the furthe peni mot to the kynge.[1]

In 1402 the House of Commons accused by name the Welsh minstrels as fomentors of trouble and causers of rebellion :

Item : That no westours and rimers, minstrels or vagabonds, be maintained in Wales, to make kymorthas or quyllages on the common people, who by their divinations, lies, and exhortations are partly cause of the insurrection and rebellion now in Wales. Reply : Le roy le veut.[2]

The songs of the Peasant Wars are known examples of such 'exhortations.'[3] Outstanding among them is " The Cutty Wren " which, it is interesting to note, is composed in an ancient Church mode (Mixolydian).[4] Robin Hood, the friend of the poor and ordinary folk, was a favoured champion of minstrels' songs and ballads :—[5]

I can rymes of Roben Hood and Randal of Chester,
But of our Lord and our Lady I lerne nothyng at all.
(Piers Ploughman)

The " Scholares vagantes " were considered to be particularly

---

[1] *The Political Songs of England*, ed. Th. Wright, Edinburgh (Bibliotheca curiosa), 1884 Vol. II p. 78 ff. Ibid. songs against the clergy, the King's taxes, etc. (Vol. III, pp. 30, 60, and others).—Here is a rough translation of the above song :

> I heard men on the land making much moan,
> Mournful they are, anxious over their tilling,
> Good years and corn are both gone,
> and here there is no talking, nor no song sung.
> Now we must (seek) work, there is nothing else for it,
> I can no longer live with my loss (my gleaning ?)
> Yet there is still a bitterer burden to their complaint,
> For every fourth penny must (go) to the King.

[2] *Rolls of Parliament III*, 508 (quoted by Jusserand, p. 212). A German musician (piper), the shepherd Hans Boeheim of Niklashausen, usually called Pfeifferhans, actually started the movement of the Peasants' Revolts in Central and Southern Germany (1491). In this country the great ecclesiastical and historical writer Giraldus Cambrensis (Gerald de Barri ; see below, p. 37) was once accused of inciting the Welshmen to rebellion (see *Encycl. Brit.* under Giraldus Cambrensis).

[3] Full text of John Ball's sermon in G. G. Coulton's *Social Life in Britain*, 1919, p. 359.

[4] See also A. L. Lloyd on " The Hunt of the Wren " (Manx) and other songs from the Peasant Wars (*The Singing Englishman*, London, 1944.) The " Cutty Wren " has been published and recorded by the Workers' Music Association, London, 1939.

[5] See also J. Ritson, *Robin Hood Ballads*, London, 1865.

dangerous and anti-clerical. One of them (late 13th century, presumably English or Northern French) lets fly thus :

> . . . Rome that is the head of the world, but this head is unclean, and unclean is whatever it touches. . . . It is but a great market where they sell and buy prebends. . . . If you come before the Pope, always remember : the poor has no position before him, his favour only goes to him who brings gold and silver with him.[1]

From the middle of the 14th century onwards, it was particularly the Jig which was connected or associated with oppositional and even seditious anti-Catholic plays.[2] In the 15th century, the Jig (later Gigue) was a dance in fast and stirring rhythms, well suited for the purpose of inciting people to disaffection.

One might gain the impression from the number of references quoted that instrumental music was, after all, just as much in the foreground of official medieval life as poetry or singing in the churches. But this is not the case. Let us state then once again quite unequivocally that instrumental music as a whole was of small importance in *official* medieval life compared with vocal music, especially vocal religious music.

True, in later medieval England the instrumental music of the popular classes was never quite so repressed as for instance in Germany and Spain. But even in England instrumental music, hampered and pursued by continual ecclesiastical attacks, could advance only slowly and painfully.

Yet the ordinary folk in old England succeeded in keeping instrumental music alive and active all the time. Popular instrumental music, which was kept down through all the centuries of the middle ages, thus appears as a matter of great importance as an *unofficial* and often underground musical activity.

A 14th century village poet[3] confesses bashfully that sometimes when idleness overcomes him—and only then !—he takes to playing musical instruments. Thus speaks Idleness :

> I teche hem daunce,
> And also, ffor ther lady sake,

---

[1] From a poem " Utar contra vitia carmine rebelli," contained in Brit. Mus. MS, Harley 978. See also O. Hubatsch, *Die lateinischen Vagantenlieder des Mittelalters.* Goerlitz, 1870, p. 52 f., and J. A. Schmeller, *Carmina Burana,* 1883.

[2] Ch. Read Baskervill, *The Elizabethan Jig,* Chicago, 1929, Ch. 1.

[3] Quoted by H. S. Bennett, *England from Chaucer to Caxton,* London, 1928, p. 91.

Endyte lettyrs, and songys make
Up-on the glade somerys dayes,
Balladys, Roundelays, vyrelayes.
I teche hem ek, (lyk ther ententys,)
To pleye on sondry Instrumentys,
On harpe, lut, and on gyterne,
And to revelle at taverne,
Wyth al merthe and mellodye,
On rebube and on symphonye.

This passage shows that instrumental performance was popularly regarded as an accomplishment even while it was discouraged by the Church. Instrumental music grew up original and healthy in the atmosphere of natural naivety which only popular practice could provide. In Germany the minstrels of the central middle ages were expected to be able (apart from throwing little apples and catching them with knives, imitating animals' voices, etc.) to play not less than nine string and wind instruments.[1] Pictures from this country suggest a parallel development over here. The minstrel accompanied his singing by playing the vielle[2] and other instruments, or he played purely instrumental music.

Chaucer was fond of playing harp and dulcimer and of listening to purely instrumental music of which he talks as of something well-established :

Many thousand tymes twelve
That maden loude menstralcyes
In cornemuse, and shalmyes
And many other maner pype,
That craftely pype
Both in dulcet and in rede,
That ben at festes with the brede ;
And many floute and lilting-horne,
And pypes made of grene corne.[3]

A considerable variety of instruments appeared and disappeared

[1] J. Wolf, *Geschichte der Musik*, I, 1930, p. 34 f.

[2] " Emisit cantum viellando," as it says in a Latin story of the 14th century ; see *Latin Stories*, ed. Th. Wright (Percy Society), 1842, p. 83.

[3] From *House of Fame*, book III, 1199 ff. For more quotations from Chaucer, see Sister M. E. Whitmore, *Mediæval English Domestic Life and Amusements in the Works of Chaucer*, The Catholic University of America, Washington, 1937.

in the course of the middle ages. We find almost all the names that are familiar to us now, together with names of instruments like ' nabulum,' ' tintinnabulum ' (presumably a small set of bells), ' pennola,' ' bombylium,'[1] the exact identity of which is difficult to define. There are the predecessors of the violin and viol, such as gigue, rebec, rubebe or rybyb, rota (or rotys of Alemayne, probably imported from Germany), vielle and fiddle. The metamorphosis of the crwth can be followed up in the long series of lyras, clarsechs or telyns and other harp instruments, while there are innumerable forms of lutes and cythers like the cytele or cythol, with a variety of hurdy-gurdy instruments. The forerunners of the pianoforte as well as of the harpsichord, such as dulcimer, dulsate, psaltrie or tympan, are found to have been played in England just as much as on the continent ; and there are many wind instruments : bagpipes such as the cornamuse (also called tympanum, symphony, or sambuca), reed instruments such as the shepherd's pipe, oboe, wait, shalm, pommer and others, instruments of the flute and recorder family, such as pipes or fyfes (tibiæ), sordines, rackets ; furthermore horns, cornets, trumpets, trombones, and percussion instruments like bells, drums, tabors, nakers, and triangles.[2] The rich variety of the instruments invented in the middle ages shows clearly the vigour of the popular musical interest that produced them. Several of these instruments were introduced from Moslem and other non-European and pagan sources (though certainly not by the Church authorities).

During the earlier centuries of the middle ages large wind instruments with majestic and far-reaching sounds were everywhere more highly esteemed than stringed instruments. This was obviously because horns and trumpets were more in use at the courts, especially at hunts, and in the army. The change in the respective valuation of instruments seems to have occurred during the 11th, 12th and 13th centuries. Johannes de Grocheo found that stringed instruments " occupy first place among all instruments." It was the vielle which was most popular among stringed

---

[1] Mentioned in Cotton MS., Tiberius C 6 (beginning of 11th century). Explanation of some of the names is given in " De proprietatibus rerum," see Hawkins, p. 268 ff.

[2] For details, see G. Hayes, *Musical Instruments and their Music*, London, 1930 ; Canon F. W. Galpin, *Old English Instruments of Music*, London, 1910 ; also K. Schlesinger, *Modern Orchestral Instruments and Early Records of the Precursors of the Violin Family*, London, 1910.

instruments, and a stringed instrument was considered to be able " to move the souls of those listening much more than trumpets or drums could have affected them."[1]

And what of the nature of the music itself?

There is little to be said of the instrumental practice of the earlier middle ages. No traces of any music have so far been found in our libraries, with the exception of a 17th-century MS.[2] containing notations of harp music which the writer of the MS. claims to be ancient Welsh (unfortunately he does not state how he obtained this music).

Only about 1250 does more reliable information appear, and it seems that from the 14th century onwards instrumental music developed along its own lines. We hear more and more often of instruments played not only in accompaniment of singing but also without singing.

Giraldus Cambrensis, famous writer (1146–1220), praises popular music in Ireland, Wales and Scotland in the most enthusiastic terms. He has a low opinion of the Irish of his time, but thinks that their instrumental music is superb and that " their musical skill is better than that of any other people."[3] Reading his essay one must assume that instrumental music was very much alive. In England it is said to have been of a less vivid character at this time,[4] although towards the end of the 13th century we learn from another source that popular instrumental playing in England was developing as elaborately as anywhere : Anonymus 4 (Coussemaker, *Scriptores*) talks about the division of longer notes into many small ones in instrumental music as opposed to vocal music, obviously meaning fast passages, scales and figuration.[5]

[1] *Sammelbände der Internationalen Musikgesellschaft*, 1899–1900, pp. 96 ff.

[2] British Museum, MS. Add. 14905.

[3] *Giraldi Opera*, vol. V, p. 135 (Descriptio Hiberniæ) : " In musicis solum instrumentis commendabilem invenio gentis istius diligentiam. In quibus, præ omni natione quam vidimus, incomparabiliter instructa est." Giraldus also says that the Scots knew citharas, bagpipes and crowds, the Welsh citharas, tibias and crowds, and the Irish citharas and the tympanum.

[4] Ibid. " . . . in Britannicis quibus assueti sumus instrumentis, tarda et morosa est modulatio . . ."

[5] Coussemaker, *Scriptores* I, p. 328 : " Iterato sunt et alii modi prout modi supradicti frangunt brevem vel breves in duas, tres vel quatuor, etc., prout in instrumentis. . . . Sonus sub uno tempore dici sonus acceptus sub tempore non minimo non maximo sed medio legitimo breviter sumpto, quod possit frangi veloci motu in duobus, tribus vel quatuor plus in voce humana, quamvis in instrumentis possit aliter fieri." Ibid. : " Et ulterius per consuetudinem raro frangimus, videlicet non monimus quatuor pro brevi in voce humana, sed in instrumentis sepius bene fit."

The same writer even speaks of the chromatic possibilities of instruments (" falsa musica "), as does John de Garlandia, another English writer on music, at the beginning of the 13th century.[1] A later theoretician discusses consonances (he only admits thirds, 'fifths, sixths and octaves) and continues : " Such treatment is obvious whether voices are used or instruments, either stringed instruments or the organ."[2]

The general observations of such theorists are particularly valuable in view of the almost complete absence of written examples of the music of the times ; on the whole the transmission of folk music through the tradition of mere practice is part of its essence. Least of all was any kind of instrumental music of the earlier and central middle ages preserved by writing, in view of the small value attached to it and the low social status of its bearers. But towards the end of the 13th century Anonymus 4[3] describes among other things that " simple dots " were used in notation of music for every sort of instrument. This means that at that time there was not only a firm tradition of instrumental playing but possibly also a system of notation. Then, towards 1300, there is evidence that instrumental music *was* written out, a fact which indicates that it was holding its ground, and that even theorists were beginning to take an interest in this popular art which proved so obstinately immune to the antagonism of the Church.

There is a tune from the same period still preserved in the Bodleian Library at Oxford[4] which gives at least some notion of what popular instrumental tunes must have been like towards the later middle ages. It is a dance-like piece in unison which spreads into three-part harmony shortly before the end ; here are a few extracts from it :

[1] Coussemaker, *Scriptores*, I, p. 166 : " Videndum est de falsa musica (i.e. chromatic alterations) quæ instrumentis musicalibus multum est necessaria, specialiter in organis."

[2] Fauxbourdon Anonymous 9 (from Brit. Mus. MS. Add. 21455), quoted by M. Bukofzer, *Geschichte des englischen Diskants und des Fauxbourdons nach englischen Quellen*, Strassburg, 1936, p. 138. The treatise was presumably written about 1400.

[3] Coussemaker, *Scriptores*, I, p. 339 (the treatise is shortly after 1272) : " Simplicia puncta quedam accipiuntur, prout . . . utuntur in quolibet genere omnium instrumentorum." See also J. Wolf, *Notationskunde*, II, p. 5 f.

[4] MS. Douce 139 (about 1270) ; facsimile in Stainer's *Early Bodleian Music*, London, 1902. See also L. Schrade, *Die handschriftliche Ueberlieferung der ältesten Instrumentalmusik*, Lahr (Baden), 1931.

Example 4 : 13th century dance tune.

How unlike the music of the Church !

Most conspicuous is the rhythmical simplicity of the piece. Its structure has nothing in common with the intricacies of contemporary vocal (i.e., ecclesiastical) compositions. At the same time this music requires quite a high degree of dexterity on the part of the performer, and the musical language is outspokenly instrumental in several respects if we consider the unvocal leaps of fifths up and down, the tone repetitions, and the rows of sequences throughout the piece. Such instrumentalisms are completely missing in all medieval music apart from instrumental composition.

The rhythmic qualities of the tune raise important problems of the relationship between medieval music and poetry. In the earlier centuries of the middle ages the boundaries between music and poetry must have been vague, as vague as those between vocal and instrumental music. The instrumental accompaniment of the singing of the Anglo-Saxon scop was presumably based on the same non-metrical, rhetoric-rhythmic style as the verses themselves, and the continental production shows that secular

vocal music until 1000 was on the whole most closely related in
style to religious music.

An important change occurred in certain 11th- and 12th-
century forms of Latin poetry, chiefly the " sequentia " of these
centuries which consisted of Latin rhymed verses with words set
to the freely improvised melodies of the " Allelujah " in the Mass.
These words were rhythmically and metrically regular, imitating
the poetic style and form of the older Christian hymni.   The
music was accordingly rhythmically regular and based on equally
long repeat periods :—

Example 5: Sequence " Prosa de Sancto Dionysio," by Adam
of St. Victor.[1]

The influence of Latin hymns, tropes, and sequences on the
development of rhythm and metre in France as well as in England
was most marked.   The songs of the troubadours and trouvères
used the metres of the ancient Greeks : trochæics, iambics,
dactyls, etc., thus bringing rhythmically measured music with
‘ bars ’ in the modern sense a stage nearer.

These changes are not peculiar to English or even to French
history, but since England was part of the Christian world of that
time they have to be mentioned here.   The change from the
non-metrical to the ‘ measured ’ rhythmic structures of the ‘modi’
clearly corresponds with the change from Anglo-Saxon alliterative
and declamatory poetry to Middle-English accent, rhyme and
metre, with Latin quantitative and accented measures representing a transitional period ;   and again popular music, as
closely linked up with popular poetry, was bound to be most
strongly affected by this change.

With metre and rhyme comes a greater degree of clarity within
the secular melodies themselves.   We observe the appearance of
parallel lines and periods in many songs and tunes.   The ‘melodic
energy ’ is more and more concentrated into the *end* of each
melodic period.   The melodic development of each melodic line

[1] From Joh. Wolf, *Geschichte der Musik*, I, p. 22.

is to be rounded off satisfactorily, in conformance with the rhymes in the poetry.

The final stage in this vital process of shaping rhythm and metre is the so-called ' mensural ' music (from the 13th century) which provides definite time values for each single note (maxima = 2 longæ ; longa = 2 breves ; brevis = 2 semibreves ; semibrevis = 2 minimæ ; etc.) as well as definite bar measures (triple rhythm, common time, etc.). Mensural notation is, of course, quite indispensable as part-singing and part-playing (especially polyphonic part-singing) develop and the parts have to be rhythmically co-ordinated.

Popular instrumental music, wherever it was least affected by the more artistic treatment of musically more educated individuals, seems to have been far ahead of both Church and secular vocal music in the evolution of rhythmic clarity and metrical decision. It is as though the theorists who laid down the new systems of practice, performance and notation, were in fact guided by the rules and customs of the wandering minstrel. There are clear parallel periods and distinct phrases. Similar vocal forms such as the Northern French ' lay ' and ' rondo,' seem here reduced to the utmost metrical simplicity.

A further change is that our little dance tune is in common time (two-in-a-measure) which in the 13th century is still little used in Church music. The Church prescribed 'triple rhythm' (three-in-a-measure) as a symbol of the Holy Trinity.[1] Two-in-a-measure at that time is almost invariably non-Church and often enough anti-Church.

Yet at least as important as the rhythmic and other instrumental peculiarities of this tune is its harmonic and tonal structure. The whole popular approach to music, as opposed to the ecclesiastical use of the art, is here illustrated in one simple example. For the frequently observed phenomenon that early English popular music uses full-grown major and minor ' modes '[2] is clearly confirmed in this little tune, and the question of these melodic modes is of the utmost importance.

The Church did not employ major and minor, although towards the end of the middle ages they were theoretically

[1] See below, p. 68.

[2] The term " mode " (modus) has a variety of meanings in medieval music. In this case " mode " means " type of scale " and should not be confused with the use of the word as characterising " rhythmic patterns " as it did in the previous paragraphs.

admitted in the modal system as ' Ionian ' and ' Æolian.'[1] The
Dorian, Lydian, and other modes of the Gregorian choral
suited the purpose of the Christian liturgy best, for the following
reasons.   First, these basic modes of the medieval chant, are
based not on a complete scale ranging from prime to octave
but rather on hexachords.[2] They have no ' leading note ' which
like b to c, leads back to the ' finalis,' the tonic note of a piece,
by a half-tone, the shortest possible interval of the scale.   That
means that the close functional relationship between dominant
and tonic (in the sense of modern harmony) is foreign to the
Church modes ; which again signifies that the most important
means of building up emotional developments is denied to the
Church modes.[3] Secondly, the Church modes are not organised
(and cannot be organised) upon the harmonic base of con-
sonant triads, consisting of prime, third, and fifth, upon which
all recent music (except some of the most recent) is built.   The
Church modes are usually based on two melodic ' axis ' tones :
the ' finalis ' on which the song starts and ends, and the ' repercussio,' the tone round which the melodic line mainly circles
during the song.   The ' repercussio ' is in the main modes either
a fifth (Dorian, Lydian and Mixolydian) or a sixth (Phrygian)
above the ' finalis.'

Example 6 : Antiphon " Statuit."[4]

The melody is in the Dorian mode.   ' D ' is finalis, ' a ' is reper-

[1] Notker Balbulus names the tones of the scale " A " to " G " which suggests
minor ; but it is interesting to note that in doing so he refers to *instruments*
(psalterium and lyra).   See Gerbert, *Scriptores*, I p. 96.
[2] Scales that consist of only six tones, e.g. the Dorian hexachord consists of
d, e, f, g, a and b.
[3] As late as the 15th century the seventh (i.e. the leading note) is considered
an evil by some theorists ; e.g. the author of *De Origine et Effectu Musicæ* (cf.
Burney, II, p. 416).   Many players and singers, however, sharpened the sevenths
in the old modes as they played and sang, even though church composers continued
to write strictly ' modally.'   See E. Blom, *Music in England*, 1942, p. 14.
The Lydian mode on F (modus quintus) which also contained the E as a possible
leading note to F, was by far the least frequent among the *permitted* modes of
medieval Church music.
[4] From Cod. 339, St. Gallen, p. 27 ; published in Adler, *Handbuch der Musikgeschichte*, II, ed. 1930, vol. II, p. 112.

cussio. It must be emphasised that although the repercussio is mostly the fifth tone of the hexachord scale, its relationship to the finalis is *not* harmonic in the sense of our modern dominant. The ancient repercussio is a kind of second ' home ' note for the melody. It ' dominates ' the *melody* of the Gregorian chant, but it is not the *harmonically* functional dominant.

How absolutely foreign the harmonic triad was to all early Catholic Church music will become clear if one considers the fact that the ' third '—major as well as minor—was considered and treated as a dissonance or, at best, an ' imperfect consonance ' up to the 13th century.[1]

It is these two qualities of the Church modes, the *absence of the* ' *leading note* ' (which denied the dramatic dominant-tonic progression to the music of the Church) and the *non-chordal structure* (which did not allow for the forming of those colourful major and minor triads), which make all medieval Church music appear so neutral, ethereal and passionless. Only the major and minor modes could express secular joy or distress, and for such elements there was no room in Church music. At the same time, the major and minor modes contain the ' leading note ' which held out the possibility of providing the dramatic tension of the dominant and the satisfactory solution of the tonic. Therefore the major and the minor, the step-children of the system of Church modes, became the modes of the secular, the popular forces of society.

The secular musicians . . . had a special predilection for the tonality on C. . . . For this very reason it was looked at askance by the ecclesiastical teachers and designated as " tonus lascivus." The itinerant musicians were more progressive than the theorists.[2]

---

[1] Two English theorists of the second half of the 13th century, Walter Odington and Anonymus 4 (Coussemaker), advocated for the first time the recognition of the thirds as consonances. See Coussemaker, *Scriptores*, I, pp. 200 and 358. The great influence of the popular modes (major and minor) and harmonies on ' official ' music in England during the 14th and 15th centuries is shown in Guilelmi Monachi *De preceptis artis musice* (15th century ; see Coussemaker, *Scriptores* III, p. 289 f.). See also below, p. 48.

[2] Carl Nef, *An Outline of the History of Music*, New York, 1935. Tonus lascivus : " the wanton mode."

Already Glareanus remarked in his *Dodekachordon* (1547) on the *popular* nature of the major key ; it was, according to him, the key of folk-songs and folk-dances. It would be interesting to find out whether the development of major and minor was directly assisted by the playing of certain wind instruments. The ancient horns, trumpets, etc. produced the *natural scale* (harmonic series) in which the first five harmonics constitute the major triad.

One of the new features which developed together with and within the major scale is the *melodic cadence*. The feeling of finality at the end of a melody in the major scale is strengthened by certain melodic formulæ which appear with increasing frequency in the secular music of the late Middle Ages. They laid the foundations of the later *harmonic cadences* which were to play such an important part in all post-Reformation music.

Is the major key found more frequently in medieval English than in continental music? The answer is in the affirmative. Indeed we may justly speak of it (together with the harmonic-melodic technique of the ' fauxbourdon ' which will be discussed later on) as one of the first signs of a national character in the music of this country, as Gerald Hayes suggests in his analysis of the problem.[1] There was, moreover, a growth of nationalism among the people of England during the 14th and 15th centuries, due chiefly to the gradual permeation of feudal life with new social elements, more individualistic and less cosmopolitan in character, largely derived from new developments in trade and manufacture at home, particularly in relation to wool and cloth. In fact this new nationalism was expressed in the field of music towards the end of the 15th century by such men as John Major (born 1469 in N. Berwick), when writing of Cambridge where he was in 1493 :

> The bells of St. Osenay are the best in England, and *as in music the English excel all other nations*, so they excel in the sweet and artistic modulation of their bells.[2]

National characteristics in the cultural life of a country are and always have been chiefly determined by the characteristics of its *popular* art, and it has invariably been the transition from feudal to modern society that brought these characteristics to the surface. The secular gaiety chiefly of the major key remained one of the typical features of English music for centuries.

John Cotton (about 1100) was the first to consider beautiful a melody based on major and minor triads.[3]

Among the numerous instances of major and minor in early English music we refer once again to the Summer Canon (Example 2). After 1400 major and minor tonality as well as melodies

[1] *King's Music*, London, 1937, p. 39. Hayes mentions Welsh influences in connection with the spreading of the " modus lascivus."
[2] *A Miscellany Presented to J. M. Mackay*, 1914, p. 249.
[3] See Gerbert, *Scriptores*, II, p. 254.

based on triads, are found more and more often in the works of Church composers, for instance, in those of John Dunstable.[1]

To the major scale we have to add the pentatonic scale which has been the other mainspring of English and Scottish folksong ;

the scale on which " Auld Lang Syne " and so many other songs are based. It is difficult to say, at the present stage of research, what part the pentatonic scale played in medieval instrumental music, but it is a fact that the pentatonic scale is a very ancient feature of English and Scottish music in general. This is not the place to discuss the possibility of prehistoric connections between this scale and the Chinese and other Far-Eastern scale systems which are also pentatonic.

Recent analysis has also stressed that there exists a certain pentatonicism in the Gregorian melodies and that it is connected with the pentatonic elements in ancient Greek music. It seems to be a fact, however, that the pentatonicism of medieval English folk music has other roots and developed quite independently of the Church.[2]

Out of the popular practice of instrumental playing there also grew the tendency to group several instruments together, as is shown in the three-part episode towards the end of our 13th-century dance tune.

We know from Giraldus Cambrensis that part-*singing* was known in popular vocal music as early as the 12th century. He states that " in Wales they made descants to their tunes, in the same way that singers did to the plainsong of the Church," also that " singing in two parts was common in the North of England, and children tried to imitate it." The latter statement, which suggests singing in simple parallels, has been confirmed by the discovery of a Northern hymn to St. Magnus :[3]

Example 7 : Hymn to St. Magnus.

No--bi-lis hu-mi-lis magne martir stab-i-lis

---

[1] In Stainer's list of Dunstable's works, thirty-three among forty-six pieces are in the major, the others mostly in the minor. See *Sammelbände der Internationalen Musikgesellschaft*, II, pp. 1–16.

[2] It is mentioned by John Cotton ; see M. Gerbert, *Scriptores*, II, p. 234, also Lederer, *Über Heimat und Ursprung der mehrstimmigen Tonkunst*, Leipzig, 1906, I, pp. 287 and 348, and J. Yasser, Mediæval Quartal Harmony, New York, 1938.

[3] From Wolf, *Geschichte der Musik*, I, p, 62.

Furthermore Giraldus says in his frequently quoted *Descriptio Cambriæ* that the Welsh not only sang in two but often in many parts.

Instrumental group music—chamber music—is first foreshadowed in such purely popular activities as the already mentioned ' bordune ' practice,[1] i.e. the holding out of one sustained note while all kinds of melodic figuration took place in other instrumental or vocal parts. Originally these activities represented quite a casual co-operation of several instrumental players. As far as can be seen these tendencies were at first confined to the peasantry and the independent popular minstrelsy.

Again, the Abbot of Rivaulx's sermon[2] seems to have been directed against a still further advanced stage of combination of several instrumental parts when he denounced the " harmony of the pipes and cornets." Further, several pictures of very early times show in a primitive way ensembles of such instrumentalists ; for instance, there is a picture of a procession of musicians (11th century) where we can see rote, rebecs, and psalteries together, and a particularly beautiful scene from the 12th century where not less than nine musicians are active : chime-bells, harp, rebec, viol, recorder, pan-pipes, organistrum, psaltery and hand-bells. In a picture of an acrobatic performance from the 14th century there are two musicians, obviously ' ioculatores ' (jugglers), playing pipe and tabor, while a third person performs a dangerous acrobatic trick.[3]

Now we need not necessarily conclude from these instances that instruments appearing together in a picture were actually played together, although the possibility that that might have been so has to be admitted.[4] But certain it is that wandering minstrels meeting casually or travelling together *did* increase the fun (and the art value, for that matter) of their activity by playing on different instruments in consort (at first presumably they played in unison). There is some contemporary evidence to that effect.

---

[1] See above, p. 21, footnote about Anonymus 4. Giraldus Cambrensis gives this description of such instrumental ' ostinati ' (pedals) : " . . . sub obtuso grossioris chordæ sonitu, gracilium tinnitus licentius ludent, latentius delectant, lasciviusque demulcent " (*Descriptio Cambriæ*, VI, 189).

[2] See above, p. 26.

[3] F. W. Galpin, plates 21, 20 and 28. Similar scenes are on reliefs of the 11th century ; see Duncan and Crowest, *The Story of the Minstrelsy*, 1907, pp. 22–23.

[4] Ibid., p. 274. Canon Galpin himself has doubts whether the instruments shown together in some pictures have really been used together. Quotations from literary sources to this end are, of course, more convincing.

In a parable translated by Wycliffe there is this sentence : ". . . when he cam neere, he herde a symphonie and a crowde."[1] Ensemble music extended to brass instruments. In the *Confessio Amantis* Gower speaks of the " sounds of bumbarde and of clarionne with cornemuse and shalmele " (1393). In the *Sqyr of Low Degree* (about 1400) we are told that :

> Ther was myrth and melody,
> With harpe, getron, and sawtry,
> With rote, ribible and clokarde,
> With pypes, organ and bumbarde,
> With other mynstrelles them amonge,
> With sytolphe and with sawtry songe,
> With fydle, recorde, and dowcemere,
> With trumpette and with claryon clere,
> With dulcet pipes of many cordes.[2]

It seems that groups mostly (and more or less naturally) formed within similar categories of instruments : trumpets do not often occur in the company of dulcimers ; string instruments are usually mentioned together—soft with soft and loud with loud.

But for the evidence of the continuous growth of instrumental group music in the middle ages we are not dependent only upon pictorial and literary references.

There are three more dance tunes still in existence, from which we can get an impression of the character of 13th-century instrumental group music, in particular of the polyphonic technique of the early forerunners of chamber music. These dances,[3] which are all in triple rhythm, are to be considered as music of the rising middle classes ; such and similar types are described by Johannes de Grocheo[4] as Stantipes, Ductia and other dance forms.[5] They are all in two-part harmony ; there is always a consonance (either a perfect consonance such as a fifth, octave or unison, or a so-called ' imperfect ' consonance, which means a third or sixth) on the *main* beat of the bar, while all sorts of

---

[1] F. W. Galpin, p. 106.
[2] Ibid., p. 64.
[3] Brit. Mus. MS. Harley 978 ; MS. after 1225. Full transcription of the dances by J. Wolf, *Die Tænze des Mittelalters*, Archiv. f. Musikwissenschaft I, 1918–19, pp. 10 ff.
[4] See J. Wolf, *Die Musiklehre des Johannes de Grocheo*, Sammelbände der Internat, Musikgesellschaft I, 1899, pp. 93 ff. See also above, p. 22.
[5] These forms were used in Italy about 1300 ; see above, p. 22.

dissonances, consecutive fifths, consecutive octaves, etc., may occur during the latter part of the bar. The movement of the two parts is very largely opposite. Everywhere there are dance-like periods of 8 or 16 bars. One part has the real dance tune ; in the following example the tune is to be found in the bass, while the counterpoint in the superior part was obviously composed *after* the bass melody :

Example 8 : 13th century dance tune (for two instruments).

There follows a repetition of the whole of the three sections in the bass while a different counterpoint appears in the top part. There are simple periods ; there is always a ' question ' (*a*) and an ' answer ' (*b*), without much artificial complication or embarrassment. The speed is moderate. Again here is the radiant major key, as familiar in early English folk music as it is rare in Church music of the same time.

Church or no Church, in all its simplicity popular instrumental music appears as an art which had its own logic and its own laws of æsthetics. Yet the example just shown is only the first indication of the style which instrumental music was finding for itself. About the middle of the 14th century it became evident that the struggle of instrumental music for legitimate acknowledgement had entered a new phase.

Indeed, much was being altered in the public estimation of instrumental music as well as in the organisation and development of the ministrelsy itself. Approximately up to the first part of the 14th century instrumental music was ' unofficial ' in every respect : always kept down though sometimes tolerated and never successfully suppressed. After this time it became more and more respectable.

The close fabric of medieval society was gradually loosened.

Not that the secular power of the Church had gone ; its loss of moral prestige did not prevent it from retaining, for the time being, its privileges, its wealth and its mighty organisation.

But freedom of the individual, freedom of the mind—these basic demands of later English life and culture began to be announced in earnest. With the increasing influence of secular circles, as opposed to the overwhelming power of the Church, instrumental music gained, first of all, more recognition among the middle classes. In this development the influence of the peasant movement was of great importance : the cultural life of the peasantry, so vital for the development of instrumental music in the middle ages, was made known to the inhabitants of the towns. True, throughout the middle ages there had been a continuous trickle of villeins escaping to the towns. Invariably they had taken with them on their flight the tunes of the wandering minstrel, the dances and rounds of the village green.

But the art of the peasantry and the art of the townsfolk mingled to a far larger extent when both classes achieved a greater degree of emancipation from feudal rule. The cultural life of the towns in particular became more intensive and independent as they became powerful factors in the country's social life, especially in the 15th century when the textile industry was spreading into the rural districts and the great manufacturing colonies of Yorkshire, Gloucestershire, Wiltshire, and East Anglia.

The ' franklins ' or free yeomen were of particular importance for the development of music. Much of the balladry came from them, and certainly many of the early folksongs. They remained a vital cultural force for centuries and laid the foundation of much of the musical greatness of the 16th century.

These independent peasants were closely akin to the craftsmen in the towns. The towns, on the other hand, had developed their own forms of instrumental playing. In some of them (e.g. London, Coventry, Bristol, Norwich, Chester, York, Beverley, Lynn, and Leicester) the consolidation of a musical profession is expressed in the formation of guilds of ' waytes ' or ' waits.'

These watchmen of the 14th, 15th, and 16th centuries were employed by the town councils. They had oboe-like reed instruments which were also called waits.[1] About 1500 they also used sagbuts, horns and even strings. It was their duty as municipal bands to perform musical functions on great occasions, such as public plays, pageants, and other festivities (among them the mystery plays mentioned earlier), but they also had to do actual watchmen's service.

. This day it is agreed . . . that the waytes of this Citie . . . shall betwixte the hours of 6 and 8 of the clok at night, blow and playe upon their instruments the space of half an houre, to the rejoicing and comfort of the hearers thereof.

This order of Norwich city council[2] indicates an important part of the regular duties of the waits.[3] In view of the nature of this kind of performance as well as of the number and variety of instruments (" blow and playe ") it must be assumed that not only unison music was produced but also some kind of harmonies, preparing the ground for chamber music in yet another aspect.

Yet not only the rising merchant class but also feudal noblemen of various kinds began to take to the enjoyment instrumental music could provide. It found its way into the houses of more and more counts, dukes and princes, as a kind of secondary pleasure. In fact, in the 13th century minstrels had become quite welcome guests at many castles of the aristocracy, for they could entertain the knights as well as glorify in song their deeds and those of their ancestors.[4] Feudal lords, in particular of the 14th century, borrowed the popular music of the peasantry and towns, and only too often misused it. At that time instrumental music served, in such houses, as the seasoning of meals. During these dinners of the rich the music was frequently interrupted by the loud conversation and roaring laughter of the diners, but

---

[1] Medieval instrumentalists were often named after their instruments : pipe, drum, etc.   In the case of the waits the instruments were named after the function of the players. ,

[2] See J. C. Bridge, *Town Waits and their Tunes*, Musical Association Proceedings, ·1927–8.

[3] Rewards for the work of the waits increased during the 15th century.   The town council of Lynn decreed in 1431 " that the three players shall serve the community this year for 21 sh. and their clothing to be had of every house."   A few years later they received 20s. each, and clothing ; in return they had to " go through the town with their instruments from the festival of All Saints to the Feast of the Purification."   See Mrs. A, Green, *Town Life in the 15th century*, 1894, p. 65.

[4] For details, cf. Jusserand, p. 199.

also by the " crunching of the bones gnawed by the dogs under the tables, by the quarrels of the same, or by the sharp cry of some ill-bred falcon ; for many noblemen kept during dinner these favourite birds on a perch behind them."[1] Some distinguished people took a more active part. A highly-placed traveller of the second half of the 14th century was reported to have had great pleasure in listening to musicians at an inn. " Then come forward into the lord's presence the trumpeters and horn-blowers with their frestles (pipes) and clarions, and begin to play and blow very loud, and then the lord with his squires begin to move, to sway, to dance, to utter and sing fine carols till midnight, without ceasing."[2]

On the whole the medieval courts showed more tolerance towards the minstrelsy, vocal and instrumental, than the Church did. There are certainly numerous instances of early medieval courts having followed the Church in its denunciation of minstrels. To mention only one of them, Louis the Pious (d. 840) decreed that minstrels (histriones) should not be admitted to the palace, and in his edict minstrels are called " vile and infamous people " and ranked with thieves and prostitutes.[3] Yet from the time of the ancient scop to the wandering minstrel of the 13th century, stories tell of many musicians visiting courts and castles, and of kings offering the minstrels generous rewards.

" Sir Orfeo " in the famous 13th century romance is the symbol of the wandering minstrel. He is admitted to the " fair high castle of gold and silver and precious stones " and brought before the King and Queen. " How do you come here ? " said the King ; " I never sent for you, and never before have I known a man so hardy as to come unbidden." " It is our manner," Sir Orfeo said, " to come to every man's house unbidden,

> And though we nought welcome be
> Yet we must proffer our game or glee."

Then he played on his harp, and the King offered him whatever he should ask :

> " Minstrel, me liketh thy glee."

[1] Ibid., p. 203.
[2] *La Manière de Langage*, composed by an Englishman in French in the 14th century ; ed. P. Meyer, *Revue Critique*, Vol. X (1870), p. 273. See also Jusserand, p. 202.
[3] Boretius, *Capitularia*, I, p. 334.

Orfeo asked for the lady bright. " Nay," said the King, " that were a foul match, for in her there is no blemish but thou art rough and black." " Fouler still," said Orfeo, " to hear a leasing from a king's mouth " ; but the King let him go with good wishes.[1]

The story of instrumental music in the service of medieval kings has recently been described so exhaustively by Gerald Hayes that we may confine ourselves to a few summarising remarks.

In the earlier middle ages Court music was supplied chiefly by trumpets and trombones[2] apparently in mere fanfares which cannot really be called composed music.

But from the times of Henry III and Edward I (both 13th century) more and more is heard of musicians of all instruments gathering at the court. True, trumpeters, shalmists, and pipers alone appear to have at first belonged to the permanent staff of the royal music. But slowly viellists, harpists and others are engaged for certain occasions. In 1252 there is for the first time a mention of " the harpist of the King."[3]

And after instrumental music had staged its spectacular return to public life in the 13th century, it never vanished again from the royal households, but found indeed one of its main strongholds at the Court. Some kings even took an active interest in the art as composers or players, notably Richard II and Henry VI.

In the absence of any musical examples little can be said about the instrumental music itself which they loved and played, Certainly Court representation, display of pomp and might. always played a vital part :

> The princes, that war riche on raw
> Gert nakers strike and trumpes blaw
> And made mirth at thaire might.[4]

However, the vigorous dances of the peasantry, too, the homely tunes of the town waits, and the dainty rounds and virelais o French troubadours—they all were practised at the English courts by English, French and Spanish artists. The chronicles report occasional musical events on a considerable scale, such as

[1] Retold by W. P. Ker, *Medieval English Literature*, p. 125.

[2] See above, pp. 36 and 37. Galpin gives a number of early references to instruments used at court.

[3] Hayes, *King's Music*, p. 30.

[4] From a Song on King Edward's Wars, by Laurence Minot ; about 1352. See *Political Poems & Songs*, ed. Th. Wright, London, 1859, I, p. 69.

the Westminster Feast of 1306 where 25 harpers, 22 trumpeters, 9 violists, 8 crowders, 6 taborers, 3 gigours, 2 organists, 2 psaltry players, 2 bagpipes, and one lutenist, gitarist, citoler, nakers and chimes player were employed.[1]

Another famous instance is Richard of Maidstone's description of a great musical show given in 1393 on the reconciliation of Richard II with the City of London. On this occasion these instruments are said to have co-operated :

> Fistula, cistula, tibia, timpana, cum monacordo,
> Organa, psalteria, cimbala, cumque lyra,
> Zambuca, citharæ, situlæque, tubæque, viellæ,
> Buccina cum nablis, simphonicisque choris.[2]

In 1377, at an entertainment for young Prince Richard,

> in the night, one hundred and thirty citizens, disguised and well horsed, in a mummery, with sound of Trumpets, Sackbuts, Cornets, Shalmes and other minstrels . . . rode from Newgate . . . to . . . Kennington.[3]

And in 1502, to mention only one more event among many, a ladies' orchestra, consisting of 12 musicians (playing on " Clarycordis, dusymers, clarysymballs and such other ") entertained a distinguished audience at a pageant in Westminster Hall.[4]

The English Kings between 1250 and 1500 patronised instrumental music :

> . . . and he called for his pipe,
> And he called for his bowl,
> And he called for his fiddlers three.

But did an original, independent art of its own derive from the English courts before Henry VII, comparable to the art of

---

[1] Hayes, p. 31.

[2] Davey, *History of English Music*, p. 42. The exact meaning of some of these names is doubtful. Fistula is the recorder ; cistula the citola (pear-shaped guitar with flat back) ; tibia is a pipe ; timpanum (timpan) is not yet the kettle-drum but either a bagpipe or (more often) an Irish psaltry, just as psalterium and cimbalum, lyra (lyre) is a form of rebeb (rubebe, bowed instrument) ; zambuca (sambuca) is either a psaltry or a bagpipe (symphony) or even a trombone (saquebout = sagbut) ; cithara may be any harp, lyre, cither ; situla probably again the citola ; tuba a non-specified trumpet, probably straight ; viella is the vielle (bowed minstrel's viol) ; buccina is the old Latin trumpet which was usually curved, (but in the middle ages the buccina is straight and has a short tube) ; nablum may be either a string or a percussion instrument (nakers ?) ; symphonicus chorus is presumably a hurdy-gurdy.

[3] Burney, II, 368.   [4] Galpin, p. 64.

the Church on the one side and that of the peasantry on the other, or to the achievements of later absolutism ? Hayes believes that " if outwardly the Court led and the people followed, subconsciously the Court was influenced by the cultural tendencies of the people."

Throughout the centuries of the middle ages it certainly does not appear that the Court ever led in the field of *instrumental music*, or did more than make use of the art of the secular forces. And it never completely renounced its musical dependence on France—not even (or perhaps least of all) during the 100 years' war.

It was indeed fortunate for English music that the all-too-precious beauty of the Machaut or Landino type did not spread from the Court to popular music to such a degree as to drown it completely. Popular music never lost its originality and independence. It was always healthy, strong, and sensuous in the tonal-harmonic simplicity of its triads, in contrast to so many of the abstract, orderly constructions of the contemporary de Vitry and Bartolomeus de Padua. *It was the music of the popular forces in England which contained the elements that were to be decisive for the musical development of the whole nation.*

To recall the " Summer Canon," we recognised French influences as well as traces of ' polite ' art and of a highly technically and musically skilled mind in this amazing and prophetic little piece.[1] Here, too, we want to state again that it is the *popular* qualities of the tune which make it appear so vigorous and, after all these centuries, so delightful to sing and listen to. It is the gay beauty based on triads, thirds, and sixths which is the most conspicuous feature of this canon—this extraordinary synthesis of the simple and the complex, of the ' popular ' and the ' precious.'

However, materially the instrumental minstrelsy gained much by the increasing favour of the kings. The formation of chapels especially (particularly during the 14th and 15th centuries) assisted the consolidation of the instrumentalist's profession. In the towns the minstrels had long ago formed their brotherhoods, but in 1469 permission was granted also to the minstrels at the Court to "maintain, continue and augment a fraternity or guild."[2]

But with the increasing patronage of the courts, coinciding with the increasing demands that were being made on the

---

[1] See above, p. 23.   [2] Jusserand, p. 436.

minstrelsy in the towns, a very profound change came over the social structure of the minstrelsy itself.

By 1400 those minstrels who had been able to find permanent positions in either Court or municipal service, had become well-behaved and respectable citizens with regular (and sometimes very substantial) incomes, with servants, and valuable privileges, and with the outlook of well-established guildsmen—the " higher minstrelsy " who often accompanied the newly-elected Lord Mayor at his show through the town, and the navigator on his journey on the seas. At the same time the great mass of independent wayfaring minstrels began to degenerate. The 15th century saw on the one hand the evolution of the musical profession, on the other hand the rapid decline of the minstrelsy in the old sense.

It is certain that the development of the " liveries " considerably assisted this process. The great houses especially of the 15th century kept huge bands of liveried retainers (private armies)— the feature of the century and of the Wars of the Roses. With these retainers a great number of minstrels were gathered and maintained by the great houses—another step towards the settlement of part of the minstrelsy and the degradation of another part.

The guilds of the town waits and of the established royal musicians watched jealously over the activities of the ' lower ' or independent, non-established, and unlicensed minstrels, whom they kept away from their own places of work by rigorous means. In the efficiency of their measures against the independent minstrelsy these guilds sometimes surpassed the Church.

The wayfaring minstrels of the original medieval type kept themselves alive during the 15th and 16th centuries. But they were driven lower and lower, as they were wandering up and down the island as " common fyddelers," " trompoteres " or " systolyrs," amidst a world of firmly organised guilds and professions. Their existence became increasingly difficult, and also narrowed in scope and function, with the rise of the ' higher ' minstrelsy to settlement, recognition and wealth, brought about chiefly by the growing strength of the development of the burgherdom. A new class distinction made itself felt in the practice of the minstrelsy and of instrumental music itself. It expressed the rapid advance and consolidation of the towns as against the very unsettled conditions on the land ; it reflected the gradual dissolution of the villeins' medieval pattern of living.

The independent minstrel was lowered to the stage of a vagabond and beggar.

This process had already begun at the time of Edward II who, in 1315, decreed :

" . . . to the houses of meaner men that none (no minstrel) come unlesse he be desired, and that such as shall come so, holde themselves contented with meat and drynke, and wyth such courtesie as the maister of the house wyl shewe unto them of his own good wyll, without their askying of any thyng."[1]

This already struck hard at the independent minstrels. In 1467 the town of Coventry issued an order :

" . . . also yt ye wayts of yis Cite yt now be and hereaft to be shall not passe yis Cite but to Abbot's and Priors within 10 myles of yis Cite."[2]

Finally, by Edward IV's order the guild of the minstrels was authorised to " examine the pretentions of all such as affected to exercise the minstrel profession ; and to regulate, govern, and punish them throughout the realm."[3] The invention of the printing-press further accelerated the downfall of the itinerant minstrel who was formerly welcome as bringer of the latest news from all over the world.

Both classes of minstrels, however, the higher as well as the lower, derived from the same source, the old picturesque juggler, the man of the common people. These itinerant musicians of the earlier middle ages up to the end of the 13th century—law-breaking, rebellious, scandal-mongering, dirty, scraggy and utterly useless in the opinion of many rulers—were the real fore-fathers of our occidental instrumental art. They accompanied and assisted the rise of a new class of citizens to power ; they entertained and cheered them, and they contributed a good deal to their enlightenment. We have to express our admiration for their independence, their uncompromising courage, and their partisanship for the people and their ways and doctrines : an attitude which, in the end, led to higher and higher organisms of literary and musical forms, styles and practices.

During the 14th and 15th centuries with the rise of instru-mental music from the depths of anonymity to a more honour-able position, more complicated forms developed. Certain

[1] Poole, *Music in Early Drama*, p. 25.   [2] Bridge, *Town-Waits*.
[3] Poole, p. 25.

15th-century literary references to instrumental music suggest already a remarkable advance of instrumental composition on the path towards respectability. In many English chansons and motets that were practised at the Court and in other high society circles about and after 1400 the performers must have played single parts of the vocal score on instruments—at least *ad libitum*.

The beginning of this practice of playing some of the voice parts on instruments can already be seen in certain 14th-century compositions.

There are many motets, secular and religious, which contain contrapuntal parts without words. In the following piece[1] it appears not at all unlikely that the two lower parts were played by instruments :

Example 9: English Motet with two presumably instrumental parts ; time about 1375.

[Continued on next page.

[1] From J. Stainer, *Early Bodleian Music*, reprint from MS. Bodl. 264. It would be useless to transpose this music into a piano score with two systems ; if played on the piano it would not appear to make any sense at all. To those who would like to get an impression of the music a performance with two voices (alto and baritone) and two stringed bass instruments, preferably bass viols, is recommended. Speed of the piece is moderately slow.

Example 9—*continued*

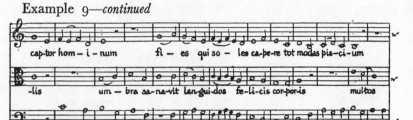

The two parts without words keep to the style of the vocal parts in similar motets. The piece is again closely related to French motets of the time, and it is of the kind that could only have been practised by musically educated persons.

In the 15th century the evidence of instrumental playing in highly evolved compositions increases considerably. The famous MS. Pepys 1236 (first half of 15th century) contains among its many vocal motets a four-part piece without words and wtihout religious or literary references (pp. 73b–74a). It might have been played by instruments, although it differs in no way from the usual style of vocal motets. The piece is in common time (four minims to a bar) which once again suggests secular use.

But there are also examples of parts in polyphonic music of which there can be no doubt that they were performed by instruments. In several 15th-century chansons there are so-called ritornells which bear, it is true, still few traces of instrumental peculiarities but are, nevertheless, certainly intended for instrumental execution. Incidentally they prove that most instruments were used in very aristocratic surroundings[1]:

Example 10: Ritornello to "Now wolde y fayne sum merthis mak."

[1] Examples 10 and 11 from Stainer, *Early Bodleian Music*, II, pp. 51 and 68. Stainer remarks : " Is it possible that the passages without words were intended for instruments alone ? I think so, and if this is the case, these songs present us with very early examples of symphonies " (p. 51). Example 10 is about 1425, Example 11 about 1445.

Example 11 : Ritornello to " O kendly creature of beaute perles."

We find in these Ritornells all the complications of the vocal music of the time : imitations, difficult counterpoint, rhythmicised fauxbourdon[1] and other features. They are obviously influenced by French and Italian models—again : the music of the aristocracy was more liable to be influenced by foreign elements than popular dance tunes.

From the point of view of instrumental interest the most important form of the century was, however, the non-aristocratic (or at least only partly aristocratic) carol or carolle. Its history in this country actually begins in the 12th century. It was originally a dance either accompanied by singing or by instrumental playing (instruments were used, for instance, by the " Sacrilegious Carollers " at the beginning of the 14th century).[2] If sung it is divided between a leader and the rest of the chorus ; where instruments were available they came in with the chorus, but at least some of the lines and verses were also accompanied by instruments. The form was extremely popular. Not only did it provide the formal material for the *ballad* but it also must have become an important field for the further development of instrumental playing.

---

[1] A 15th-century technique of harmony which is mainly based on the consonance of the prime, the third, and the sixth ; in modern terminology, " block harmony " :

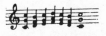

See Manfred Bukofzer, *Geschichte des englischen Diskants und des Fauxbourdon nach englischen Quellen*, Strassburg, 1936.

[2] See above, p. 25.

Here is an old Christmas Carol (time about 1460)[1] :
Example 12 : 15th century Christmas carol.

And here is the first part of a dance in the same style and rhythm as the carol.   In the copy that has come down to us it has words with it ; but originally it was quite obviously instrumental, for the words are awkwardly adapted and the phrasing in the text is irregular and unsymmetrical.[2]

Example 13 : English dance tune (time about 1425).

*   *   *   *   *

So there are indications that instrumental music was developing parallel with vocal motets and chansons, with the ballads and romances.   We recognise the vigorous advance of instrumental music during the 14th and 15th centuries and its importance for the future of the art.   And yet it cannot be repeated too often that even during that period, Church music was still *the* official art which absorbed most of the energies and talents of the community, even though instrumental music was, historically seen, on the increase.

In the course of the 15th century, the material and social basis of English musical life was slowly transformed.   The years

---

[1] From Chappell, *Popular Music of the Olden Times,* p. 42.
[2] From Stainer, *Early Bodleian Music* (reprint from Oxford Bodl. MS. Douce, 381).

between Henry IV and Henry VII were a time of preparation, of transition, a complicated and contradictory though germinating period. At a superficial glance this last stage of pre-Tudor England offers a picture of anarchy, of piracy, of noble lords imposing their will on the bewildered Commons by parading armed bands of retainers, of murderous battles fought between rival factions of the nobility, and of churchmen hunting down heretics from cloisters, castles and colleges. But in the 15th century there also appeared more numerous and more impressive signs of the coming of the new age.

Indeed the Church, after Langland and Gower, had become intellectually unproductive. Yet there were several schools of choral writing flourishing in 15th-century England. This, to be sure, was not due to any spiritual strength in the Church. It has already been mentioned that there was a cleavage within the Church organisation itself.[1] These schools resulted from the apparently paradoxical fact that the ancient polyphonic tradition of the Church was temporarily rejuvenated by the intrusion of just those reformatory elements which the Church endeavoured so hard to keep down. Such elements are easily recognised in the music itself : the stiff motet style (as exemplified on p. 57) gave way to greater freedom of writing, as seen chiefly in Dunstable's[2] work. The popular, tonal-harmonic fauxbourdon (faburden),[3] which was closely related to all the gay dances and rounds of the previous centuries, gained enormously in importance. Here, then, we have a parallel development to the one which was going on in instrumental music itself. The elements of secular emotion gained ground—there must have existed a strong ' human element ' especially among the lower clergy. The progressive, emancipationist forces of the time certainly affected the activities of the rank and file of Church musicians.

The great feudal lords who were busy cutting each other's throats had become an anachronism, and their basis of justifiable existence was crumbling. This condition they attempted to hide by ostentation and pretended refinement in their homes.

But on the other hand commerce and the cloth trade developed at an incredible pace. In spite of its still essentially corporate character the advance of the bourgeoisie increased the demands for individual freedom ; a process which is felt in all the cultural

[1] See above, p. 32.   [2] See above, p. 45.   [3] See above, p. 59.

spheres of the 15th century.   Besides, the new mercantile classes
were far more educated and literate than their ancestors.   They
could study things for themselves and think them over by
themselves.

The cultural forms of the old age decayed with the Church
and crisis-stricken feudal institutions, while on the other hand
the conditions for the great spiritual renaissance that was to
rise in the towns were being created (though by no means yet
fulfilled).   This applies to literature and art as much as to music.

For instrumental music, too, the 15th century was a time of
preparation.   Unfortunately, it must be said again, we have few
musical examples (beyond the instances quoted)[1] which could
give us more clues as to the nature of the music of the waits in
the towns and of the minstrelsy at Court.   This makes it very
difficult, for the time being, to assess the actual state of instrumental art especially in the second half of the 15th century.

Only one thing can be stated as certain.   Instrumental music
could not develop freely until the road was opened to its chief
promoters :   the progressive popular and mercantile classes, the
new forces.

[1] There is an instrumental piece (apparently a ground tenor) with the name of
Dunstable added to it in the British Museum Add. 31922 (fol. 36b).   If the piece is
really by Dunstable it would be his only known instrumental composition.

CHAPTER II

ON THE THRESHOLD OF MODERN TIMES

IT was the time of Henry VII and Henry VIII that brought the great change.

The virtual completion of the process of liberating the serfs and the subsequent fluidity of labour ; the " triumph of the sheep " (the transformation of the land from growing corn to producing wool) ; the upward surge of trade and industry ; the discovery of distant fair lands offering unlimited possibilities for trade ; and last but not least the invention of gunpowder to blast the ancient castles of the feudal nobility—these factors had spelt death to the middle ages.

The universal adoption of the reformed English language, the reappearance of Lollardry, the revived study of Greek and Roman ideas, the growth of English nationalism and finally the invention of the printing press to enlighten new masses of citizens—such were the spiritual expressions of the great revolution that was going on.

During Henry VIII's reign a stage in the development of England had been reached where a national emancipation had to take place. In 1536-40, in what is called the English Reformation, the secular power of the Catholic Church was challenged. The monasteries had been dissolved and their property, together with that of some of the older feudal noblesse, confiscated by the King in what might be called a ' revolution from above ' and distributed among merchants and certain representatives of the aristocracy. This was part of the struggle by which the national independence of England was established against the power and exploitation of the Catholic Church, and so was enthusiastically supported by the bourgeoisie and Parliament.[1]

---

[1] See Christopher Hill, *The English Revolution*, London, 1940, p. 21. Mrs. A. Green gives a lively picture of the social developments towards the end of the 15th century : " As soon as the village weaver began to make cloth for the Prussian burgher or the trader of the Black Sea instead of for his next door neighbour, the old conditions of his trade became absolutely impossible. The whole industry was before long altogether reorganised both from the commercial and the manufacturing side. The exporting merchants drew together in a new and powerful association known as the Merchant Adventurers. Meanwhile the army of workmen at home was broken up into specialised groups of spinners, weavers, larders, fullers, shearers and dyers. The seller was more and more sharply separated from the maker of goods. Managers and middlemen organised the manufacture and made provision for its distribution and sale." (*Town Life in the 15th Century*, London and New York, 1894, Vol. I, p. 67).

The merchants quickly gained decisive influence. Vital rights for the merchants were established, a kind of merchant nobility settled on the land and strongly consolidated itself in the towns. With them the whole mass of middle-class citizens in the towns achieved increasing importance. The growth of the Reformation during the first half of the 16th century was the main spiritual indication of this change in society. But the cultural outlook of this new society was entirely different from that of the older feudal classes.[1] The attitude of the new individual towards life was no longer to stabilise the world in its status quo but, on the contrary, to change it, to create possibilities of personal freedom, of individual development, economic, political and cultural.

This atmosphere of vitality and progress could certainly leave no sphere of life and culture untouched. Quickly the outer appearance of all cultural life changed. While during the middle ages the main cultural centres in England were the churches and, to a lesser degree, the aristocratic courts, the 16th century, especially after the dissolution of the monasteries, brought the establishment of many new centres, the town and country seats of the new gentry.

In the middle ages town and country were as far apart in their cultural outlook as in their geographical distance, which appeared enormous in face of the primitive travelling facilities of the time. Yet when, through the settlement of the new nobility of the towns in the country, and the intermarriage of merchants and aristocracy, the two spheres were brought together, a new cultural vitality developed throughout the country with amazing rapidity.

The insularity of the medieval manor house was broken down. Before the 16th century " a great house provisioned itself with little help from the outer world ; the inhabitants brewed and baked, churned and ground their meal ; they bred, fed and slew their beeves and sheep and brought up their pigeons and poultry at their own doors. Their horses were shod at home, their planks were sawn, their rough ironwork was forged and mended."[2]

Not that self-sufficient economy in England had ended by the

---

[1] See also L. C. Knights, *Drama and Society in the Age of Jonson*, London, 1937, pp. 103–8 and p. 115.

[2] Frances P. Verney, *Memoirs of the Verney Family during the 17th century*, London, 1925, I, 5.

middle of the 16th century. But a great change in the way of housekeeping was beginning to make itself felt after 1500 and continued to do so to an ever increasing degree as the 16th century and the revolution on the land progressed (particularly around London). Of Anne, second wife of Thomas, Lord Berkeley (d. 1534), we are told : " Country huswifry seemed to be an essential part of this lady's constitution," while already the " huswifry " of her daughter-in-law began to decline, and she " seemed to betake herself to the delights of youth and greatness. . . ."[1] The influence of the elegance and luxury of the great towns on the country seats became very noticeable. Many gentlemen even began " to take another course, and falling from the use of their ancestors, do now either altogether (or very much) leave to dwell in their country houses, inhabiting cities and great towns . . ."[2]. London itself during Henry VIII's reign is described thus :

> From the Tower to Westminster along, every street is full of luxuries, and their shops glister and shine of glasses, painted cruses, gay daggers, etc., that is able to make any temperate man to gaze on them and to buy somewhat, though it serve to no purpose necessary.[3]

So the spirit and tempo of life in the new cities invaded the former centres of patriarchal agrarianism. Leisure, luxury, and at the same time, a keen sense of art, science and philosophy developed in the country seats, as the gap between town and country diminished. The new " gentlemen of importance " patronised painting (especially did they commission the best continental artists to paint their portraits) as much as architecture; numberless precious manors and castles were modernised and completely rebuilt during the 16th century. The country manors became comfortable living-places ; they were no longer merely centres of agricultural production. Witness the wonderful beauty of many small Tudor country houses that are still in existence to-day. In 1577, towards the end of the century, William Harrison[4] could write :

[1] Berkeley MSS. II, p. 254. Quotations by Knights, p. 112.

[2] *Cyvile and Uncivyle Life*, 1579, Sig. B. i., V.–B. iii. Quoted by Knights, p. 115.

[3] Traill and Mann, *Social England*, III, p. 226, quoted by Knights, p. 118.

[4] *Elizabethan England*, p. 11 ; quoted by H. S. Bennet, *The Pastons and their England*, Cambridge, 1932, pp. 87 ff.

The furniture of our houses . . . is growne in maner even to passing delicacies and herein I doo not speake of the nobilitie and gentrie only, but likewise of the lowest sort in most places of our south countrie, that have anything at all to tak to. Certes, in noble mens houses it is not rare to see abundance of Arras, rich hangings of tapestrie, silver vessell, and so much other plate, as may furnish sundrie cupboards, to the summe often-times of a thousand or two thousand pounds at the least. Likewise in the houses of knights, gentlemen, merchantmen, and some other wealthie citizens. . . . But as herein all these doo far exceed their elders and predecessors, and in neatness and curiositie, the merchant all other ; so in time past, the costlye furniture staied there, whereas now it is descended yet lower, even unto the inferiour artificers and manie farmers, the most part learned also to garnish their cupboards with plate, their joined beds with tapestrie and silke hangings, and their tables with carpets and fine naperie.

The homes of the new half-town-half-country gentry all over England henceforth became the centres of art and culture. Here the vitality of the young and ascendant mercantile class was translated into cultural reality.

With the new standards of comfort and taste there arose a vivid musical culture. The production of instrumental music in particular increased with great speed.

Of great importance in this connection were the Royal Chapels. While the Church gradually lost its position as the centre of the country's musical activities, the absolutist Court of the early Tudor kings took over this function. The great innovator Henry VII contributed essentially to the revolutionary increase of instrumental music in particular. Once again we can refer to Hayes' representation of the music of the Courts of the early Tudor kings. Simultaneously with the increasing amount of music composed for instruments the percentage of instrumental players, compared with singers, increased rapidly at the Courts of Henry VIII and Edward VI (who, incidentally, added two " makers of instruments " to his chapel).

After 1500 many private families, too, even the less wealthy, already had their private establishments of harpists and violists.[1] A favourite instrument in many country houses was the portable

---

[1] See Chappell, *Popular Music of the Olden Times*, pp. 55 ff.

organ or regal, the very existence of which constituted a challenge to the Church—not to mention the music played on it, which ranged from secular arrangements of religious songs to popular tunes.

A study of the social past of the young merchant nobility reveals that many of them came from the lower middle classes, or at least had very close associations with them ; that is to say with artisans, craftsmen, small merchants and yeomen. The rise of these people meant at the same time the rise of music of a popular character, for the representatives of the new merchant nobility took their tunes and harmonies with them, introducing the melodies from the village green into the private gardens and drawing-rooms of the higher society.

*   *   *   *   *

The chief feature of instrumental music in England around and after 1500 is rhythmical definition, and this is the quality which most clearly shows its secular origin and purpose and sets it most obviously aside and apart from contemporary choral music, the music of the Church. Now it has been pointed out that 15th and early 16th century English Church music was generally less obscure and abstract than many continental Masses and motets of that time, especially those of the Dutch and Flemish schools. But compared with popular instrumental music, even English Church music—though very beautiful and highly evolved—appears over-complex and rhythmically blurred, like all art of hyper-cultivated, over-developed and declining societies. Syncopes and rich ornaments in all voices make it all but impossible for the listener to discriminate between arsis and thesis in a bar[1] :

Example 14 : from " Adoramus " by Hugh Aston (died 1521).

The new instrumental art, with its simplicity, shows on the other hand the qualities we found in the little folk tune in Chapter I. It has very clearly marked 2/4, 3/4 and 4/4 rhythms,

[1] *Tudor Church Music*, Vol. X, No. 1.

and exhibits distinct accents at the beginning of bars and periods.[1]
The structure, too, is outspokenly homophonic :

Example 15: Dance tune a 3 by Henry VIII.[2]

    In this instrumental music, it is interesting to note, the common-
time rhythm had now risen to an importance unknown in Church
music. As we have seen in the first chapter, these rhythms
2/4 and 4/4 had always been outstanding rhythms of folk music,
even at times when common-time was kept out of all Church
music. Then triple rhythm, the three beats of which were
for a long time considered symbolic of the Holy Trinity, was
sacred, all other rhythms profane.[3] About 1500, at
a time when rhythmical complications of all kinds dominated
the ' mensural vocal ' music of all countries alike as never before,
in instrumental notation each note almost without any exception
subdivided into *two* of the next smaller units : a breve into two
semibreves, a semibreve into two minims, etc. The whole
apparatus of ' ligatures,' ' perfection,' ' alteration,' etc., in
mensural music was foreign to instrumental art.[4]

    The music of Henry VIII's court is typical of the art of the

---

[1] This applies to contemporary organ music as well (which may be mentioned
here though it is not part of our subject), except, of course, to organ arrangements
of choral church pieces.

[2] Brit. Mus. MS. Add. 31922.

[3] See also P. F. H. Radcliffe in Mus. Ass. Proceedings, 1930–31, and above,
p. 41.

[4] See also H. Riemann, *Geschichte der Musiktheorie*, pp. 213 ff.

new bourgeois aristocracy ; and music written for or at the
Court was widely used outside it.[1] In and around the Court,
dance tunes and dance forms constituted the main bulk of
instrumental music, at least up to 1550, and indeed, of all the
rapid developments of musical forms in this fast-moving century,
the triumph of dance music is certainly one of the most striking.

Most of the new dance pieces of the Court and of the new
aristocracy and merchant bourgeoisie were melodically fresh,
simple and rhythmically clear. The easy-going melodies of the
lower middle classes and peasantry of the later middle ages,
worked into a slightly stylised form, were the musical material
of early Tudor Court and society :

Example 16 : " Blow thy horn, hunter. . . ."[2]

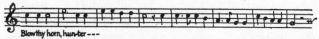

Blow thy horn, hunter ---

Tunes of this and similar kind, known as country dances from
Chaucer's time onwards, were taken from the huge reservoir of
true " music of the people."[3] The young bourgeoisie whose
interests were so largely represented by Henry VIII wanted this
kind of simple and jolly music and took it over, having no use
for the highly architectonic contrapuntal combinations of the
learned scholars in the cloisters.

Among the new Court dances there appears a species which
attracts our special attention : the domps, dumpes or dompes.
They were of particular significance for the development of
independent chamber music. For it was the domps which, as a
form of instrumental music, appear chiefly to have been performed by an ensemble of instruments rather than on a keyboard.
These pieces, like the rest of Henry VIII's Court dances, were
rhythmically square and melodically simple. But they lacked
the gaiety of the other forms. The name was always applied to
slow dances of a sombre and somewhat sinister nature. Some of
them must have been used at funerals ; an atmosphere of mourning or solemn reflection had to be created in these pieces ; it
could best be brought about by a group of instruments.

[1] There are numerous references to the use of court music in the houses of
wealthy citizens in Galpin's book.
[2] See Chappell, *Old English Popular Music*, I, 41–53. Tune from p. 40.
[3] Mrs. Walter Carr, in *Grove's Dictionary*, Vol. I (article on country dances)
rightly emphasises that the country dances were English folk tunes from the very
beginning, as against the notion that the country dances were in reality " contre-
danses."

Domps are built on this rhythm :

as shown in Example 17 : " My Lady Carey's Dompe."[1]

They consist of three, four or five strains of a varying number of
bars.   In the later strains the movement becomes livelier, and
sometimes certain variations modify the original melodies
of the dances.   In these variations, we may fancy, instrumental
expression is struggling to be born.   On the whole the domps
are stately, important and expressive in a musical sense.[2]   There
are pieces, for instance, like " the Duke of Somerset's Dumpe "[3]
whose particularly solemn character suggests that they were
used on prominent occasions.

Later in the 16th century the domps lost much of their mourn-
fulness, and some of them took on the playful character of
Elizabethan tunes ;   witness " Queen Marie's Dumpe " for
two viols,[4] an arrangement for virginal of " Lady Carey's Dump "
towards the end of the century,[5] and an " Irish Dump " from the
Fitzwilliam Virginal Book.[6]   The latter even changes the slowly

[1] Brit. Mus. MS. Roy. App. 58 ; time about 1520.

[2] Literature of the time makes frequent references to the domps.   Naylor
(*Shakespeare Music*, 1912, pp. 5 ff.) reminds us of the " doleful dumps " in the
first verse of Richard Edward's poem which Peter sings in *Romeo and Juliet*, IV,
5, 125.   Peter's request to the musicians to " play a merry dump to comfort me "
(earlier in the same scene) is in reality an allusion to the sad character of the dump.
It is not a " merry " dance—he calls it " merry " mockingly—but it is tragic and
depressing.
" Where gripping grief the heart would wound
And doleful dumps the mind oppress . . ."
In *Lucrece*, line 1127, we find :
" Distress likes dumps, when time is kept with tears."
In Humphrey Gifford's *Gilloflowers* there is another poem called " A dolefull
Dumpe " and two more, " A Dumpe " and " A Dumpe by his friend C.C."
(See J. Pulver, *Dictionary of Old English Music*, 1927).   A piece named " Ye
Quenes dumpe " is mentioned in a list of dances of Henry VIII's time (Brit. Mus.
MS. Sloane 3501, fol. 2b).   A " doleful dump " is mentioned in *Chevy Chase*, the
famous ballad of the 15th century, re-told by a 17th century writer, see *Ballads
and Poems*, ed. Frank Sidgwick, Cambridge, 1913, p. 38, line 194.   In Shake-
speare's " Sigh no more ladies " a " dull and heavy dump " is mentioned.

[3] MS. Roy. App. 58, fol. 51b.

[4] Brit. Mus. MS. Add. 15118 (Bass part only).

[5] Naylor, p. 5.

[6] *Ibid.*, p. 7.

striding rhythm into a ' merry ' 6/8, quite in accordance with the change towards greater gaiety that so many dance forms underwent about 1600.[1]

Although the domps are of purely English origin and, as far as can be said, confined to the musical repertoire of this country, they have a certain similarity to the more widely known ' basse danses ' of the Continent which, in their very earliest stages in Spain, were called " danzas de la muerte " (dances of death)[2]. Both domps and basse danses were slow dances which included a great variety of movements and steps, and both died out towards the end of the 16th century. Yet it is essential to recognise the importance of the domps, which, as purely English pieces, not only give proof of the productivity of the regenerated society of this country but also prepare the ground—in their demand for *sostenuto*—for a new instrumental technique.

Another dance form, the hornpipe (Hornpeype) played a similar, though less important part in the development of instrumental technique in chamber music. It was of greater importance to organ and virginal music, as is shown in the well-known " Hornpype " by Hugh Aston (d. 1521), composed for a keyboard instrument, an exceedingly lively and richly figured piece of considerable technical difficulty.[3] Only a few hornpipes for chamber music combinations are known to have been written during the 16th century ; several are included in a list of compositions of Henry VIII's court.[4] The hornpipe was a dance in vivid 3/2 or 3/4 rhythm ; in the 16th century it consisted of many small symmetrical periods of two, four or eight bars. The small melodic units were as simple as those in Aston's piece.[5]

[1] Two " thumpes " in Add. 38783, entitled " Alphonso Waye " (presumably by Alfonso Ferrabosco, jun., 1575–1628) are rhythmically simple and in common-time, like the earlier dumps (the MS. is from the beginning of the 17th century) but different from them in their general outlook, being just ordinary cheerful dances without the interesting qualities of the old domps. There are two more domps for lute, both anonymous. One is called " Militis dumpe " (Add. 31392), the other one " A thumpe " (Add. 15118). Both are from the end of the 16th century.

[2] See C. Sachs, *A World History of the Dance*, New York, 1933.

[3] Complete reprint in J. Wolf's *Sing- und Spielmusik*, 1925–6. See also Grove's *Dictionary* II (3rd edn.), p. 670, on the origin of the hornpipe, and Davey's *History of English Music*, 1921, p. 98, on domps and hornpipes.

[4] Brit. Mus. MS. Sloane 3501.

[5] On the whole, chamber music and music for keyboard instruments developed fairly independently of each other during the first half of the 16th century, as they belonged to entirely different spheres of life. The interplay of styles between keyboard and ensemble music became, however, livelier after 1550 when the brilliant technique of the virginal pieces helped to prepare the way for a more typically instrumental technique on instruments used in chamber music.

Apart from these two purely English dances, domp and horn-pipe (to which the already mentioned jig and some odd forms[1] would have to be added), we can count a great variety of dance forms of continental origin among the compositions played at Henry VIII's court. Most of them are lively, replacing the old and stiff court dances of the 15th century, and many are not named but are easily recognisable as early saltarellos, courantes, bransles, pivas, etc., on models familiar in contemporary French, Italian and Dutch collections such as Atteignant's editions of dances in 1529 and 1530.[2] French influence is particularly conspicuous in the formal structure of many of these dances, but the melodies are almost invariably of the popular English type which was shown to be prevalent in the music played at Henry VIII's court.[3]

It is difficult to form an opinion as to the approximate number of dances composed at Henry VII's and Henry VIII's courts. Among the composers of such music we meet most frequently the names of Richard Pyttins, Thomas Fardying, W. Cornysshe, John Floyd (Flude), Robert Fayrfax and Thomas Churcheyarde ; there are also instrumental pieces by Bramston, Banastir, Heywood, Ludford, R. Cooper, Dygon and Johnston.[4]

[1] There is a piece called " Mrs. Winter's Jumpp " in Add. 31392 (lute only). also several other dance pieces without titles or names in Add. 31922, Roy. App, 58, 74, 76, etc.

[2] 6 galliardas and 6 pavanas, Paris 1529 ; 18 basse danses pour lute, Paris, 1529 ; 9 basse danses, 2 bransles, 25 pavanas, Paris, 1530.

[3] It must be mentioned that Henry himself was a very active composer. His works, which include many different forms from the contemporary repertoire, are characteristic of the whole period. There are little episodes of 4, 5 or 6 bars ; each of these episodes finishes on a long sustained chord and is repeated, in the same way as in the continental pavanas, galliardas, etc. The setting of the pieces is remarkably homophonic, with the top instrument carrying the chief melodic part all the time. This marks already a most important difference from vocal items of the time as well as from the few known instrumental pieces of the 15th century such as the polyphonic two-part fragment in Brit. Mus. MS. Add. 5665, fol. 54. Notwithstanding their comparative simplicity, Henry's works are skilfully written and pleasant to listen to. The only question is whether Henry completely worked out these pieces. It is certain that he was at least a very able amateur as a player and inventor of melodies (see also Chappell, *Old English Popular Music*, I, 41 ff.). Yet sometimes one is tempted to assume that some of the king's court musicians were employed to arrange these melodies invented by him in several-part-harmony and to write them out properly. This appears likely in view of the fact that they vary so greatly in style, now resembling works of this, now of that composer of his court.

[4] Many compositions of these masters are in Brit. Mus. MS. Add. 31922 ; others in the already mentioned MSS. of the time. There are 2 pieces a 3 and 23 a 3–5 in Roy. App. 58 ; among the numerous instrumental pieces contained in Brit. Mus. Add. 31922, there are 30 a 3–4 by Fayrfax (d. 1521), Fardyng (d. between 1514 and 1524), Cornysshe (d. 1523) and unnamed composers.

During Henry VIII's reign some pieces are found which are actually called pavanas (pavins) and galliardas (galliards).[1] They appear either as single dances or in pairs, pavana and galliards being coupled as one and the same item in a performance of dances at the Court. The pavana then provided a majestic introduction in common time while the galliarda followed suit in a faster triple rhythm. It is difficult to say at what part of this period the English musician adopted the continental habit of basing both dances on one and the same tune (the galliard appearing as a variation of the pavana at greater speed, with still stricter and stronger accents on the arsis of each bar, and usually in triple rhythm). But we can guess the reason for this economy of thematic material. As the general demand for entertainment for the common people increased and dances and similar diversions received more or less official recognition, the composers of dance music were often unable to cope with the enormous calls that were made on them. So variety and enrichment of the repertoire of dance music was achieved by simply repeating a dance tune in a different rhythm. Thomas Morley alludes to this " Variation Suite " (the couple of pavan and galliard) :

After every pavan we usually set a galliard (that is, a kind of musicke made out of the other). . . . This is a lighter and more stirring kinde of dauncing.

Morley then gives as basic rhythm of the galliard the " foot

Trochæus " :   ♩♪♩♪♩♩♪   etc.[2]

How much of the continental practice itself was known in this country is hard to say.[3] But in the connecting-up of different dances in this way, the principle of the later dance suite is recognised in these early arrangements.

Some pieces called pavanas (about 1550) are technically rounds or canons.[4] This suggests that there are certain tendencies in

---

[1] Pavanas and galliardas in Brit. Mus. Stowe 389, Roy. App. 58, 74–6, etc. Some have names :. " The emperorse pavyn," " King Harry 8th' Galliard " and others. Thomas Churcheyarde (1520–1604) appears among composers of the dance tunes of Roy. App. 75.

[2] *Plaine and Easie Introduction to Practicall Musicke*, 1597, p. 181.

[3] There seem to be some examples of this principle in Roy. App. 74–76 : " Ronda " with ," la represa " and similar pieces which include two versions of the same piece in form of variations on each other.

[4] Pavan " in subdiatessarum," " Per aliam viam reversi sunt in regiam suam " in MS. Roy. App. 74–76.

the pavana to 'stylise' the dance piece ; probably under the influence of the polyphonic technique of contemporary church compositions.[1] But up to 1550 this feature is still of minor importance.

Towards the end of Henry VIII's reign another continental dance appears in English collections, the allemande (almand),[2] which even on arrival bears the main features of its standard 17th-century form : a certain gravity modified by the possibility of changing the character of the music as the dance changed. Like most other dances, the almand consists of three or more parts which are separated by complete cadences with pauses. From the beginning it is slightly more polyphonic than the domp or galliard, although in Henry's time it was still simple, hardly stylised and quite obviously essentially a 'dancing dance' and not a ' dance to be listened to ' (as indeed are all but a very few of the dance forms of the period 1500-1558). Morley defines the almand : ". . . a more heavie daunce than this " (the galliard), " (fitlie representing the nature of the people, whose nam it carrieth), so that no extraordinarie motions are used in the dauncing of it."[3]

Finally there is the courante (coranto), the 3/4 dance in moderately quick time and in simple binary form. It made its appearance in England about the beginning of the reign of Elizabeth, and Shakespeare mentions it frequently. The courante became a vital factor in 17th-century dance music, especially in the suites.[4]

As for non-dance instrumental music, it had scarcely begun to exist ; such specimens as are found are chiefly preludes and voluntaries for keyboard instruments.

*   *   *   *   *

Instrumental music had developed with vast energy within half a century, but it was not yet able to claim for itself an independent existence in its own right. It was still largely functional, chained to the dance and to the observances of the court. It was just about 1558 that chamber music in the new

---

[1] See below, Chapter III.

[2] Allemande d'amor for 4 and 5 viols in MS. Roy. App. 74–76. One allemand in this MS. is by R. Pyttins.

[3] *A Plaine and Easie Introduction*, p. 181. Morley also mentions bransles, voltes and other dances.

[4] Ibid., p. 181.

meaning—as an independent art—began its conquest of England. What was behind this triumphant rise ? For a triumph it was if ever there was one.

The sudden development of the art was due to rapid and important changes in the spirit and ' tempo ' of the times.

From about 1558 onwards a life of increasing activity developed : the spirit of enterprise, adventure, progress and intensified labour affected all parts of the population engaged in the various spheres of the new commercial life. A greater freedom of competition prepared the ground for a musical activity which was not tied by a thousand bonds to a non-musical function, but was based on the initiative of the individual composer. During the middle ages all professions, including the musical, were organised into guilds, so that the isolated individual could never have achieved full consciousness of his power, nor have protected himself and advanced. The individual was only a link in a chain which was composed of equal parts, a member of a corporation or fraternity which stood for his rights, but at the same time held him captive. Now, after 1558, music moved away from the medieval way of functioning at court and church, or on municipal occasions, towards the much more independent ideal of pure chamber music.

And what part this music played in the awakening of the new age ! How alive and varied it became ! It had to respond to the immense and ever new, ever increasing demands of that fast-growing public of educated musical amateurs—the first stage of the ' general public ' as we know it to-day. It has to be repeated that the chief centres of chamber music were at first the country manors of the new merchant-nobility. But more and more chamber music was called upon to counterbalance the increasingly strenuous life in the towns that developed so quickly (particularly in London). For although the growing freedom of life in the new cities offered more and more possibilities for the advance of the individual, it brought also increased strain ; men became more and more entangled in its allurements and enchained by its promises, which only meant new and ever new endeavour, haste and exhaustion.

In this situation music became a means of providing recreation and pleasure. Towards the end of the 16th century English music shows an increasing tendency to develop quite new features pointing in that direction : in music there now is ' sweetness,' 'charm,' 'loveliness,' 'magic'—and the minds of the listeners are carried away into an unknown sphere of harmony and immaterial beauty.

We in the 20th century are so used to listening to music in this way that we often do not realise that it is of a comparatively recent growth, and that in the middle ages the attitude of the listener was entirely different. The predominance of the element of pleasure and diversion did not become apparent in musical life until the end of the 16th century. William Byrd, the greatest of Elizabethan composers, was the first to express the wish that his music "might happely yeeld some sweetness, repose and recreation."[1]

Chamber music offered an almost ideal medium for providing just this mental and spiritual recreation, by virtue of the privacy of the practice, its apparent remoteness from any perceptible purpose, and the opportunity it gave for the expression of a more subjective emotionalism.

Let us consider for a moment instrumental music in general. It is the realm of 'absolute' sound, in which are no limits or boundaries. It addresses man's emotional life most immediately and directly; and in so doing does not rely on 'roundabout routes' as do other arts; it does not represent concrete objects from real life as painting does; nor deal with symbols of reality as literature and poetry do. In instrumental music man's emotional life is most purely reflected. Therefore man found here a practically unlimited field for developing his imagination.

With the new conception of life the artist's imagination was freed from its medieval fetters. It was instrumental music which offered itself to Elizabethans as a perfect field for the realisation in ideal terms of all those demands which the Reformation and Renaissance put forward, and in particular we shall see how in the following century instrumental music, this kaleidoscope of changing visions and emotions, became an important vehicle for the expression of the new life—modern life with its wrongs and hopes.

It must not be overlooked that this new development in the field of music, the evolution of instrumental music, contained a potential element of danger. In instrumental music the imagination of the artist could develop in two directions : he could indeed draw up plans for the battle of life which would stimulate and

[1] Introduction to *Psalms, Songs and Sonnets*, 1587–88.

inspire his fellows with new energy and optimism ; but he could also (and here lay the element of danger) dream himself away from life to a world of passive wish-fulfilment. It must be made clear from the start, however, that during the days of the childhood of instrumental chamber music there was hardly any question of escapism. Elizabethan composers chose the first way, for society (as will be shown in a later chapter) was more active, and more united and balanced than in most other periods of English history ; and there was no need to escape from reality. There was much optimism and vitality in Elizabethan art which was in itself a healthy reaction to the religious escapism of medieval Church art.

So it was historical necessity that brought about the evolution of chamber music and of chamber music instruments. It was not (as some still suppose) through the means of ' invention ' that chamber music came into being[1] ; the preparation of this art was a painful process that dragged on for centuries. Nor did some individual genius conjure this art out of nothing— some Aladdin who had only to rub his magic lamp—a whole people participated in the creation of its chamber music. Talent is indeed a necessary prerequiste of creative art, but the artist's talent is directed and developed by the fact that he is not an isolated but a social being. The individual ' creative genius ' is only creative because he recognises most clearly and deeply and magnificently (though not necessarily consciously) the spiritual necessities of the society to which he belongs. His work is a factor in the development of the human community as a whole, but it is itself a product of this development,[2] and only as a result of the influences of events upon him can a creative genius himself influence them. Least of all is it blind chance or the caprice of some dark, cold destiny that is responsible for the appearance and disappearance of great periods of art. *It is the creative power of human society itself that makes the history of art.* All the finest qualities of the human race, all its warmth and beauty will be recognised in the great age of music that now begins.

[1] H. Davey in his *History of Music in England*, 1922, writes on p. 88 : " It is this MS. (Roy. App. 58, Brit. Mus.) which enables us to claim for England the glory of having invented instrumental music as well as vocal composition."

[2] How far the whole conception of a ' genius ' is dependent on historical necessity is most clearly shown in our own art, for the cult of the great, all-conquering ' genius ' of music is a creation chiefly of the 18th and 19th centuries—the time of great careers and great personalities who struggled to rise far above their fellow-human-beings, in accordance with the general trend of society which was based on industrial conquest and individualism.

CHAPTER III

THE EMANCIPATION FROM THE CHURCH

In the new type of instrumental music which was developing under Henry VIII, we have seen that its connection with Court functions and dancing was still essential; pleasure in instrumental sound and playing, so essential to chamber music, was not yet the chief purpose.

After all that has been said it may seem surprising that the decisive step to accomplish this was made in music that originated in the Church. The earliest real chamber music had, indeed, the form of religious works and was written by Church composers. There were important reasons for this peculiar situation.

Humanism and the Renaissance in England, propagating personal, social and cultural freedom, advanced in the cultural sphere essentially on religious grounds. It was no contradiction if instrumental music, another expression of a progressive social outlook, was connected with the Reformation. But further, Anglican Reform pursued a peculiar policy regarding music in the church. The 16th century was a time of fierce religious and social struggle. In all such times the emphasis in vocal music laid upon the *words* (and the text in general) becomes stronger. In all countries the movements of the Reformation and Counter-Reformation alike endeavoured to convey their messages through the medium of vocal music; this endeavour established the temporary triumph of the words and their meaning in the Musica Reservata on the Continent, in the Florentine Camerata, in the opera, and in the choral Laudes of the Jesuits—all this after the long predominance of the hyper-complex old motet-style, in which the music was all-important, drowning the text. We think further of the clarity of the declamation in the operas and songs of the French Revolution, re-acting against the primacy of the purely musical element in other 18th-century French music which was crammed with ornaments and coloratures. We can also find similar tendencies aiming at greater distinctiveness and more effective interpretation of the text in the music of modern political movements—as against the intricate and twisted counterpoint of contemporary " l'art pour l'art " composers.

The words must be clearly understood by the listener who is to be converted or convinced of the rightness of a new theory, philosophy, gospel or policy. So we find in 16th-century England, too, a stronger elaboration and clearer interpretation of the biblical words of a vocal work. In 1559 the Anglican Church decreed the simplification of the vocal score. The 49th Injunction in Cranmer's Reform asks for a " modest and distinct song so used in all parts of the prayer that the same might be understanded as if it were read without singing." There should be but one note to one syllable, and the whole choral arrangement should be homophonic. Simultaneously the organ was temporarily silenced (organists hitherto provided excessively florid accompaniments).

It is evident that such a style offered little scope for the composers to continue in the Church their tradition of artistic and polyphonic motets. True, they wrote vocal Church music according to the new regulations, and they tried to give of their best in it. But they also had to find an outlet, another field where they could employ their technical skill and pacify their ' polyphonic consciences.' Some of the composers went on composing Catholic music in the old sense, occasionally with the disapproval of the Anglican authorities. They were, however, in the minority. But to what field did the main body of composers direct themselves? To instrumental music which, as shown, contained so many elements of attraction for the musical world of the middle of the 16th century. So it was the Church composers themselves who developed instrumental music from out of the environment of the Church.

This tendency has already been seen in the " Canon Pavanas " of the first half of the 16th century. But these were minor examples ; much more important were the instrumental works which grew directly out of the choral Church art. The old choral polyphony determined the form as well as the style of the early chamber music. Immediately before and during the early stages of the Reformation by far the most important form of Catholic church music, apart from the mass, was the *motet*, an authorised though not liturgical vocal species. This was in essence a polyphonic setting of a biblical text, having as a rule one voice reserved for the enunciation of the Gregorian chant proper to the words, the other parts moving freely in counterpoint to it. English composers of chamber music took hold of the motet, and by a kind of act of collective creation metamorphosed it into chamber music. Let us study the form and the process.

The standard type of motet of the English school during the first half of the 16th century was influenced by the works of the contemporary Dutch polyphonists Josquin des Près, Pierre de la Rue, Gombert, Mouton and others. This influence, it must be emphasised, was certainly very moderate compared with the subjection of the whole Continent to the Netherlandish cathedral style. But it was noticeable over here, too ; just as Dutch spiritual movements, both orthodox and reformatory, moral and intellectual, made a deep impression on the English in the general sphere of religous thought.

At that time the standard type of motet still appeared mainly as ' Cantus firmus ' motet or ' Tenor '[1] motet, characterised by the maintenance of a cantùs firmus in one of the parts of the score throughout the piece. Every one of these cantus firmi was solely based on one of the flourishing melodies of the Gregorian Chant which from the 7th century onward were the choral material of the Catholic service. The Gregorian melodies were considered as sacrosanct in the Church. The succession of the notes was therefore strictly kept whenever they were used as the thematic backbone of the polyphonic motets. The rhythm was altered, though ; usually the plainsong in the motet of the 16th century moves along calmly in one of the parts in long, equal notes, regardless of all the polyphonic happenings in the other parts :

Example 18 :

(a) Plainsong :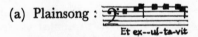

(b) Motet Cantus firmus :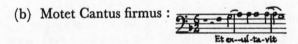

---

[1] Tenor originally meant " ea vox quæ tenet " the voice that " holds " the main part in the motet ; the term must not be confused with " Tenor " meaning the upper part of the male voice chorus which only up to the 13th century really was " ea vox quæ tenet."

(c) 4-part Motet by John Taverner[1] (cantus firmus in the first
bass) :

Otherwise the form of the motet depends on the formal arrangement of the sentences of the text.   While the cantus firmus is
smoothly running along
  Taverner (1495–1545), Tedeum[2] :

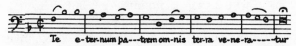

a close polyphonic net is being woven by the other parts.
  The scheme of the polyphonic structure of these contrapuntal
parts is usually as follows.   One clause of the Latin text, " Te
eternum patrem omnis terra veneratur," is sung by one voice
which introduces a melodic phrase :

A second voice enters, mostly *imitating* the melody of the first,
although often pursuing a more independent course after a few
notes in the beginning, while the first voice carries on a counterpoint of its own.   A third voice comes in, then a fourth, until the
full polyphonic stream of the whole choir is reached.   A final
cadence concludes the first ' section ' of the motet.[3]

[1] *Tudor Church Music*, III, p. 3.
[2] Ibid. pp. 26 ff.
[3] In this particular case each of the first sections consists of two sub-sections :
Te eternum patrem—omnis terra veneratur, and : Tibi cherubin et seraphin—
incessabili voce proclamant.

Now a new sentence starts : " Tibi cherubin et seraphin incessabili voce proclamant." A new phrase starts in the musical composition accordingly :

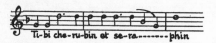

Fugal imitation and the whole polyphonic construction take place again, and again a cadence concludes the development. A third section begins :

and so on, until the text finishes.[1]

It is true that this scheme is not always strictly followed, the fugal imitation especially, is rarely regular in all voices during the first half of the 16th century ; there are also homophonic parts, and sections in which there is no imitation but every voice has an entirely independent contrapuntal line of its own. The sections, moreover, mostly overlap : the melody of a subsequent section comes in before the cadence of the previous section has finished.

It may be said that it was a common practice long before the middle of the 16th century to reinforce or even to replace one or several of the voice-parts by the organ (or perhaps by some soft stringed instruments as shown in Chapter I). But only about 1550 do we find it a general practice for all parts of a vocal score to be performed by instruments. The special attraction of the instrumental performance of a vocal piece must have been very great, for there are hundreds of instrumental arrangements of vocal works of the time—secular as well as religious—still in existence.[2] The reader may try for himself, by having any motet of the time first sung by a choir and then played by instruments.[3]

[1] See also the author's *Form in the Instrumental Music of the 17th Century,* Proceedings of the Musical Association, 1938–1939, pp. 45–61.

[2] There are many titles with indications that music may be used either for voices or instruments. E.g., Thomas Whythorne's *Duos or Songs for two voyces* bear the sub-title : " playne and easie to be sung or played on Musicall Instruments " (1590).

[3] Parts of William Byrd's *Psalms, Songs and Sonnets* of 1587 were originally composed for one voice with instrumental accompaniment and rearranged for *a capella* choir only when published. See also H. Davey, *History of English Music,* p. 147.

He will be surprised at the discrepancy in the two performances.[1]
There are hundreds of arrangements of this kind in one large
collection alone.[2]

The instrumental arrangements of cantus firmus motets follow
the vocal line strictly. Some types of vocal motets seem to have
attracted instrumental performers more than others. For instance,
there are many instrumental motets based on the Gregorian
" Miserere,"[3] most of which one could identify as literal transcriptions of vocal pieces. Yet among the numerous genres of instrumental pieces appearing in 16th-century manuscripts there is one
which cannot be considered as a mere ' arrangement.' It is the
so-called ' In Nomine.'

The In Nomine is a cantus firmus motet written for instruments. The cantus firmus of all In Nomines is identical :

Example 19 : " In Nomine " (Cantus firmus).

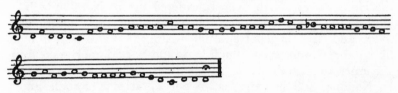

This cantus firmus is not only common to all In Nomines ;
it is peculiar to them, for it occurs in no vocal scores. In Nomines
are thus original compositions *for instruments*. The In Nomine is
the first definite form of composed instrumental music, the fore-
father of all English chamber music up to the present day.

The origin of the species is totally obscure. True, the melody
of the In Nomine itself was part of the service and can be traced
as such. The melody belongs to the festival of the Holy Trinity.[4]

[1] In the old MSS. the texts of vocal and instrumental versions are identical,
apart from minor variants that occasionally appear. In a piece by Taverner,
Brit. Mus. MS. Add. 31390, 107, the music is identical with the vocal motet
" Dum transisset," cf. *Tudor Church Music*, III, 37–45, except for the fact that
in the instrumental version several parts have double stoppings in the final chord !

[2] Brit. Mus. Add. 31390. Many are also in Add. 30480, such as " Levavi
oculos " by Wyllyam More, " harpour to Ed. VI." A reference to the work is
found in G. Hayes' *King's Music*; the whole piece is published there on pp. 26–27.

[3] There is one instrumental " Miserere " for 4 parts, anonymous, in Brit. Mus.
Add. MS. 36484, one a 5 by Bramley in Royal Coll. of Music, MS. 2049, one a 2
by Nathaniel Giles in The King's Library RM. 24 d. 2, one a 5 by Mallorie in
Oxford, Bodleian D. 212–16, one a 5 by Lupo in Oxford, Christ Church, MS. 2
and several other libraries, one a 5 by Stoninges in Brit. Mus. Add. 31390, one a 5
by Chr. Tye in Oxford, Bodl. Ms. Mus., School e 1–5. Morley speaks about the
" Miserere " in the *Plaine and Easie Introduction*, p. 115 (1597).

[4] See Gevaert, *La mélopée antique*, Gand, 1895, Thème six.

Yet we are neither able to state why the words " In Nomine " (or " In Nomine Domini " as written on one or two occasions) were put to this melody, which originally had quite a different text in the Gregorian Chant,[1] nor do we know the text beyond the three words In Nomine Domini. And, worst of all, we do not know why this melody, before all others, has made history as the thematic material of the first form of real chamber music. It is certain that the In Nomine did not make its appearance until the middle of the 16th century when the Church went through its deepest crisis and when instrumental chamber music began to be the fashion. Most probably the instrumental In Nomine never had a place in the service. But why was a sacred melody used ? Why was it performed instrumentally ? And why was it used by so many composers up to as late as the second half of the 17th century ? Is the right explanation that given by the Hon. Roger North, who considered the In Nomine to be a kind of test piece among composers to prove their accomplishment and skill in contrapuntal writing ?[2] This seems most likely, for almost every English composer of importance from Taverner to Purcell wrote In Nomines. There are about 150 In Nomines still in existence in our libraries ; of these about 100 are of the 16th century. The composers of the 16th century turned to the In Nomine with an exalted intensity which can really only be understood if we imagine what panic the Anglican Reform must have caused among the composers of polyphonic Church music.

The mystery of the almost legendary origin of the In Nomine, despite the attempts of various scholars to elucidate it, remains unsolved.[3] But one thing is clear : the In Nomines are not only historically the first harvest of the new art of chamber music, but they also exhibit items of striking musical value from the very beginning.

From the purely historical point of view the importance of the In Nomines goes far beyond the academic interest which it shares with other ' first-borns ' of the history of music such as the dry experiment, Peri's " Eurydice," which was the first real

[1] Gloria tibi trinitas, cf. Gevaert.

[2] " If the study, contrivance, and ingenuity of these compositions, to fill the harmony, carry on fuges, and intersperse discords, may pass in the account of skill, no other sort whatsoever may pretend so more." *Memoirs of Musick*, 1728.

[3] See list in the author's article on *The In Nomine and the Birth of Instrumental Style, Music and Letters*, January, 1936.

opera, or the primitive attempt on the harpischord by the obscure Dutch composer Sybrandus van Noordt which he called " Sonata for Cimbalo Solo "—the first piano sonata in history.[1] These are single compositions, but the In Nomine was a cult, a fashion. It became the field in which an instrumental style was first developed. Freed from the vocal past, the independence of instrumental playing was established here, and the vast possibilities of a chamber-music style were first recognised in the In Nomines written by the composers of the 16th century.

Certainly in the oldest In Nomines the original vocal character of 16th-century polyphony is still very obvious. In the In Nomines by Taverner (1495–1545) and Tallis (1505–1585) we find hardly any difference from other instrumental cantus firmus motets of the time. The cantus firmus is always strictly kept ; its individual notes are all of the same duration : long notes, ranging from longæ (𝄽) to semibreves (𝅝).[2] The In Nomine cantus firmus is usually in one of the middle parts : only towards the end of the 16th century do all parts of the score become possible candidates for the honour of playing the most outstanding—yet most monotonous—part. The sectional development of successive themes is the same as in the vocal motets, although without relation to any verbal sentences. The single parts are vocal in character : any choir could have sung these pieces had they had texts. The melodies of the contrapuntal parts flow softly in a neutral and continuous stream :

Taverner, In Nomine[3]

But after Taverner and Tallis the In Nomines give a different impression. In the hands of the composers during the third quarter of the 16th century, Robert Parsons (d. 1569), Christopher Tye (d. 1572), Robert White (1530–1574), Osbert Parsley (1511–1585), Nicholas Strogers (d. about 1585) and Alfonso

---

[1] Printed in 1690 in Amsterdam ; copies in the British Museum and the Bibliothèque Nationale, Paris. See also my essay on " Die Vorherrschaft der Instrumentalmusik im niederländischen Barock," *Tijdskrift van de Vereeniging voor Nederlandsche Muziekgeschiedenes*, The Hague, 1938–9.

[2] This is a feature common to all In Nomines up to the end of the 17th century. With a few exceptions composers resist the temptation to drag the In Nomine cantus firmus into the magic polyphonic movement of the other parts ; then the medieval rigidity of the equal note values melts into softer ornamental counterpoint.

[3] Add 31390.

Ferrabosco, sen. (1543–1588), the In Nomine underwent a decisive change.   The *style* was instrumentalised.

An entirely new flexibility of the parts grew out of the nature of the instruments on which this music was mainly played. These instruments were viols. The viols are a family of differently-shaped instruments with 6 strings, pitched a fourth apart, except for the two middle strings which are separated by a third[1] :

They were played with a bow much softer and more curved than that of the violin family which was altogether different in style and appearance.   In the viol family frets indicate the pitch of the notes on the finger-board.   Still more important, the viols have a quality of sound which is fundamentally different from that of the modern violins and 'cellos.   The sound is slightly nasal and rather soft but much more distinctive.   While modern instruments respond to the utmost subjective expression (accentuation, vibrato and cantabile), the viols speak by themselves. Quite naturally so, since the music which is to be played needs an objective and somewhat neutral interpretation, compared with a violin concerto, say, by Tchaikovsky, which is nothing without the interpretation of the performer and his violin, with its extremes of emotion.   In the art of the 16th century, the influence of the middle ages, when art was functioning in accordance with the much more static general outlook of things, is still very close.   These viols, on which the music of the 16th century was mainly played, offered, however, innumerable new possibilities for the introduction of extensive scales, quick figures, tone repetitions, jumps and slurs.

Several facts indicate that the In Nomine had finally left the Church in the second half of the 16th century.   The main MS. which contains In Nomines[2] has a peculiar form of arrangement of the different parts which points to chamber music, not to Church music.   The parts are written on each side of the open book so that a whole company of from 4 to 12 people sitting round the table on which the book was lying could play the piece simultaneously from one single volume.   This may have been

---

[1] For details about the viols see Gerald R. Hayes, *Musical Instruments and their Music* (1500–1750), London, 1930.

[2] Brit. Mus. MS. Add. 31390 ; date about 1575.

done in private houses as an after-dinner-recreation, but surely not in a church[1] :

Bᴀꜱꜱᴜꜱ.	Mᴇᴅɪᴜꜱ.	Aʟᴛᴜꜱ.
	Tᴇɴᴏʀ. Cᴏɴᴛʀᴀᴛᴇɴᴏʀ.	Cᴀɴᴛᴜꜱ.

Some instrumental pieces are called " In Nomine Pavin " and " In Nomine Galliard "[2] which again shows the process of secularisation to which the In Nomine was subjected. The In Nomine melody is also used as the thematic-harmonic backbone of Orlando Gibbons's merry Quodlibet, called " The Cries of London."

The music itself, especially some works by the most outstanding composer of In Nomines, Christopher Tye, shows most clearly this process of secularisation.

Tye may be called the first great English composer of chamber music. There are 19 In Nomines for 5, one for 4 and one for 6 parts known to be by him. Most of them have characteristic titles, such as " Rachell weepinge," " Weepe no more Rachell."

The chief importance of these pieces lies in the change of the polyphonic structure which they all underwent. The melodic lines of the instruments—apart from the In Nomine cantus firmus which never altered—are no longer so extended. The phrases are no longer so indefinite. The motifs[3] are shortened and, at the same time, more characteristically shaped. We find here the first attempts at " thematic work "[4] :

---

[1] A similar arrangement of the parts is also found in the original printed edition of Dowland's " Lachrimæ," London, 1605. See below, p. 121. On this occasion it may be mentioned that 16th and 17th-century composers did not often write the scores of their compositions—they thought and composed naturally in parts.

[2] An In Nomine Pavan and Galliard in Cambridge University Library, both for 2 recorders, and without the In Nomine melody. A piece for 6 parts, also called " In Nomine Pavan," is in Morley's *First Book of Consort Lessons*, ed. 1611 after the master's death.

[3] I am applying this term for the basic figures of a piece or a section of a piece, as far as they represent the thematic material on which the contrapuntal work is based—as against the Wagnerian meaning of the term " Leitmotiv " which always associates musical themes with non-musical subjects, ideas or situations.

[4] From " Weepe no more Rachell," In Nomine a 5 by Tye (Add. 31390).

We note, too, that the cadences are becoming more definite. The technique of ' overlapping ' which veils the structure of the pieces and creates the impression of an ' eternal ' melody still exists, but it is no longer so absolutely dominating as before. It happens occasionally in Tye's In Nomines that the sections are kept apart—the motif of a new section begins only *after* the cadence of the previous section has been heard distinctly. We further find the first signs of a tendency to unite the pieces in a-b-a formula by returning to the initial motifs towards the end of the piece ; the motifs

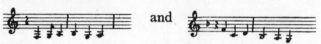

reappear slightly modified (in normal position as well as reversed) in the last section of this piece. The full importance of this phenomenon will be discussed in a later chapter.

Instrumentalisation is developed to quite an astonishing degree in another of Tye's In Nomines, called " Trye."[1] This piece is based on a purely instrumental theme :

It must be said that themes like this are extremely rare at this time (ca. 1560) anywhere in Europe. Tone repetitions as such are part of the technique in Jannequin's, the contemporary Frenchman's chansons ; but the combination of such very fast tone repetitions with octave and fifth jumps is unique at that time. Yet even more astonishing, the whole piece consists of only two sections, each of which is a complete *fugato* development of considerable length such as was done 100 years later ! Moreover the second section is a variation of the first in different rhythm :

(Moderate ; ♩ = 76)

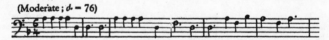

The derivation of the second part from the first is quite in line with the habit of connecting up a pavana in common time and a galliarda in triple rhythm. We have already discussed this practice in 16th century dance music. But it is difficult to account for the thematic and structural novelties in the piece. Themes like the one mentioned are surely much more likely to

[1] Add. 31390.

be encountered in a Scherzo by Bruckner than in a 16th-century In Nomine ! Yet at a time when progress was so to speak in the air, when innumerable musicians were trying to find new ways and styles and possibilities, results were occasionally anticipated by some daring individuals which were generally arrived at only centuries later. The principle of independent instrumental music being once established, sometimes possibilities of instrumental technique were touched which, although they were the logical consequence of the instrumentalisation of music, could be generally acknowledged only a long time after the more elementary novelties had been absorbed. In France and Germany men like Jannequin or Regnart were free to break a good many rules of the ' good old times.' Approximately at the same time colleagues in Italy reached an even more advanced stage of the revolutionary spirit of conquest when anything within the reach of the composers was tried out ; even the ' modulating passion ' of the post-Wagner era was anticipated, as for instance in works by Gesualdo da Venosa. And did not Bacon in this country even speculate about quarter-tones and other experimental schemes ?[1]

Some other composers of In Nomines are hardly less daring than Tye. Robert Parsons appears as an innovator (as well as a charming personality whose works have much more of the ' human touch' than those of his contemporaries). One In Nomine of his is of a particular warmth of sentiment which was rare at that time : the famous " Parsons' In Nomine " (it is only one out of a whole series, but it was very famous in its time and was played all over the country for many years)[2] :

Example 20 : In Nomine a 5 by Robert Parsons.

[1] " We have Sound Houses where we practice and demonstrate all sounds, and their generation. We have Harmonies, which you have not, of Quarter sounds, and lesser slides of Sounds. Diverse Instruments of Musick, likewise to you unknown, some Sweeter than any you have, together with Bells and Rings that are Dainty and Sweet . . ." (*New Atlantis*, 1627, ed. Harold Osborne, London, 1937, pp. 39 ff.).

[2] Add. 31390 ; also in many other MSS. in the British Museum, and Oxford libraries. It also appears as " A Dial-song " for 4 parts, composed by W. Syddael in imitation of Parsons' original, in Charles Butler's *Principles of Music*, London, 1636, p. 42. Some MS. arrangements of the piece are for 4 and 7 parts. Another In Nomine a 4 by Parsons and one by Parsley were edited by Sir R. R. Terry, 1923.

It has an especially fine conclusion, with its touching little descant figures above the compact harmony of the other instruments. This use of the top part is an important advance beyond the technique which we found at Henry VIII's court. Then a tune was simply a top melody with accompaniment ; here is anticipated *in nuce* the technique of the concerto where one single instrument operates against a more or less independent body of instruments of equal importance.

Parsons wrote six In Nomines, among them two for seven instruments.

All these In Nomines are harmonically in the old idiom. The Church modes are still dominant, especially Dorian and Mixolydian. This is the main reason why they still sound somewhat archaic to us, in spite of the momentous changes contained in them.

The In Nomines of the 16th century are generally on a very high average level of skill, contrapuntal ingenuity and variety of themes. There are many composers of In Nomines in the 16th century, of whom we know little more than their names. Here are some of them : Alcock, Allison, Baldwine, Bevin, Brewster, Buck, Cobold, Corke, Eglestone, Edward Gibbons, Gibbs, Goldar, Hake, Johnson, Mericocke, Mudd, W. Munday, Picforth, Poynt, Preston, Randall, Sadler, Stanner, Stoninge, Strogers, Thorne, Wayser, Whitbrooke, White, Woodcocke, Woodson and Th. Work.

An In Nomine a 5 by Picforth deserves special mention. Here contrapuntal mannerism—a remnant of 15th- and 16th-century Netherlandish church music—goes far beyond the Pavin canons of Henry VIII and his fellow-composers. In this curious piece one part (the In Nomine cantus firmus) has only breves (𝄹) throughout the piece : the second part has only equal dotted semibreves, the third simple semibreves, the fourth dotted minims, the fifth simple minims. These values are strictly kept in every one of the parts to the bitter end : an acrobatic polyphony is the outcome.

So in the In Nomine a genuine chamber-music style was established which derived straight from the Church service. Although the 16th-century In Nomine still shows many traces of the pre-Reformation cantus firmus motet its importance for the subsequent blossoming of chamber music simply cannot be

overrated.   There is nothing like the In Nomine in other countries
or schools in Europe.   It is a purely English form.

*   *   *   *   *

In the meantime a parallel process of instrumentalisation was
going on within another kind of Church motet.   Apart from
the cantus firmus motet with its " tenor ", another polyphonic
vocal form had come into being which may be called the ' free '
motet.   This species had the sectional arrangement of all motet
compositions, but the Gregorian melodies which formed the
melodic material of this kind of motet were dissolved into little
segments and distributed among all the voices taking part in the
performance.[1]   Thus towards the middle of the 16th century all
voices of this ' free ' motet had their thematic material taken from
one or other of the Gregorian melodies.   The practice of imitation
was practically the only method of achieving a polyphonic result.
In this form the greatest triumphs of English polyphony were
celebrated.

It is true that the free motet represents, on the one hand, a
more rigid control of the composers, for the thematic material is
now finally confined to the Gregorian melodies, while before all
kinds of secular tunes could be used to make up the polyphonic
texture.   But on the other hand there is a strong new element of
individualism and independence in the free motet.   The cantus
firmus in equal long notes had become a burden on the composition.   The 15th- and 16th-century composer had to carry this
heavy weight along as Sindbad carried the Old Man of the Sea.
Now at last greater freedom in the polyphonic texture was made
possible.

The musical profession itself had become more independent ;
it had developed, in accordance with the increasing freedom of
competition in the social and economic field.   The more the
musical profession was emancipated from the Church, the more
freely could the composer treat the thematic material, even
though he was not yet in a position to *invent* his motet melodies
freely.

[1] Certain signs that this process was going on can be noticed as far back as in
the 15th century.   Some motets by Dunstable show a greater degree of freedom
in the treatment of the cantus firmus.   See H. Davey, *History of English Music*,
p. 36, and M. Bukofzer, *Geschichte des englischen Diskants*, Strassburg, 1936.   The
Old Hall and the Pepys MSS. (see above, p. 29) also contain some motets in
which the cantus firmus has the same speed and is of the same strongly ornamental
character as the other voices.

In a motet by Robert White (1530–1574), for instance, the melodic material is taken from a Gregorian melody in the Æolian mode.[1] This melody forms the fugal subject of the motet,[2] without a cantus firmus running through the whole piece.

Fugal imitation of this theme takes place in all parts of the score, and a conclusion in form of a cadence rounds off the first section as in the cantus firmus motet :

Example 21 : from *Ad te levavi*, 6-part motet by R. White.

A new section is built up in a similar way ; altogether there are eight sections in this motet.[3]

The distribution of the cantus firmus among the various parts and sections had begun to show a much rougher handling of the sacrosanct material of the Gregorian choral. The emancipation of an instrumental style advanced far more radically in this kind of motet than in the still rather ancient and scholastic cantus firmus motet. To watch the birth of another vital form of instrumental music out of this free motet is a fascinating study.

When, through the purely instrumental performance of a motet

---

[1] Gevaert, *La Mélopée antique*, p. 235 ; characterised as belonging to the " third type of Gregorian melodies " (thème 3) :

[2] *Tudor Church Music*, V, pp. 48 ff.

[3] Eight in part I ; an independent second part with more sections begins with the text " Miserere nostri."

of this kind,[1] the motet was deprived of its immediate religious significance, the next step was to dispense with the holy melody as thematic material altogether. As all that instrumental playing sounded so new and independent and as no reminder of the sacred origin was retained in the playing, there was no more need to stick to the old melodies of the service.

At first the composers used many secular melodies as thematic material.[2] But the next step was decisive : *the composers began to invent instrumental melodies themselves.* At first this was done in a purely tentative way. So difficult was it for the old masters to get away from their old-accustomed technique of using already existing melodies that they at first used the most obvious and simplest motifs : fragments of the scale !

The scale was at that time named not with our letters, C, D, E, etc., but as in the Tonic-Sol-Fa system, with syllables like ut, re, mi, fa, sol, la, si. This scale itself provided the thematic material in numerous instrumental compositions of the second half of the 16th century. Ut-re-mi or similarly elementary motifs, such was the new thematic material of a piece.

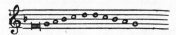

The scale motifs ut-re-mi-fa-sol-la and backwards were especially in fashion as ' themes ' in contrapuntal instrumental works before and also shortly after 1600. Many great composers such as Byrd,[3] Baldwine,[4] Ferrabosco, sen.,[5] Th. Woodson,[6] Robert Parsons,[7] later also Ferrabosco, jun.,[8] Tomkins,[9] and others[10] wrote ' Ut-re-mi's.' This fashion is an important indication of the growing popularity of the major key which began definitely to

---

[1] There are many instances of this kind in Add. 31390, e.g., " Dum transisset Sabatum," " O Luna," " Aspice, Domine," etc., by several composers.

[2] " Une bergère," " O dulks regard," and many others in Add. 31390. The use of secular melodies as basic thematic material of instrumental pieces represents a step beyond the practice of the 15th century when secular melodies were used in religious works (Mass " L'homme armé," etc.) ; see above, p. 61.

[3] Add. 32377 (partly lost).

[4] One a 2 and one a 3 in King's Library RM. 24, d. 2.

[5] Ibid.

[6] Ibid.

[7] Add. 32377 (one part only).

[8] Oxford Christ Church ; one Ut-re-mi and one La-sol-fa.

[9] Called " In Nomine Ut-re-mi," Dublin, Marsh's Library, Z.3.4. 1–6.

[10] There is an anonymous piece called Re-la-re in Add. 31390 ; more are in Royal College of Music, 2036 and in Add. 36484.

replace the Church modes towards the end of the century in the work of the instrumental composers.

The next and last phase of the development is easily established. The primitive scale motifs are extended and enriched. Real themes are invented, independently of any vocal origin—with free *fantasia*. The final stage of the metamorphosis has been reached.

Fantasia, or fancy—this was the name given to these new pieces which were to play such a vital part in the history of English music. Thomas Morley, one of the leading Elizabethan composers, recognised its importance even at the time. In the instrumental fantasia he says " may more art be showne than in any other musicke."[1]

The name and the principle of the fantasia are not exclusively of English origin. There are fantasias in continental publications such as those which are contained in Milan's *El Maestro* (Madrid, 1535), *Fantasie Ricercari Contrapunti a 3 voci di M. Adriano* (Willaert) & *De Altri Autori*, Venice, 1559,[2] and Giuliano Tiburtino's *Fantasie et Recercari a 3, Accomodate da Cantare et Sonare per Ogni Instrumenti*, Venice, 1549.[3] Yet the continental influence did not go very far beyond the name and the basic formal structure. On the whole the English works are of English evolution. The earliest fantasia in England which I have been able to find is a piece called " Fansy" by " Mr. Newman," contained in the famous Mulliner's Book[4] as an organ piece. There are other fantasias composed before 1600 for several instruments, for instance a fantasia a 3 and one a 6 by William Daman (d. 1593),[5] Thomas Wilson,[6] Alfonso Ferrabosco, sen.,[7] and the great William

---

[1] *A Plaine and Easie Introduction to Practical Musicke*, 1597, pp. 80 ff.

[2] See R. Eitner, *Bibliographie*.

[3] Ibid.

[4] Add. 30513, written by Th. Mulliner, Master of St. Paul's Choir before the middle of the 16th century. Fantasias by early masters like Strogers (d. about 1585) and Wm. Munday (d. 1591) are also in the Fitzwilliam Virginal Book.

[5] The one a 3 is printed in the collection *Konyncklyche Fantasien* (Amsterdam, 1648 ; now in Royal Library, Uppsala and Scheurleer Library, The Hague).

[6] Add. 36484.

[7] Add. 32377 (Cantus only). The subject of the first section of this fantasia:

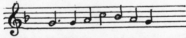

occurs many times throughout the instrumental literature of the 16th, 17th, and 18th centuries, up to Bach's famous E-major fugue (Wohltemperiertes Klavier, Vol. II). See also " Et exultavit " by Taverner, quoted above, p. 81.

Byrd (1543–1623) ; students of Byrd's music may be referred to one of his earlier pieces, a fantasia for three strings[1] which exemplifies the earliest English chamber music at its best.

The fantasia a 3 by William Daman (d. 1593) must have enjoyed special popularity abroad, for it was given the honour of being printed in a continental collection.[2]   It is more of an ' Ut-re-mi-fa-sol-la,' on the model used in the middle of the 16th century ; the only progress compared with the older species being the introduction of much shorter note values, for the piece starts in breves and semibreves and works itself up to a lively second half with crotchets and quavers. A fantasia a 6 by the same composer[3] is less interesting.

Thomas Morley's only 5-part fantasia[4] (he wrote many in two parts) is kept in the traditional motet style. It is, however, unusually homophonic and bears certain traces of the influence of the vocal madrigal. This piece is not typical of the great master's instrumental compositions, which will be considered later on.

Thomas Whythorne (1528—after 1590) wrote several instrumental fantasias which are contained in his *Duos or Songs for 2 voices* (London, 1590).[5] The purely instrumental pieces form the third part of this collection of duets. In the first part the composer leaves it to the performers to play the vocal items of his work on " Instruments of Musicke that be of the like compasse or distance in sound," while those of the second part, also originally intended for voices, may be played on two treble cornets.

Technically these duos introduce a kind of practice which was very fashionable on the Continent during the 16th century. Such duets for voices or all kinds of instruments of equal pitch were a favourite form especially in Germany and Italy where they were called Bicinia. In all these pieces the two parts perform a concertant and fugal counterpoint. No difference appears to have been made between vocal and instrumental duos either in style or in form. In England the technique of the Bicinium was

[1] Add. 34800.

[2] In the already mentioned 20 *Konyncklyche Fantasien*, Amsterdam, 1648.

[3] Oxford Christ Church, MSS. 979–83.

[4] Brit. Mus. Add. 37402–6 (no composer's name), also Royal College of Music MS. 2.049 (with the name, but incomplete).

[5] Copy in the British Museum.

neglected until Whythorne and his far more important immediate successor Morley published their collections.[1]

Although Whythorne's compositions for two instruments have been condemned as very poor indeed by almost every scholar who has written about them,[2] they are interesting and important as the earliest printed collection of instrumental music ever published in this country. They cannot be considered, however, as in any way essential or typical from the point of view of the development of chamber music in England, being weak copies of the continental masterpieces. True, they are contrapuntal compositions,[3] but they lack special characteristics, scale motifs up and down being the chief melodic feature.

It was the fantasia, even more than the vocal madrigal, which subsequently formed the main basis of the home-music which became so immensely popular towards the end of Elizabeth's reign. When the fantasia swept the homes of the new gentry and middle classes, the two historical sources of instrumental chamber music became equally visible : Church motet and dance tune.

[1] Whythorne himself refers to this fact in the preface to his publication (which, incidentally, was paid for by the author himself) where he says : " Having understanding . . . that neither before nor since that I published in print Musick for 3, 4 & 5 voices, which is now almost 20 yeeres past ther hath not any of our nation published in print any Musick for 2 voices (as divers strangers in forrein countries have don heretofore)."

[2] P. Warlock, *Thomas Whythorne*, London, 1925 ; see also Ch. Burney, H. Davey and E. Walker in their books on the history of music.

[3] Whythorne calls them " canons of 2 parts in one."

CHAPTER IV

CHURCH MOTET AND DANCE TUNE, THE PARENTS OF ENGLISH CHAMBER MUSIC

SUCH was the state of instrumental music at the beginning and during the first years of the Elizabethan age : a dualism in musical practice, resulting from a class division in cultural life— the growing power of a new class while the old one was still rather firmly entrenched. The early In Nomines and fantasias, both deriving from vocal Church forms and practices, contain the relics of the feudal age that formerly ruled supreme. Dance music, on the other hand, was derived from the tunes of the people and now progressed vigorously as the music of the rising merchant class.[1]

In spite of the considerable advance achieved in the struggle for greater independence of style in instrumental music, almost all the In Nomines and fantasias of the 16th century still showed important features of the vocal style of an earlier aristocratic society. Those which survived most obstinately were the long-drawn-out, motet-like melodic lines by which the neutral character of the Church motet was still maintained, and the device of ' overlapping ' the sections, by which the formal structure of the whole was blurred. We have seen how even in William Byrd's piece clear-cut cadences were avoided by the technique of ' overlapping.' The " eternal melody " of the Catholic age was still suggested.

At the same time dance music during Henry VIII's reign and part of Elizabeth's was chiefly practised in its genuine and pure form, as rhythmical music to which people really danced. The practice of dancing to regularly phrased yet tuneful melodies, continuing the age-old popular art of the minstrelsy, was thriving in the second half of the 16th century in England as much as anywhere.

During the last twenty years of that century the popularity of dance music broke all previous bounds. Practically the whole of Europe was held, as never before or since, in the spell of a rage for dancing. There, mankind was virtually racing through life in a whirl of gliding, stamping and hurrying rhythms. Innumerable editions of dance collections appearing year by

---

[1] Most composers of the time actually wrote *both* types of music, Church motets and dance tunes.

year bear witness to the consciousness of the newly-won freedom
—too early, one is tempted to say, in view of the ordeals through
which following generations had yet to pass.

Here is an example of such a ' dancing-dance ' (time about
1570) ; it is by the famous Robert Parsons :

Example 22 : Galliard for 5 instruments[1], Robert Parsons.

In later Elizabethan England, dancing was cultivated with
special gaiety, no doubt because the threat of the Counter-
Reformation was more effectively checked over here than in
other countries. With the defeat of the Ármada the menace of a
return of the dark ages seemed to have been finally removed.
Dance music was even encouraged by some clergymen, such as
Hugh Kinge who wrote a treatise in defence of music and
dancing.[2]

Pictures as well as literary works of the time give evidence of
the great popularity of dancing during the Elizabethan age.
One recalls Sir Toby's exuberant variations on the theme :

  " Wherefore are these things hid ?   Wherefore have these
  gifts a curtain before 'em ? are they like to take dust, like
  Mistress Mall's picture ?   Why dost thou not go to church in
  a galliard, and come home in a coranto ?   My very walk

[1] MS. Add. 30480–85.
[2] Brit. Mus. MS. Harley 2019 (date about 1575).

should be a jig : I would not so much as make water but in a sink-a-pace. What dost thou mean ? is it a world to hide virtues in ? I did think, by the excellent constitution of thy leg, it was formed under the star of a galliard."[1]

Dance tunes were whistled in the streets, then as now. Gay melodies in popular style can be found among the galliards and almands of Anthony Holborne and John Dowland, two of the most famous composers of religious and other ' serious ' music :

Example 23 : A. Holborne, *The Night Watch.*

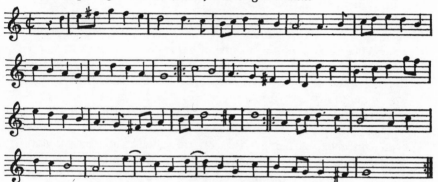

Tunes such as " Mr. George Whitehead his Almand " by Dowland remind us of " Lucie Locket lost her pocket "—or even " Yankee Doodle " :

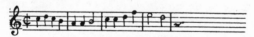

These dances are completely homophonic, as may be seen in this typical galliard by Holborne (conclusion) :

Example 24 : from A. Holborne, Galliard for 5 instruments.

---

[1] *Twelfth Night*, Act I, Scene III. This passage has been freely, though mostly incompletely, quoted (e.g., H. O. Anderton, *Early English Music*, 1920).

There is an immense number of such tunes, some of them as popular up to the present day as " Green Sleeves."[1]   Of particular importance are the Country Dances and ' Morris ' Folk Dances, originally tunes from the village green (in two or four-in-a-measure time) which became popular at Elizabeth's Court.

Dancing was inseparable from the people's life during the age of Elizabeth.   Some 16th century critics may have noticed " a certain deformity and insolency of mind " among their fellow countrymen, dress, food and luxury in general may have been sumptuous ;   Italian extravagance and flamboyance may have been aped by the English ;   there may have been exaggeration, vehemence of action and licence of expression in pageantry and many stage plays ;   manners may have been naughty or the English italianate " a devil incarnate "[2]—the Elizabethan age was wonderfully and insolently alive.   And hundreds of dance melodies still bear witness to this exuberant intensity of living.

The development of instrumental music so far discussed has been conceived as being based on the dualism of clerical and secular (middle-class) elements.   During Elizabeth's reign this dualism gradually disappeared, and was succeeded by an astonishingly uniform and homogeneous musical life.

In particular, a new form of chamber music developed, to which all authoritative parts of the community contributed, and in which a singular *rapprochement* of styles was achieved. Fantasias and In Nomines were more and more secularised and influenced by the elements of dance music, and dance music itself was stylised, taking on many a feature of the complicated and contrapuntal fantasias and In Nomines.   Dances and fantasias henceforth were only two aspects of one and the same musical era.

This amalgamation of two kinds of musical practice which had once seemed irreconcilable ;   this incorporation of the best elements of the art of the old age in the vigorous cultural drive of the new time, proved immensely beneficial to English chamber music.   The resulting hybrid style gradually developed more and more in a secular direction, and the music became more typically instrumental and more independent.

[1] See Chappell, *Old English Popular Music*, p. 239.   Chappell also gives numerous other tunes.   Most popular dances of the time appear just as often with texts as without.

[2] J. B. Black, The Reign of Elizabeth (1558–1603) in *The Oxford History of England*, Oxford, 1936, p. 237.

In many spheres of musical practice the small man distrusts the so-called ' good music ' which he has not the education to understand. At the same time sophisticated people regard the music of the masses as vulgar and over-simple, an attitude that mostly springs from the upper-class standard of better and more complete musical education. In the middle ages up to the reigns of Henry VII and Henry VIII, the gap lay between clerical motets, the art of a feudal society, and the music of the popular minstrelsy.

Why did this gap close at the time of Elizabeth ? How was it possible for an art that originated in the Church and another that arose out of popular activities to come together ?

The answer is : because the Elizabethan age witnessed a remarkable unification of hitherto warring forces of society.

For one thing Elizabeth succeeded in rallying a large part of the population on the issue of resistance to foreign invasion and Spain's reactionary power.

National unity was further strengthened by the success of Elizabeth's policy on the constructive economic side, for example her patronage of commercial and colonial expansion and the encouragement which she gave to industrial - development. Successes in these fields silenced the criticism and thwarted the opposition of the Catholics.

Furthermore the growing acceptance by the nation of the Anglican Church and the cultural *rapprochement* of town and country, described earlier, are clear indications of the unification of these leading cultural elements under Elizabeth's control.

It is true that there was within the state another ' opposition ' class (apart from the Catholics). There were certain radical sections of the growing capitalist bourgeoisie whose creeds were expressed in the gradual spreading of Puritan doctrines. So with the defeat of Spain, the greatest enemy, and therefore England's entry on to the European stage of power, there came not only the height of national glory but also the young beginnings of a clash between state power and just this rising bourgeoisie (which could only end in revolution, since the state power was in form feudal and absolutist and therefore unsuitable to an expansionist bourgeoisie). However, Elizabeth's state power suited the bourgeoisie up to the great turning point of the Armada. The vital problems of foreign policy that confronted the country between 1558 and 1588 effected a temporary

solidarity, and the struggle between absolutist-Anglican conservatism and Puritan ambitions was postponed.

The cultural life of the nation reflected its social and political
unity. The cultural features of the different groups of Elizabethan
society became assimilated to a high degree. Hence also the
unity in the practice and production of chamber music.

But what was the position of the popular masses, especially the
small peasants, manufacturing artisans, agricultural labourers,
and shop-keepers ?   Did they cultivate an art of their own ?   If
so, did they contribute to the development of chamber music
which was from now on considered an accomplishment among
" Gentlemen and Merchants of good accompt " ?[1]   Or did a
new split appear between official and popular cultural activities
with the rise of the merchant monopolists to increasingly powerful
positions in the country ?

The answer to these questions reveals perhaps the most imposing
feature of Elizabethan cultural life : an astonishing mutuality of
influences between popular and official music.

It is true that the 16th century as a whole was a terrible one
for many dispossessed peasants.   But the free yeomanry played
an important part in cultural life.

So it was a veritable two-way traffic reflecting the close bonds
that existed between free yeoman and prosperous townsman in
an age when the majority of the people of England still depended
on the land.

On the one hand, then, the masses consumed the cultural
fruits that came from the higher strata of society.   On the other
hand the new wave of musical activity in singing and playing in
the second half of the 16th century proves most eloquently that
the ordinary folk, especially the peasantry, were not only not
incapable of creative thought, but a very important part of
Elizabethan musical life.   In turn the art of the higher regions
of society was most strongly influenced by the vigour in the
cultural activities of the common people, in their popular
pageants, folk songs, and dances.

Aristocratic music lovers did not consider it at all beneath
them to listen to or indulge in such activities, even though it
may not have occurred often (as it did occur fifty years later)
that a gentleman confessed :   " even that vulgar and Tavern-
Musick, which makes one man merry another mad, strikes in

[1] Introduction to *Musica Transalpina* by Nicholas Yonge, London, 1588.

me a deep fit of devotion and a profound contemplation of the
First Composer."[1] And a study of Elizabethan virginal music
(e.g., the Fitzwilliam Virginal Book) reveals how very close the
bonds between aristocratic or intellectual and popular music
were. In virginal music there are innumerable folk-song
melodies used by composers to build up sets of variations, dances
and fantasias.

The influence of folk music is most impressively documented
in the general use of the popular idiom in the works of all composers, even the most intellectual and sophisticated, as the
examples of Dowland and Holborne show.

So Elizabethan and early Jacobean chamber music, though it
chiefly originated and was mainly practised in the circles of
' polite society,' was not quite such an exclusive and aristocratic
affair as is often imagined. If a man could afford any degree of
luxury, musical instruments were among the first things he
would acquire. Instrumental music, especially the smaller
combinations, such as solos and duos, had a comparatively wide
appeal among artisans, small producers, shopkeepers, and well-to-
do yeomen, and continued to do so during the age of James I.

In the midst of all these activities stood Elizabeth's court. It
combined, furthered, and co-ordinated all the productive forces
which had been springing up in the cultural life of the country
ever since the beginning of the Reformation. Musical life in
particular profited from Elizabeth's broadmindedness in all
matters of science and art. Apart from being personally fond
of music, the Queen was a great organiser of musical activities
in all quarters.[2] Her personal patronage of music and musicians
is proverbial. This patronage did not indeed create the mar-
vellous musical life of the end of the 16th century, but it assisted
and advanced it enormously.

*   *   *   *   *

Among the old instrumental motets, fantasias as well as In
Nomines, we find a tendency to take on more and more the
elements of popular music—even dance music. The fantasias
of Thomas Morley (1557–1603) provide the most lively instances
of the secularisation of the instrumental motet. It is chiefly his
two-part fantasias which we have to consider as representative
of this process.

[1] Sir Thomas Browne in his *Religio Medici*, 1642.
[2] See Hayes, *King's Music*, p. 55.

There are nine fantasias a 2 in *The First Book of Canzonets* of 1595[1] and six in *A Plaine and Easie Introduction* of 1597.[2]   Here an important advance has been made, not only beyond Why-thorne's duos but also beyond the general style of the previous period.   For the first time the ' overlapping' of the sections is, if not entirely given up, yet everywhere reduced in its veiling effect ; after isolated attempts to the same end had been made by earlier composers such as Tye.[3]   Each one of the small sections of the pieces expires on a clear cadence, before the next section starts :

Morley, " La caccia " a 2 (1595).

Morley, " La girandola " a 2 (1595).

The only trace of the earlier ' overlapping' here is that in most cases one of the two parts does not pause immediately after the final note of the cadence is reached, but holds the final note of its section while the other part introduces the new fugal theme, thus still bridging over the transition from one section to another.

Altogether Morley pays much more attention to cadences and clearly noticeable conclusions than any of his predecessors.   In the *Plaine and Easie Introduction* he treats the problem of cadences in detail,[4] differentiating between " middle closes," as " com-monle taken at the ende of the first part of a song," and " finall closes," ". . . whereof such as bee suddaine closes belong properlie to light musicke, as Madrigals, Canzonetts, Pavins and Galliards, wherein a semibriefe will be enough to cadence upon, but if you list you may draw out your cadence or close to what length you will."   Other music is classified as " grave music," including fantasias ; here " you must in them come with more deliberation in bindings and long notes to the close."

[1] Brit. Mus., printed music and MS. Add. 23625.

[2] Brit. Mus.   [3] See above, p. 88.   [4] pp. 132–44.

A similar tightening-up of the form appears in some works of Morley's contemporaries, such as Edward Blanke.[1] Here, too, the sections are differentiated from each other.   Blanke's fantasia a 5, which seems to have been written before 1578,[2] thus being one of the earliest pieces of chamber music in England so called. is moderately vocal in outlook, being at the same time fairly homophonic rather in the way of certain contemporary madrigals. But in the middle of the piece, which is in common time, we find a short episode that is entirely homophonic and has 3/4 rhythm, clearly dividing two rather long sections :

Example 25 :   from fantasia a 5 by Edward Blanke.

An early In Nomine a 5 by William Byrd[3] has the last section in a galliard-like triple rhythm as against common-time in the earlier sections :

Example 26 : from In Nomine a 5 by William Byrd.

---

[1] Add. 31390, p. 31.
[2] See Catalogue of MS. Music in the Brit. Mus., Vol. III.
[3] Add. 31390, p. 44.

A similar arrangement of various rhythms can be found in the 5th duo of the *Plaine and Easie Introduction* by Morley.

Clarification of form seemed now to be the general aim of composers.

Thus a technique was being attacked that had been one of the chief characteristics of Church polyphony for centuries. It was largely by means of the technique of overlapping that musical art under declining feudalism was kept in such a state of complexity and turgidity, many highly ornamental voices winding around each other in slow-moving counterpoint. The psychological effects of this weaving of continuous close tissues of independent parts, impossible to disentangle from each other and from the whole, was one of neutrality and lack of definition (which does not mean that many of these pieces were not singularly beautiful and powerful).

The ' overlapping ' had first appeared in some motets and other vocal forms of the 13th and 14th centuries. The Catholic Church, from that time, had to make a stand against Humanist and Renaissance tendencies in all spheres of spiritual life. These tendencies were always towards clarity of thought, enlightenment by education, and recognition of the rights of the individual. As against them, the Church cultivated mystical complexity in its art. The desire of the Church to keep in particular its music neutral and opaque became most noticeable in the choral works of the Netherlandish School towards 1500. Certain reforming tendencies can, it is true, be found again and again in this music, such as the use of secular melodies as cantus firmi in the motet (officially discouraged by the Catholic Church about the middle of the 16th century), and the elaboration of a more elegant and comprehensible melodic and formal structure, as for instance established by Josquin des Près and his pupil Mouton (but Josquin's intentions were counteracted by composers like Gombert, De la Rue and others on the Continent, and by Taverner in this country, also by Merbecke and Aston). Yet in spite of the fact that such Renaissance tendencies even penetrated into the sacred motet, the ' medieval ' character of the motet was, on the whole, maintained throughout the 16th century. This was effected to a high degree by avoiding cadences, in particular by the welding together of the sections, i.e. by the ' overlapping.'[1]

---

[1] Here is another example of a fantasia in the old style ; it is by Mich. Guy and must be dated just about 1600 (Brit. Mus. Add. 40657–61). The overlapping is very strongly noticeable, the continuous flow of polyphony obstinately kept—while at the same time the liveliness of the parts increases (example opposite):

(continued from footnote 106)

The abolition of the overlapping of the sections in the motet form represents an assault on the very stronghold of the music of the old Church. After having developed forms of art of their own in the dances of the first half of the 16th century, the young bourgeoisie in England now took hold of the forms of the old age and transformed them while absorbing them completely.

Just as important as this process of growing clarity and transparency of the form is another interesting development, on the melodic side. Morley occasionally interrupts the continuous flow of the melody, cutting it up into little fragments :

Example 27 : from a duo by Morley (1597).

We have already seen the beginnings of this technique in Robert Parsons' famous In Nomine a 5.[1] But Morley in his duo goes much further.

Morley's duos are on the whole far less monotonous in structure than those of his predecessors. Each melody consists of several more or less independent short sub-melodies. For instance in " Il Torello " (1595) the initial theme clearly consists of four little segments : a thematic lead (a), a cadence (b), a figure (c) corresponding to (a), and again a cadence (d) :

Example 28 : " Il Torello " a 2 by Morley (1595).

Compare this melodic structure with that of works of his fore-runners, even of progressive composers like Parsons :

Parsons, In Nomine a 4[2]

Parsons, In Nomine a 4[3]

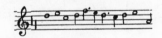

[1] See above, p. 89.
[2] Oxford, Bodleian Library, MSS. D. 212-6.   [3] Ibid.

so the essence of Morley's advance in the spirit of the new age
becomes manifest. The whole atmosphere in Morley's duos is
one of greater freshness and popular simplicity :

Example 29 : Morley, Duo III (1597)[1]

Morley's nine fantasias a 3[2] as well as several more pieces a
3 and 4 from the *Plaine and Easie Introduction* are even more lucid
and popular. Some elements of the form of contemporary
popular songs have been taken over, for instance the repetition
of the last part of a piece.

Finally, the treble melody becomes more important, being
worked out more elaborately and strikingly than the other parts
of the score. This happens even in Morley's polyphonic pieces :

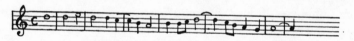

Yet Thomas Morley's work was itself only a beginning.

Some composers before and about 1600 gave the fantasia form
a further secular meaning by connecting it up with amusing
non-musical subjects, sometimes even going so far as to play
about with it in the form of programme music. John Baldwyne
(d. after 1615), author of In Nomines and fantasias a 2 and 3 in
Morley's style, wrote a fantasia based on the " Coockow's "
motif.[3] There is a ' battle ' fantasia for two lutes in Pickering's
Lute Book,[4] and another battle piece by Byrd.[5] Munday wrote

[1] *Plaine and Easie Introduction*, pp. 60–61.
[2] Add. 34800. The MS. also contains 6 fantasias a 3 by Blanke, similar to
Morley's but without the freshness of those of the greater master. They bear more
traces of Church music.
[3] Brit. Mus., Roy. MS. RM. 24, d.2.
[4] MS. Egerton 2046 (Brit. Mus.).
[5] See H. Davey, p. 171 ; also E. H. Fellowes, *Byrd*, London, 1935.

a " storm " fantasia.[1] Certain programmatic ideas also appear
in Morley's duos, for instance in " La Caccia " where a little
motif is ' chased ' over the whole scale in unusually long
sequences[2] ; similar instances can be found in some pieces by
Tobias Hume (shortly after 1600).

*   *   *   *   *

How on the other hand popular dance music began to change
into something much more artistic and stylised is most impressively shown in the works of Anthony Holborne (d. about
1615). Much of the elaborate style of the In Nomines and fantasias has been incorporated in these pieces which were once
famous on the Continent as well as in England.[3]

Holborne published a collection *Pavans, Galliards, Almains and
other short Æirs for five Instruments* (1599) which contains 65 items.[4]
Throughout the collection a galliard follows a pavan, except in
the last part which contains almains, rounds and gavots. Most
of the pieces have literary, religious or fanciful names, such as
" The Tears of the Muses," " Paradizo," " Infernum," " The
Image of Melancholy," " Mens Innovata," etc.

Holborne's dances are strongly influenced by the style of the
abstract fantasias of the day. There is nothing vulgar or strikingly
obvious in them ; they are lyrical, long-drawn and always highly
civilised and elegant, avoiding literal sequences and too obvious
analogies :

Example 30 : from " Moretta " a 5 by Holborne.

The structure of the melodies is similar to that of Morley's
themes, with the natural differences necessitated by form of the
pavan ; (the pavana consisting of several ' strains ' each of

---

[1] See H. Davey, p. 171.

[2] From the Canzonets, 1595. There are also programmatic pieces for virginal
in the collections of the time.

[3] Four of Holborne's dances were printed in Zacharias Fuellsack's and Christian
Hildebrand's collection of dance tunes, Hamburg, 1607.

[4] Examples from Holborne's *Pavanas, Galliards, Almaynes, Corantes*, London,
1599, in Brit. Mus. h. 267 (printed music in photocopy), and P. Warlock's publication of dances by Dowland, London, 1926.

which finishes on a full stop at a double-bar). There is first a
' thematic lead ' (*a*), then a series of sequences which, however,
are never mechanical and literal (*b*), and finally a long cadence
(*c*) :

Example 31 : from " Patiencia " a 5 by Holborne.

Sometimes the distinguished character of the melodies in
Holborne's stylised dances appears most beautifully in a kind of
melodic structure in which a thematic lead is repeated several
times, again not literally but in extensions and rhythmical
variations :

Example 32 : from Pavan 41 a 5 by Holborne.

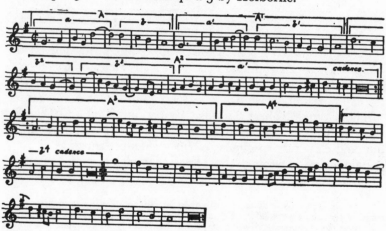

Here the originally neutral character of the thematic lead is
enlivened through the insistent phrase repetitions. The melodic
ups and downs are very carefully balanced ; climaxes are
reached slowly, to avoid either too dramatic or too obvious
effects.

Even more intimately influenced by the technique of the
fantasias is the *counterpoint* in Holborne's dances. All parts of
the score are independent, making up a moderately polyphonic
counterpoint, as opposed to the homophonic character of the

pure ' dancing-dances ' before mentioned.[1] Imitations are often
used to create polyphony ; they are mostly based on scale motifs :

Polyphony in the dances is, however, not as dense as in the
fantasias of the time, for the parts nearly always play on without
breaks in their melodic lines, so that there is not as much scope as
in the fantasias for imitations at entry and re-entry.[2]

Between 1580 and 1600 there was one particular vogue which
illustrates very well the birth of the new style of secular music
out of the unification of popular elements and aristocratic art.
This was the sudden popularity of the " Browning," an instrumental form containing sets of variations on a certain folk tune.
This song[3] is based on a simple rhythmical and melodic scheme.

Example 33 : The Leaves be greene.

The leaves be greene, the nuts be browne, they hange so high, they will not come downe.

Composers produced complicated and artistic variations on this
tune, weaving contrapuntal nets in all instrumental parts, including very lively passages and all kinds of polyphonic tricks. Among
the composers of Brownings were John Baldwyne,[4] Elvay Bevin,[5]
William Byrd,[6] Robert Parsons,[7] Henry Stoninge[8] and Clement
Woodcocke.[9] Those by Byrd and Woodcocke are particularly
fine and elaborate specimens of early chamber music.[10]

Baldwyne also wrote a set of variations which he called ' fantasia
upon a ground '[11] thus opening the long series of ' grounds ' that

[1] See above, p. 98.   The German theorist Michael Praetorius expressed his
surprise that there were left in England pavans to which people still danced. At
that time the complete stylisation of pavans was already an accepted fact on the
Continent. See Michael Praetorius, *Syntagma Musicum*, III, 1619, p. 24.
[2] An anonymous piece called " Frayse Gallyard " (Add. 31390, fol. 115b–116)
is an extreme case of a polyphonic dance piece, having contrapuntal imitations
among all the parts nearly all the way through.
[3] See Chappell, pp. 154 ff.
[4] a 3 (1600) ; Royal MSS. RM. 24 d.2.   [5] a 3 ; ibid.
[6] a 5 ; Add. 31390 ; re-edited by Sir R. R. Terry, 1923.
[7] a 4 ; ibid.   [8] a 5 ; ibid.
    a 5 ; Oxford, Christ Church MSS. 984–8.
[10] An admirable description of Byrd's Browning is found in E. H. Fellowes's
biography of Byrd, 1936, p. 196.
[11] a 3 ; Roy. MSS. RM. 24 d.2.

were popular during the 17th century as music for bass viol. The technique of variations on a ground was, however, in existence before Baldwyne in the continental ' differencias,' ' folias ' and organ arrangements of chorals, as well as in the variations of many English virginalists.

* * * * *

So much for the *rapprochement* of styles and forms in chamber music towards 1600. This combination of styles characterises the work of the whole generation of composers between 1580 and 1615. There remains the other problem : how to explain the amazing intensification of activity, particularly in the practice and composition of chamber music, and at the same time to account for the high general level of artistic value and the profundity of feeling that gave the musical life of Elizabeth's time and her successor's the character of a ' golden age.'

One of the most conspicuous features of the time was that the general economic standards of the country were advancing. With rising prices and expanding markets commercial enterprise, large new manufacturing houses and commercial centres developed quickly. The East India Company established regular connections between England and the Orient. Virginia and other colonies were planted which gave England access to the riches of the new world. Wealth accumulated especially among the merchants and landed gentry who in due course laid the foundations of a new nobility. It became more and more essential for the citizen of the realm to form his life in accordance with the recently established ideal of the ' complete gentleman ' as we know it from Henry Peacham's revealing description of a slightly later date.[1]

For a considerable number of citizens among well-to-do classes there was plenty of opportunity for repose, and inclination to enjoy it, and with the consolidation of economic welfare came increased demand for valuable musical instruments as items of elegance—a fact that itself strongly favoured the further extension of musical life. From the last decade of the 16th century onwards we find an increasing number of printed publications of music both vocal and instrumental.[2]

The co-operation of the new and musically educated general

[1] *The Compleat Gentleman*, London, 1622.

[2] A list of publications appears in Davey's *History of English Music*, pp. 157–9 and 168–9. We know of 2 publications of secular music before 1587 as against 88 from 1587–1630 (E. Walker, *History of English Music*, p. 56).

public in the development of musical life must have been astonishing, especially in London. Under the direct sponsorship of Elizabeth herself the influence of her Court and the vigour of its musical life greatly assisted this development. There was always a chapel at the Court that included the greatest musicians of the time, composers, singers, players, choir masters and teachers.[1] The houses of aristocrats and wealthy citizens such as Sir Christopher Hatton, Sir Robert Cecil, Sir Robert Sydney, Nicholas Yonge and many others closely imitated the musical life of the Court.[2] The musical activities of less prominent private individuals were in turn influenced by the stratum of society immediately above them ; and so on down the social scale. The influence of fashion assisted the general blossoming of musical life in no small way ; for by a process of conscious and unconscious emulation the musical aspirations of the aristocracy, the rich and educated bourgeoisie and the intelligentsia were transmitted to other social circles.

Whenever anyone entered the house of a friend or a shop where he was compelled to wait instruments stood ready or hung on the walls to shorten his time of waiting.[3]

Henry Peacham desired of the complete gentleman :

no more . . . than to sing your part sure and at the first sight ; withal to play the same upon your viol or the exercise of the lute, privately to yourself.[4]

The growing popularity of instrumental and other secular music was occasionally regretted by certain men who were unable to follow the trend of the age. John Cosyn complains in the dedication of his *Musicke of six and five parts* (1585) that

[1] Some of the great musicians who were employed at Elizabeth's court were : Byrd, Dowland, Ferrabosco sen., Tallis, Weelkes, Parsons. Some were at the great churches ; for instance, Morley and Cranford were employed as organists at St. Paul's.

[2] Some very well-known musicians were in the service of private individuals, such as John Bartlett who mentions in his *Book of Airs* for consort (1606) that he was in the employment of " his singular good lord and maister, Sir Edward Seymour." Michael East was in the service of Lady Hatton. See J. Pulver, *Biographical Dictionary.* Some noblemen were themselves active composers, such as Sir William Keith (d. 1581). He was one of the guardians of Mary, Queen of Scotland, during her minority ; he retired into private life about 1570. He was reputed to be the wealthiest man in Scotland. A pavan a 5 by him is in Brit. Mus. Add. 36484 (bass part only). See also Hayes, *King's Music.*

[3] W. Nagel, *Gesch. der Engl. Musik*, p. 165. For further quotations, see J. A. Westrup, *Domestic Music under the Stuarts*, Mus. Ass. Proc. 1941–2 ; also Davey, p. 156, and Crowest, p. 179.

[4] *Compleat Gentleman*, 1622.

. . . the abuse of Musike may be great when it is made an instrument to feede vaine delightes, or to nourish and entertaine superstitious devotion.[1]

But such criticisms were exceptions.

*   *   *   *   *

Yet behind this improvement in the standard of living and the code of elegance there must have been a unique forward drive in all spheres of Elizabethan life. It was this general social impetus that made the composers produce with such ardour and vigour. First of all, the age of Elizabeth was quite generally an intellectually active age. Elizabethan England was filled with a spirit of enquiry, lively in its visions and energetic in the pursuit of its Renaissance ideals. If the Elizabethan had time for contemplation and repose, he certainly hated spiritual sloth. " Otium animæ vivæ sepultura "(Sloth is the tomb of the living mind)—this assertion of an Elizabethan[2] is typical of many of his contemporaries as far as spiritual interest and activity are concerned. In Elizabethan and early Jacobean England the battle of ideas was lively and intense, not only among its politicians but also among its " metaphysicals," poets and musicians.

There was certainly no element of stagnation in the Elizabethan conception of social life ; on the contrary, there was a most determined desire for social progress throughout the second half of the 16th century and even beyond 1600,[3] and the citizens were prepared for any amount of sacrifice in their will to overcome all obstacles and dangers on the road to the fulfilment of this desire.

The age of Elizabeth was resolutely intent on developing all the forces and potentialities that had appeared on the ruins of medieval society. And it did not indulge in vague yearning and frustrated brooding—there was a very material foundation for the optimism of the age.

If 16th-century England had not yet seen the feudal order of

[1] The only existing copy of this work is in Brit. Mus., k.8.b.6.

[2] Lawrence Keymis, Raleigh's companion in the Guiana Expedition ; see also J. B. Black, The Reign of Elizabeth (1558–1603) in The Oxford History of England, Oxford, 1936, p. 239.

[3] J. A. Westrup is quite correct in stating that the intensity of musical practice and production did not decrease but continued during the early years of James I's reign. See his excellent paper on Domestic Music under the Stuarts, Musical Assn. Proceedings, 1941–2, pp. 19 ff.

the past completely demolished, it had secured a firm basis for the new mercantile and industrial forces who had written the ideal of individual freedom and expansion on their banners. Enormous prospects had opened up in the country's internal as well as its external development. Its thinkers, philosophers and artists alike, did not, it is true, exclusively write and sing of the great *material* achievements of their society : of the flourishing cities, the pompous country manors, the glories of battle on land and at sea. But they were imbued with the same spirit of activity and optimism as the builders of the new realm themselves.

" The outgoings of the spirit are conditioned by its intakings, and the imaginative reaching of the man of letters " (and art !) " keeps pace with the widening horizon of his experience."[1] And their music, too, reflects in vivid colours and patterns of sound the emotional richness of the age.

Throughout history art has received a new stimulus from socially progressive movements. Who would not feel tempted to compare Elizabethan England with the England of the present day ? As far as the art of music is concerned[2] the present phenomenal vogue of music, the enormous flowering and intensification of musical production, the deepening of public interest in our art, could hardly have been possible without the British people's heroic fight for progressive democracy and against reaction. This seems plain enough : their philosophy has been deepened, their horizon widened, and their minds have been quickened.

So there was unusually high quality and depth of feeling, beside great impetus and strength in Elizabethan and early Jacobean culture. The citizens were men of this world and of their day—passionately fond of their own time, and fully awake to the glorious possibilities of the future. The poets and artists were no exception, even though Elizabethan art and literature were capable not only of glorifying their heroes but also of expressing tenderness, and of exploring the profoundest depths of the human soul.

* * * * *

[1] J. B. Black, The Reign of Elizabeth, p. 238.

[2] The problem of the relationship of the different arts to one another must be left out of this discussion ; it has already been pointed out that there can very well be periods of great poetry and poor music, and *vica versa*. See above, p. 8.

The emotional depth of the music has its counterpart in the 'musical philosophy' of the age.

Music during the time under discussion meant for the average citizen something very high and noble. The attitude of the Elizabethan musician and music lover, as already shown by Byrd, is expressed in innumerable sayings and writings of the time. The depth of musical feeling can be judged in many passages in Shakespeare :

> O but they say, the tongues of dying men
> Enforce attention like deep harmony :
> Where words are scarce, they are seldom spent in vain ;
> For they breathe truth, that breake their words in pain.
> He, that no more must say, is listen'd more
> Than they, whom youth and ease have taught to glose ;
> More are men's ends mark'd, than their lives before :
> The setting sun, and music at the close.
>
> (Richard II)

Though the element of recreation and pleasure becomes more and more conspicuous in the dedications of publications in the second half of the 16th century, it was no superficial entertainment that the man of the Elizabethan age sought. Profound emotions resound in the works and thoughts of the century of the Reformation. Nobody found a clearer expression of the inner purpose of music during the age of Shakespeare than Thomas Morley, one of its best musical masters :

> Among so many brave and excellent qualities which have enriched that vertuous minde of yours, I know the same also to be much delighted with that of Musicke, which peraduenture no less then any of the rest hath beene to it as a ladder to the intelligence of higher things.[1]

The magical effect, the emotional power of the instrumental sound is expressed in many sonnets, several of which served the composers as favourite texts for the composition of madrigals. In them Orpheus and the supernatural power of his art are pictured again and again. Revelling in music, man might " fall asleep or hearing die."

[1] From dedication to *The First Book of Ballets*, 1595.

At this time profound emotions are stirred by instrumental music :

> O softly singing lute,
> See with my tears thou time do keep.
> Yet softly, gentle strings,
> Agree with love that cannot sleep.

> (Madrigal from Pilkington's collection, 1624)

To his Lute

They pleasing notes be pleasing notes no more,
But Orphans wailing to the fainting ears ;
Each stroke a sigh, each sound draws forth a tear ;
For which be silent as in woods before :
Or if that any hand to touch thee deign,
Like widow'd turtle still her loss complain.

> (W. DRUMMOND, 1616)

Slow, slow, fresh fount, keepe time with my salt teares ;
Yet slower, yet, O faintly gentle springs :
List to the heavy part the musique beares,
  Woe weepes out her division, when she sings.
    Droope herbs, and flowres ;
    Fall griefe in showres ;
    Our beauties are not ours :
      O, I could still
  (Like melting snow upon some craggie hill),
    Drop, drop, drop, drop,
Since natures pride is, now, a wither'd daffodill.

> (BEN JONSON, Cynthia's Revels, 1600)

For William Byrd good music is such a matter of importance that he wants it to be listened to again and again for it to be properly understood :

A song that is well and artificially made cannot be well perceived nor understood at the first hearing, but the oftner you shall hear it, the better cause of liking you will discover.[1]

In Ben Jonson's *Entertainment at Theobald's* of 1587, Genius, who had been struck dumb through his admiration of the Queen,

---

[1] *Psalms, Songs and Sonnets*, 1611, dedication.

cannot find suitable expression to tell his feelings. Rendered speechless by emotion he implores music to express his awe and homage.[1]

The musical artist at this time began to develop the first signs of that excitability in his emotional life that later became—alas ! —one of the permanent attributes of the professional musician. Shortly after 1600 Stephen Gosson speaks about " musitians whose mindes are as variable as their arte."[2] The musical profession, moreover, following the general development of professional life in the early stages of capitalism, became increasingly independent of Church and Court. ' Musician ' as freelance, as private music teacher or even as composer was one of the new professions of the time about 1600. Richard Allison (d. after 1606), composer of an excellent In Nomine[3] and several pieces for virginal,[4] calls himself " gentleman practitioner " in the art of music[5] ; he sold his music himself at his house " in the Duke's place, near Aldgate." John Farmer (d. about 1603), famous composer of madrigals, also of instrumental pieces, similarly calls himself an independent " practitioner in the Art of Musique,"[6] although he seems to have been in the employment of the Earl of Oxford as a music teacher for a short time.

This development of the profession, together with the new individualism in society, began to have a profound effect on the character of many musicians towards the end of the 16th century.

Naturally it would be going too far to characterise the musician of the early 17th century as a neurotic of the Scriabine type. And yet at that time we hear, for the first time in the history of music, of strange, adventurous careers of musicians, of composers and instrumentalists who were highly strung and hot-blooded— as Dowland expressed it : " aut furit aut lacrimat quem non fortuna beavit " (he who has been neglected by fortunè either rages or weeps).

Some musicians even got into conflict more than once with the

[1] W. McClung Evans, Ben Jonson and Elizabethan Music, 1931, p. 6.

[2] Playes Confuted in five Actions, see The English Drama and Stage under the Tudor and Stuart Princes, Roxburghe Library, 1869, p. 182.

[3] Oxford, Bodleian MSS. 212–16.

[4] Add. 31392.

[5] J. Pulver, Dictionary, p. 11.

[6] Ibid. p. 169.

law.   George Wither devotes a whole poem to these ' problem musicians ' ; a kind of poetical curtain-lecture :

FOR A MUSICIAN
What helps it those,
  Who skill in Song have found ;
Well to compose
  (Of disagreeing notes)
By artfull choice
  A sweetly pleasing sound ;
To fit their Voice,
  And their melodious throats ?
What helps it them,
  That they this cunning know ;
If most condemn
  The way in which they go ?

What will he gain
  By touching well his Lute,
Who shall disdain
  A grave advise to hear ?
What from the sounds,
  Of Organ, Fife or Lute,
To him redounds,
  Who doth not sin forbear ?
A mean respect,
  By tuning strings, he hath,
Who doth neglect
  A rectified path.

Therefore, oh Lord,
  So tuned, let me be
Unto my word,
  And thy ten-stringed law,
That in each part
  I may thereto agree ;
And feel my heart
  Inspire with loving awe :
He sings and plaies,
  The Songs which best thou lovest,
Who doth and sayes,
  The things which thou approvest.

Teach me the skill,
   Of him, whose Harp asswag'd
Those passions ill,
   Which oft afflicted Saul.
Teach me the strain
   Which calmeth minds enrag'd ;
And which from vain
   Affections doth recall.
So, to the Quire,
   Where Angels musicke make,
I may aspire,
   When I this life forsake.

GEORGE WITHER, from " Hallelujah " (1641)

Alfonso Ferrabosco, sen., the great master of In Nomines and
life-long friend of William Byrd, is a typical example of such a
restless and unstable musician ; Tobias Hume is another—he
finally went mad and spent his last fifteen years as a Poor Brother
in the Charter House. Especially were the lives and activities
of many masters either temporarily or permanently upset by the
religious strife which began to destroy the peace of many people
soon after 1600.

The life of John Dowland (1563–1626), too, was thrown out
of gear completely. First of all he was victimised in this country
for his creed. Sly priests in Rome tried to lure him into their
nets, promising to make " something extraordinary " out of him.
But he refused to be " a traitor to his queen and country " ;
later on he left Catholicism. Dowland was suffering as few others
under the strain and complexity of the time and its religious
struggles—the more so as he took an active part in them. His
reaction to a too long sojourn in one and the same place was
always violent ; he is reported to have been dismissed from the
Copenhagen court where he served for a time because of his
" objectionable mode of living."[1]

Dowland has been described as in many respects an outsider
in Elizabethan music. There are certain pessimistic tendencies
in some of his compositions which are sometimes similar in
outlook to those of Spenser, yet there is still enough that is
typically Elizabethan in his work. " Sempre Dowland, sempre

[1] J. Pulver, *Biographical Dictionary*, p. 144.

dolens " [1] : this is how Dowland himself names one of the pavanas of his most outstanding collection of instrumental works. This collection is entitled : " LACHRIMÆ, or Seaven Teares, figured in seaven passionate Pavans " ; it was published in 1605 and became so well-known that such poets as Middleton, Fletcher, Webster and Ben Jonson referred to it in their poetry.[2]   Here is, indeed, a musical language of deep effects. In several respects Dowland's music is more developed than Holborne's. Apart from having more richly figured and more interesting and varied themes and counterpoint, the movement in general is more vivid. There are short, characteristic and expressive motifs like :

and

which are used to build up climaxes. Scale motifs are no longer important ; other combinations of intervals prevail with figures which are often highly interesting. Melodies are still long-breathed, but not so smooth and abstract as in Holborne's pieces. Everything seems more personal and unusual. There are more dramatic moments brought about by sequences and repetitions of the above-mentioned expressive little phrases.

Example 34 : from Sempre Dowland, sempre dolens : Pavan, by J. Dowland.

(a)

or long pedals, which appear, by their harmonic character particularly exciting, in view of the otherwise polyphonic style of the music :

[1] " Ever Dowland, ever doleful."

[2] See also P. Warlock's edition, Oxford Univ. Press, 1926, with biographical preface. There is also a pavan by Weelkes, the madrigalist, called " Lachrimæ," obviously in imitation of Dowland. It is an expressive little piece, all in slow movements with long notes, yet rather more vocal in style. Brit. Mus. Add. 30480–84, also 30826–28 (fragments).

(b)

The passionate rising and final relapsing of the bass line, together with the conclusion on the Dominant (D) which suggests a doubtful and anxious mood, make this piece, especially at the end, one of the most emotional of the whole period.

Dowland's "Lachrimæ" are nearly all built on the famous theme[1] :

There are only very few pieces in Holborne's collection which are on a similarly high level of emotionalism. A pavan by Holborne, called "The Funeralls" flows on slowly in a sombre mood ; all instruments move about in their lowest registers :

The bass has long and dismal breves :

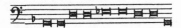

Only towards the end of this remarkable piece is there something like a mournfully sighing climax. In another obviously slow piece by Holborne, "The Sighes," a galliard, the continual

[1] Even Orlando Gibbons pays homage to his great contemporary by quoting this motif in a fantasia a 5 (Oxford, Christ Church) :

touching of the top-c, together with the slow upward movement of the melody, seems to express a programmatic idea :

Example 35 : from *The Sighes*, galliard by A. Holborne.

(Rather slow)

The works of the great masters after 1600 show even more strikingly the character of the chamber music of the great age : intimate, elaborate, expressive, distinguished, delicate and, often passionate, yet neither vague nor morbid, but always active and of transparent beauty.

CHAPTER V

THE AGE OF PLENTY

WE have watched the birth of instrumental music, with its new function in society and the rise of the new economic and social forces which made that birth possible. From the end of the 16th century instrumental music in England developed more and more on the lines and in the spirit of that particular practice which we are used to define as chamber music.

During the last years of Elizabeth's and nearly the whole of James I's reigns the production of chamber music—instrumental as well as vocal and instrumental combined—surpassed by far that of any other kind of music. There was hardly any trace of an orchestral art such as was being created in contemporary Italy and Germany. Religious choral music, though still cultivated in this country on a magnificent scale was on the wane. Chamber music was decidedly the vogue, and that more purely instrumental than vocal. Even the vocal music was often in practice instrumental, for airs and madrigals written to verbal texts could be, and, indeed, were played on instruments just as often as they were sung.[1] It is true that more vocal music than instrumental was printed, but far more instrumental music than vocal survives in manuscript, and the sum total of instrumental music composed surpasses that of secular vocal music.

It was an age not only of instrumental music, but especially of instrumental group-music—a true chamber-music era. Of the instrumental pieces intended and composed for home consumption, music for groups of instruments is far more frequently met than music for virginal or lute or guitar alone. Music for lute and virginals, though still often heard at both Court and private performances, was only a comparatively small part of instrumental music as a whole. In spite of this fact, the public to-day tends wrongly to associate virginals rather than ensembles of viols with Elizabethan and Jacobean culture. It was not so

---

[1] Peacham actually asks of the " complete gentleman " to be able to " sing his part sure and at the first sight, withal to play the same upon the viol." Very many vocal airs and madrigals are preserved as instrumental pieces. Gibbons' " Silver Swan," for instance, can be found as an instrumental piece in dozens of collections. Again the reader is referred to titles like R. Allison's " An Howres Recreation in Musicke, apt for instruments and Voyces " (1606).

much the soloist as the musical company in the private home
that was the centre of interest in Elizabethan and early Jacobean
England.

" Private Musicke," as one important collection is called,[1] was
indeed the art of the " good family." In 1599 Morley introduces
the first edition of his *First Booke of Consort lessons* :

> . . . newly set forth at the coast and charges of a Gentleman,
> for his private pleasure, and for divers others his frendes which
> delight in Musicke.

Two to six players, very rarely more, participated in such
musical gatherings. The numerous contemporary pictures
showing performances of chamber music all agree that participation was restricted to a few players. Nor was there an audience.
In several dedications of printed collections of instrumental
music it is emphasised that this art ought to be practiced
" privately " by the players. The " Clubs for Music Making "[2]
are further proof of the particular character of English chamber
music. Only a small number of selected listeners—if any at all
—were supposed to be present at these performances.

The intimacy of the art is admired and referred to in contemporary poetry, e.g., in the Pilkington collection of 1605
addressed to the " softly singing lute," the permanent companion
especially of the young lover,

> Killing care, and griefe of heart.
>
>   (Fletcher).

Contemporary poetry shows very clearly that during the
Elizabethan and Jacobean age the individual always related the
effect of music to his own intimate feelings ; music was a private
affair in its content as well as in its condition of practice.

So the country house of the gentry-nobility and the drawing-
room of the average well-to-do citizen were the chief homes of
musical activities. Music at the courts of Elizabeth and James
was music in the home of the monarch, the same in style and
substance as in the home of the subject. Elizabeth was a keen

---

[1] Martin Pierson (Peerson), published 1620.
[2] Mentioned in P. Scholes's *Oxford Companion to Music*, London, New York
and Toronto, 1939.

instrumentalist herself and liked to take part[1] or listen to, and be lost in, the " concord of sweete sounde " provided by the great composers employed by her. There are not nearly as many examples of large gatherings of musicians for the purpose of pompous display under the Tudor kings as had been customary in the castles of medieval predecessors and still were in the homes of Spanish grandees. It is true that Elizabeth on certain occasions liked to show off before important guests at her palace with twelve trumpets, two kettle-drums, pipes and cornets which " made the hall ring for half an hour together,"[2] but the use of ' quiet ' and elaborate music at her Court by far exceeded that of noisy drum and trumpet. James I maintained for a considerable time the practice of ' private music ' ; but in the course of his reign the ' Masks,' and other ostentatious musical shows with their new conception of orchestra and public, came more to the fore.[3]

The development of the royal chapel from Henry VIII to the end of Elizabeth's reign is characterised by a reduction of brass and percussion and an increase of pure chamber music instruments. At Henry's court where there were already more lutes, viols and rebecks than at his father's ; we count 4 lutenists, a virginalist, 3 rebeck players, 3 taborists, 1 harpist, 2 violists, a piper, 9 or 10 sackbut players, 4 percussionists and 16 trumpeters, the latter serving as ' waits ' on occasions like big receptions, pageants and other functions. Edward VI's chapel in turn recruits further chamber-music instruments—another harpist, 6 violists, 2 flautists, 2 virginalists and 8 " players of interludes " as well as 2 " makers of instruments," while the taborist and 3 sackbutters are dismissed. Elizabeth adds a violist and dismisses another sackbutter, although she takes in a bagpiper for special purposes, and also 7 " musitions straungers " whose identity is not known. There were, of course, always singers

---

[1] According to John Playford (11th edition of *Preface to Skill of Music*, 1687) " Queen Elizabeth herself was not only a lover of this divine science (music) but a good proficient therein," and she is said to have often " recreated herself on an excellent instrument called the poliphant, not much unlike a lute, but strung with wire."

[2] P. Hentzner, *A Journey into England in the year 1598*, ed. 1757, p. 53.

[3] Brit. Mus. MS. Harl. 2034 contains a curious item of pre-Commonwealth court representative music, called " The voluntary before the march," for drum solo, an array of very pompous rhythms, shakes and percussion-figures. Facsimile of the piece in Hayes's " King's Music." Hayes believes that the piece was used for regularisation in the army.

and organists.[1]   On the whole, it was safer to be a violist or other fiddler than a drummer or a trombone player.

Musical establishments of prominent people were equally private.   Sir Henry Unton had a violin, a cittern, a flute, a lute, a pandora and a bass viol functioning at his marriage about 1600.[2]   The inventory at Hengrave Hall, Suffolk, showed in 1602 and 1603 that the following instruments were in use (apart from a few waits' instruments like sackbuts, cornets and a serpent), 6 violins, 6 viols, 7 recorders, 4 lutes, 1 bandora, 1 mute cornet, 1 cittern, 3 oboes, 1 bassoon, 2 flutes, 2 virginals, 1 portable and 2 large organs.

All this shows the general character of the musical practice during the ' golden age '—music for the player rather than music for the listener.   It must also be remembered that according to the acknowledged code it was ' good manners ' to be able to perform upon as many instruments as possible.   Numerous representatives of the nobility and gentry are known to have been able musicians.[3]

We may perhaps digress to ask why contemporary Italy developed its musical life in a direction so completely different from that of England.   In Italy large orchestral groups competed in producing harmonic mass effects that were at the same time dazzling and exciting.   Violins, trumpets and trombones carried the full chords of great " sonatas " and " canzonas " through the halls of palaces and churches.   In Italy even chamber music itself was a medium through which composer and performer alike harangued their contemporaries, passionately expressing the storm that raged in the Italy of the conquering Counter-Reformation.   It was the Counter-Reformation that provoked the insistency and the intensity of Italian music, the ' stilo rappresentativo,' the dynamic contrasts, the dissonances and the melodic fervour, features which dominate Church and secular music alike.   In all this revolutionary art the Italy of Cosmo I and Paul V made use of and, in a sense, twisted the earlier progressive cultural traditions of the 14th- and 15th-century mercantile town-states.   The Catholic Church, especially from the time of the papal revival under Sixtus V (1585–90) onwards,

[1] Duncan and Crowest, *The Story of the Minstrelsy*, pp. 138 and 162. See also Hayes, *Kings' Music*, for music at the Court from Elizabeth to James.

[2] Galpin, p. 176, see also picture plate LIV.

[3] Examples mentioned by Westrup, *Domestic Music*.

employed every means of violent expression to accentuate her
aims. Music was to show the might of Papism in radiant
colours. It was to attract men and at the same time bewilder
them and startle them into submission—a procedure of which
pieces like Giovanni Gabrieli's famous and almost expressionist
" O Christe " are vivid examples :

Example 36 : from the Christmas Motet *O Jesu mi dulcissime*,
for two choirs, Venice, 1615.

In every respect music in unsettled early 17th-century Italy
fulfilled a propagandist function in the desperate struggle of the
old social and religious order against the new.

In the music of Elizabethan and early Jacobean England the
features which determined Italian music played a subordinate
part. England was socially much more united and safe than Italy.

The sonatas, canzonas and symphonias of the Gabrielis,
Monteverdi and the others compare with English chamber
music as paintings compare with drawings. Not the massive
effect of deep and ardent colours, but rather the tender beauty

of independent and delicately devised melodic lines, is the pride of early English chamber music. The current vogues in instrumental part-writing clearly show this pre-occupation with line as against mass colour effects.

Elizabethan and Jacobean music is not entirely uninfluenced by Italian elements of style ; although it is not so much the instrumental fantasia as the vocal madrigal and the canzonet of the Morley and Dowland type which show traces of Italian models (Gastoldi, Luzzaschi). But these influences and similarities appear small when compared with the vital differences of the two national styles as characterised above.

The name "consort," meaning a consortium of several individual players, appeared for the first time in English music about the middle of the 16th century. The chief characteristic of the consort is that it is a combination of several instruments, each with its peculiar distinguishing quality of tone. Morley's *Consort Lessons* of 1599 were written for a combination of a treble lute, a pandora, a citterne, a bass viol, a flute and a treble viol[1] ; William Holborne's edition of Anthony Holborne's *Preludes, Pavans and Galliards* (in the *Cittern School* of 1597) for cittern with viols ; John Adson's *Courtly Masquing Ayres* for 5 and 6 parts are intended for violins, consort viols and cornets (1621), Philip Rosseter's *Lessons for Consort* (1609) count on the same instrumental combination as Morley's. Charles Butler explains the consort in his *Principles of Music* of 1636 :

> The severall kinds of Instruments are commonly used severally by them selvs : as a Set of Viols, a Set of Waits, or the like : but sometimes, upon soom special occasion, many of bothe Sortes are moste sweetely joined in Consort.[2]

Butler's contemporary Walter Porter includes in his collection of airs and madrigals of 1632

> Toccatos, Sinfonias and Ritornellos, after the manner of Consort Musique. To be performed with the Harpsechord, Lutes, Theorbos, Base Violl, two Violins or two Viols.

The German composer and theorist Michael Praetorius gives a particularly picturesque description of the English consort. According to him

> several persons with all sorts of instruments, such as

[1] See also above, p. 128, where Sir Henry Unton's consort is described.
[2] Butler, p. 94.

clavicymbal or large spinett, large lyra, double harp, lute, theorbo, bandora, penorcon, cittern, viol de gamba, a small descant fiddle, a traverse flute or recorder, sometimes also a quiet sackbut or racket, sound together in one company and society ever so quietly, tenderly and lovely, and agree with each other in a graceful symphony.[1]

Such groupings of a variety of instruments are known to have been much favoured in English chamber music. They became a definite practice some time about 1575. True, we know of many examples of performances of several instruments with heterogeneous sound qualities throughout the 16th century. Apart from the above-mentioned pageant at Westminster Hall in 1502,[2] there was a dinner-music for Henry VIII (1547), which had " players on the flute, rebeck and virginalls, making the sweetest melody."[3] Yet before 1575 such variety was mostly the casual result of gatherings of musicians ; no particular combinations of instrumental sounds were demanded. One engaged whatever instrumentalists or singers happened to be available, without prescribing the use of any particular ones. Often we find the vague indication that " all sorts of instruments " may be used if those originally meant are not available, as for instance in works by Whythorne and Holborne. This ' ad libitum ' permitted in instrumental combinations in Elizabethan days is valid also for works of English chamber music of later dates ; recorders and viols in particular are known to have been freely substituted for one another down to the second half of the 17th century. But the essential principle was that a *variety* of instruments was to be employed. Only in the works by Morley, Rosseter and Dowland is preference given to a certain combination. Here we find, for the first time, something like real orchestration.

In all the combinations of instruments noted above, the fact strikes us that they all include instruments of equally moderate dynamic strength. Lutes, viols, recorders, cithers, pandoras,

---

[1] *Syntagma Musicum* III, p. 5 (1619): " ein Consort ist Wenn etliche Personen mit allerley Instrumenten, als Clavicymbal oder Grossspinnet, gross-Lyra, Doppelharff, Lautten, Theorben, Bandorn, Penorcon, Zittern, Viol de Gamba, einer kleinen Discant Geig, einer Querflöit oder Blockflöit, bissweilen auch einer stillen Posaun oder Racket zusammen in einer Compagny vnnd Gesellschaft gar still, sanfft und lieblich accordiren, vnnd in anmutiger Symphonia mit einander zusammen stimmen."

[2] See above, p. 53.　　　　　　　　　　　[3] Galpin, p. 84.

harps, dulcimers and clavichords all go perfectly well with each other. This is confirmed by Francis Bacon who gives his opinion on orchestration in one of the most famous passages in *Sylva Sylvarum* :

> And so (likewise) in that Musick which we call Broken Musick or Consort Musick[1] ; some Consorts of Instruments are sweeter than others ; (A Thing not sufficiently yet observed) : As the Irish Harp, and Base Viall agree well : The Recorder and Stringed Musick agree well : Organs and the Voice agree well, &c. But the Virginalls and the Lute ; Or the Welsh Harp and the Irish Harp ; Or the Voice and Pipes alone, agree not so well. But for the Melioration of Musick there is yet much left (in this Point of Exquisit Consorts) to try and enquire.[2]

A famous example of the attention which was sometimes paid to the balance of tone is found in the funeral music for James I, where though the numbers of players was considerable only lutenists and violists were employed (and one lone singer). We never find, say, trumpets and recorders playing together. There are a few instances in which several different instruments of equally *powerful* sound were made to perform together, such as the music in *Silenus* (1613) where the consort consisted of pipe, tabor, violin, 2 bass violins (celli), 2 sackbuts, 1 mandora and 1 tenor cornet.[3] Even in this combination of loud instruments the basic character of the consort is maintained, namely the differentiation of the parts from each other and the strongest possible independence of the individual, melodic lines, effected by allocating them to instruments of very different sound qualities.[4]

---

[1] " Broken Consort " or " broken music " means just this combination of various instruments in gatherings of chamber music where the sound is ' broken ' into various components. The name became more and more frequent during the 17th century when other forms of consort appeared, so that the original species of ' broken ' consort had to be characterised as different from the others.

[2] *Sylva Sylvarum*, Century III, No. 278.

[3] Galpin, p. 281 ; more examples ibid.

[4] Details of all the instruments mentioned and their history can be found by consulting G. R. Hayes' and Galpin's books. Here are a few general remarks. The *harp*, mentioned by Butler and Bacon and later on actually known to have been used by William Lawes in chamber music, is a variety, no doubt, of either the Welsh or the Gaelic harp, with 32 to 50 strings, running over the complete chromatic scale. The *lutes* used about and after 1600 were either alto, tenor or bass instruments (a–a^1, g–g^1, d–d^1) ; the former had 5 pairs of strings with one single string called chanterello, for the highest note in the tuning. The special colour of the lute sound is not less outspoken than that of the harp, although the sound of the lute was more nasal and slightly less loud. To facilitate the tuning

and arrangement of additional strings an additional peg box was fixed at the top of the neck; this kind of ' augmented ' lute was called archlute or archilute (a tenor archilute of smaller size was called a theorbo ; its compass was considerable, the strings reaching from Bass G to g¹). The *pandora* or bandora was a variety of the *cither* (cittern, cytherne) ; all were plucked instruments with 4–7 pairs of strings, the difference between them and the lutes being that the cithers have a flat back. The *orpharion* is a cither instrument of smaller size than the pandora. *Gittern* (geterne) is the guitar, an instrument that was very widely used in the 16th and 17th centuries ; it had 6 strings tuned in fourths and was plucked with a plectrum. *Cymbals* were not percussion instruments as to-day, but forerunners of the pianoforte. Like the medieval *tympanum* and the later *psaltery* (psalterium) and *dulcimer* the cymbal is a trapeze-shaped instrument with a wooden framing and a string-board. The strings of the cymbal and dulcimer were worked with small hammers held in the hand, while the psaltery was plucked, thus being a predecessor of the virginal and harpischord. The *viols*, bowed instruments held on or between the knees, have already been dealt with ; the bass being in particular called viola da gamba. The *lyra* family are bowed string instruments with 1 (13th century) to 12 strings and 1 to 2 " bordune " strings (see Chapter I) ; in the 17th century sympathetic strings were added on many lyras. The lyra viol is a smaller-size bass viol ; on it full chords were played after the manner of the lute. It was the solo bowed instrument par excellence during the first 20 years of the 17th century. Lyra da braccio, lyra viol and archiviola, all of the lyra family, can be considered as forerunners of the violin family ; the appearance of the latter and disappearance of the former occurred during the same space of time in the 17th century. See also K. Schlesinger, *The Instruments of the Modern Orchestra*, London, 1910. Among the wind instruments that were in use at the time in question the *pipes* were still prominent. They were whistle-flutes with 3 holes usually associated with the medieval tabor, the pipe was an open-air instrument of little relevance to chamber music, where its place as a high-pitched wood wind instrument was occupied by the descant recorder. For the state of the *organ*, during the 17th century more and more often accompanying string instruments, I have to refer the reader to Grove's list of books dealing specially with the history and varieties of this instrument. *Shalm* (shawm, schalmei, i.e. calamus-reed) is, like the old *oboe* (hautbois, hobois), a reed instrument with a conical bore and a curious shrill tone, slightly nasal but of extraordinary strength, much greater than the oboe. The shalm had a special appendix-like mouth-piece. There were complete families (sets) of bass, tenor, contralto and treble shalms, like the viol, violin and recorder families. The oboe usually occurred only in treble and rarely in tenor pitch. The *waits* or wait-pipes which were treated in the first chapter are of the shalm family and often identical with shalms. *Sackbut* (sagbut) is the forerunner of the modern trombone, usually played in a band with *cornets* and *trumpets*. *Flute* about 1600 had a twofold meaning. In many cases it meant the cone instrument which was cross-blown and held from the right to the lips (later usually called German flute or flauto traverso and flute traversière). But this flute proper was not nearly as much in use as the *recorders* which were blown into from the top, had 8 to 9 holes, and formed a family of descant, treble, alto, tenor and bass pitch. The sound of the recorders, too, is distinguished from the German flute, for the recorders have a completely unbendable, fixed, very clear and ' u '-like sound quality which always reminds one of certain high organ registers. The list of instruments, as just described, is taken from Charles Butler's *Principles of Musicke* (1636), which contains those in use at his time : " harp, bandora, orpharion, cittern, gittern, cymbal, psaltery, dulcimer, viol, virginal, pipe, organ, shalm, sagbut, cornet, recorder, fluit, wait or hobois, and trumpet." This list does not include or specially mention the lyra instruments which were so widely used, nor the violin family, for reasons which will have to be discussed later on. Otherwise Butler's list seems fairly complete. Hayes is never tired of insisting—quite properly—upon the very high degree of craftsmanship which instrument makers have lavished upon their work, from the earliest times right up to these days. Indeed, we may say that instruments were never crudely manufactured until modern commercialism corrupted artistic standards. O. Anderton mentions a list of instrument makers in the 17th century ; see *Early English Music*, 1920, p. 272.

A similar combination appears in a picture of Henry VIII's time, given in Galpin's book ; here a trumpet, a large harp, a bassoon, a pipe and a tabor are seen together.

The fact that in the consort the parts were to be distinguishable from one another is in itself clear indication that the purpose of the artist was to draw delicate and elaborate lines with all the instrumental voices. Subjective emotionalism, and that later individualism of the 18th century concert style, was as yet not so far developed in this art as to make the treble melody the carrier of the emotional message, and to reduce the other parts to the function of mere accompaniment or ' basso continuo.' It cannot be denied, however, that the treble melody was becoming more and more important in the whole harmonic structure of English music, even though Elizabethan and early Jacobean chamber music remains essentially polyphonic.

It must be emphasised that this differentiation of the parts was made possible only by the fact that each instrument in the consort had a clearly defined tone colour of its own.[1] Modern flutes, violins, pianofortes, clarinets, etc., react to any playing that is not ' made up ' with expressivo, vibrato, rubato, cantabile, sforzato and all the other refinements, by uttering completely dead sounds. Only the subjective interpretation of the artist, coupled with the accentuation resulting from the different way of bowing, makes the sound of the modern instrument breathe and live with passion and colour. The old instruments, viols, recorders, virginals and lutes are of such strong instrumental personality in themselves that they sound best and most convincing when they are played in a restrained, quiet and objective way. Their beauty lies in their ' acoustic material,' not in their capacity to reflect in a thousand details the psychology of the tortured individual in 19th and 20th-century society. To-day, when there are but few old instruments in existence and few players who can afford to buy them, there is nothing to be said against the performance upon modern violins, violas and cellos of old music intended for viols. The enrichment of the modern chamber music repertoire and the historical knowledge and understanding gained by the interpretation of old music, are too important an advantage to be sacrificed by academic insistence on old instruments for its performance. Yet the player should keep in mind that a performance of old chamber music on violins and

[1] See also Chapter III, p. 86.

cellos ought to be kept in as restrained and reserved a style as possible. Play an early 17th-century In Nomine à la César Franck and you will get a grotesque caricature, a hysterical mockery of the original.

In view of the essential nature of old English chamber music it is not difficult to understand why the violins played such a small part in its presentation. It took a complete change in the social outlook of the whole country to establish the popularity of the violin in the second half of the 17th century.

In all the consort music which we know the careful elaboration of the polyphonic lines is the most striking feature. But this artificiality is by no means based on intellectualism. The innovations which we noted in the Morley period; freshness and a new transparency of melody, and clarity of formal design, are everywhere noticeable in the music of the ' golden age ' and are carried to a high stage of development.

The classical work of the period is Morley's *First Book of Consort Lessons* of 1611, a collection of works " by divers exquisite Authors," to be performed by the six instrumental parts mentioned above. This precious work is partly lost ; we know of the existence of four parts,[1] but even this torso gives us an idea of the simple melodic beauties of the work. Morley himself refers in his foreword to the predominance of the melodic element in the consort :

> I recommend the same to your Seruants carefull and skilfull handling, that the wants of exquisite harmony, apparent, being left unsupplied, for breuitie of Proportions, may be excused by their melodious addi(ti)ons, purposing hereafter to give them more testimonie of my Loue towards them. . . .

The other works for consort of the same period are equally rich in melodic beauties and harmonic charm. Holborne's *Citterne School* (1597), which includes, among other movements, pieces for cittern, treble viol, tenor viol and bass viol ; Rosseter's *Lessons for Consort*, " made by Sundry Excellent Authors " (1609), Robinson's *New Citharen Lessons* which includes " Lessons of all

---

[1] Brit. Mus.: flute part ; Royal College : viol part. Burney attempted to add the other parts ; the full score, with the other four parts composed by Burney in the style of the time, is contained in Brit. Mus. MS. Add. 11587. The bass part, too, has turned up in a Quaritch Catalogue (1935, No. 1051 ; the price of the bass viol part was then £425 !), where reference is made to the existence of the pandora part in the Huntington Library.

Sorts " (1609), and the same author's *Schoole of Musicke* (1603) which also contains a variety of consort pieces ; some anonymous *Consort Lessons* from MS. Add. 36484, Brit. Mus. ; and so on to Adson's *Courtly Masquing Ayres*, composed in five and six parts, for violins, consorts, and cornets, which contains a number of charming pavans and galliards. An " echo " for orpharion and two bowed instruments, contained in MS. Add. 15118, is a specimen noteworthy for the melodic qualities proper to this type of music for consort. In Tobias Hume's *Ayres* of 1605[1], where there are items for the " Leero Viole with two treble viols, or two with the Treble ", the harmonic element is slightly stronger, as the character and tuning of the lyra viols necessitates. R. Allison's *Psalter* for one voice with four viols, lute, and cithern (1599) may be mentioned here too, although it is essentially a vocal work.

The parts of the consort are written as much in accordance with their peculiarities as instruments as possible. The lute part in Dowland's " Lachrymæ " is, for instance, more chordal than the other parts. At the same time we do not find in Dowland's lute parts, nor in other consorts of the time, parts for plucked instruments having long sustained notes, but long notes are always broken, by means of ornamentation. Dowland's lute part is a kind of short score of the other parts, yet adding scales, trills, mordents, etc., and rhythmicising certain passages.

The general elegance and distinction of the parts in the consorts are commended by the continental collector Besardus in his *Thesaurus harmonicus* of 1603, where he speaks with obvious delight of " those English consorts of a certain kind which are extremely sweet and elegant."[2]

The careful elaboration of every single one of the parts of the instrumental score soon led to the establishment of an instrumental solo style. The ' stylo rappresentativo ' in early 17th-century Italian instrumental music is also based on solo performance. But the essence of the Italian instrumental soli was, just as much as in orchestral music, the expressive and passionate gesture, while in English chamber music the instrumental solo was only the logical outcome of the whole style which treated all the individual melodic lines so elaborately. So combinations of lute and bass viol, bass lute with treble viol, bass viol and recorder,

[1] Hume's " Poeticall Musick " of 1609, though chiefly vocal, contains 16 instrumental items, too.
[2] " Prout sunt illi Anglicani concentus suavissimi quidem, ac elegantes." Cologne, 1603.

virginal and bass viol,[1] and also lyra viol solos were familiar features of the music of the time. Lute with bass viol was an especially favourite combination. There are pieces for lute and bass viol in Robert Jones' *Ayres* (1600), Pilkington's *Ayres* (1605), Maynard's 12 *Wonders of the World* (1611), Robinson's *Schoole of Musicke* (1603), Adson's *Courtly Masquing Ayres* (1621) ; others are found as single items, mostly in MSS., such as pieces by Norcome, and others (a beautiful example is Dowland's *Adieu for Master Oliver Cromwell*).

On the other hand, although these pieces were melodically elaborate and richly figured, they were never clumsy or over-intricate, even when written for the full consort of five or six parts. On the contrary, it must be emphasised again that clarity of structure was consciously and carefully preserved. Forms and melodies were made easy to scan and to comprehend ; it is not difficult to see why : there might so easily have been a ' mess ' of intricate parts which would have prevented the player from making any particular part heard—an overcrowded and incomprehensible polyphony. It is true that polyphony was the particular English way of building up musical forms for chamber combinations. But the jig-saw puzzles of 15th-century Church motets were not favoured in the Anglican England of 1600. Rhythmical clarity, too, prevailed in these pieces. The use of the delicate polyphonic medium of the broken consort entails a natural risk of complexity. Therefore for the sake of simplicity the broken consort exploited almost exclusively dance and similar forms, with their clear metrical and rhythmical schemes, and fantasias and In Nomines were left to other chamber combinations. The broken consort, small as well as larger ensembles, was given airs, pavanas, galliards, allemands, ' lessons ' and variation forms. The ' lessons ' in the works of Ferrabosco, Rosseter, Morley and others are pieces of easy rhythmical structure, originally presumably intended for educational purposes, with melodies easy to play, though not necessarily built in the way of existing dance types. Variations on themes already cultivated by composers of the end of the 16th century were more and more favoured, especially by viola de gamba and lyra viol players for whom were written many ' grounds ' (simple subjects

---

[1] All these combinations were often used as accompaniment for singing voices instead of virginals, e.g. Michael Cavendish's *14 Ayrs for two voices, lute and bass violl* (1598) ; similarly Dowland's *Books of Songs or Ayres* (1597–1603).

on the bass, either 4 or 8 bars in length) with ' variations ' or
' divisions ' (variations, ' dividing ' the notes of the theme into
broken chords, passages and other ornamental figures).
The viola da gamba became more and more the leading
instrument after 1600, so that it occasionally trespassed upon the
domain of the virginal, as in the " Parthenia Inviolata "[1] of 1611,
a collection of pieces for virginal solo in which the viola da gamba
goes with the virginal bass all the time.

The last consequence of these tendencies was the evolution of
solos for one melody instrument capable of producing double or
treble stoppings without co-operation of lute or virginal. In
Hume's *Ayres* of 1605 we find pieces " for the Leero Viole to play
alone " ; there are 18 dances by Thomas Ford for lyra viol solo ;
there are some pieces for lyra viol alone in Corkine's *Ayrs* of 1612,
and also Ferrabosco's *Lessons* contain items for one lyra viol.

English instrumental music in general was recognised to be
paramount in many continental countries at the beginning of the
17th century, and English string playing in particular was very
highly esteemed at this time. English music and musicians
found their way to Germany, Denmark, Holland, France and also
Italy. String music by William Brade, Thomas Simpson, Alfonso
Ferrabosco, John Dowland, Thomas Morley, Peter Philips and
many others was printed in continental collections such as
Matthysz' *T'uitnement Cabinet*, Amsterdam 1646, *Konincklyche
Fantasien*, Amsterdam 1648, Füllsack-Hildebrand's *Ausserlesene
Paduanen vnd Galliarden*, Hamburg 1607, David Oberndörffer's
Allegrezza musicale, Frankfurt 1620, Thomas Simpson's *Taffel-
Consort* and *Opusculum*, Hamburg 1621 and 1610, Brade's *Newe
ausserlesene liebliche Branden*, Hamburg 1617, Schaeffer's *Amœnitatum
musicalium hortulus*, Leipzig 1622, and others. English instrumentalists, especially string players, were particularly favoured
in the bands and chapels of Northern German towns and Courts.
The chapel of the Berlin electoral Court was transformed from
a ' Kantoreigesellschaft ' (choral company) into a chamber
orchestra under the influence of English string players. The
violist Price founded and directed a " small chamber music " in
Stuttgart between 1616 and 1630 ; the same musician continued
this practice in Dresden after 1630. In the chapel of Düsseldorf-
Neuburg where there were only three players permanently active,

---

[1] Parthenia means virgin as well as 'virginal' (" belonging to a maiden"), inviolata
means untouched as a virgin, as well as ' composed with viol.'

only once (in 1618) was a new musician engaged : an English violist and lutist.[1] Of the English musicians who went to Germany to be enthusiastically received and at once put into high and important positions many were political and religious refugees ; for instance Simpson, Brade, Norcome, Valentine Flood, Rowe, John and Clement Dixon and Jack Jordan. At least three among those mentioned were really great composers : Thomas Simpson, William Brade and Peter Philips. Among those who went to other continental countries were Maynard, Stanley, Dowland, Cuttings, and Norcome, who went to Denmark and Belgium.

*   *   *   *   *

Besides the broken consort (that very genuine and characteristic form of English chamber music) and string solo playing, *combinations of instruments of the same family* were used in 16th- and 17th-century musical England. Such combinations were also called ' consorts ' but only from the second quarter of the 17th century onwards. Naturally the independence and individuality of the parts of the ensemble was less strongly maintained than in the broken consort. But in view of the particularly tender and clear quality of tone of some families of English instruments, the delicate polyphonic character of the music was preserved or in certain combinations only slightly modified.

Robinson's *Schoole of Musicke* (1603) contains ' toys ' (as certain forms of light music were called) and a fantasia for two lutes ; some pieces for two lutes are said to be contained in J. Pickering's *Lute Book* (1616).[2] The already mentioned collection by Ferrabosco (1609) includes lessons for " 1, 2, and 3 viols tuned lyra-way " ; so does Hume's work of 1605. R. Taylor (d. 1637) wrote two Almains for " 3 liero violls."[3] There are also consorts of equal wind instruments. Butler talks of a " consort of waits " as already mentioned.[4] In *Gorboduc*, a drama of early Elizabethan time,[5] there is a pantomime before each act ; a consort of violins (viols ?) plays before the first act, cornets before the second, flutes before the third, hautboys (for the appearance of Furies) before the fourth, and drums and flutes before the fifth act.

In this kind of consort for groups of instruments of the same

[1] Details in the author's *Die mehrstimmige Spielmusik*, 1934, p. 56.
[2] Brit. Mus. MS. Eg. 2046.   [3] Oxford Christ Church Library.
[4] See above, p. 130.   [5] 1562 ; see Davey, p. 221.

family the ordinary *viols* offered the best possibilities for the peculiar type of polyphony that was demanded by Elizabethan and early Jacobean society. Throughout the 17th century there is altogether a most conspicuous preponderance of stringed instruments in the chamber music of this country, and the viols certainly represented the main contingent of stringed instruments. Viols were combined into ensembles of three, four, five, and six players ; the popular ' chest of viols '[1] consisted either of two trebles, two tenors and two basses, or of one treble, one tenor and one bass. These two combinations carried the main body of chamber music in England down to the second half of the 17th century. As late as 1676 Thomas Mace, famous musical theorist, wrote thus in his *Musick's Monument* in protest against the rapidly encroaching violins : " Your best provision (and most complete) will be a good chest of viols, six in number, 2 Basses, 2 Tenors, 2 Trebbles, all truly proportionably suited." The consort for viols became the favourite art of one particular type of cultured and musically educated family.

Compositions for this kind of chamber music ensemble appeared in a never ending flood. The amount of works printed, comparatively small, shows however that the ' music for viols ' was intended for but a comparatively small section of the musical public and not for the mass. Other combinations of chamber music, chiefly the accompanied solos, but also several kinds of broken consort, were more widely used than the pure viol ensemble. Only three collections of music for a consort of viols appeared in print between 1597 and 1638 : Gibbons' 9 fantasias a 3 (1609), East's *Third Set of Books* (1610) and *Seventh Set of Books* (1638) with fantasias a 2–5. A few single pieces appeared in vocal collections, such as two of Byrd's best pieces, a fantasia a 4 and another one a 6, which are contained in *Psalms, Songs and Sonnets* (1611). On the other hand, 13 collections for mixed combinations (in some of them the choice of the instruments is left to the player) for 2 to 6 parts appeared in print during the same period, not counting many vocal collections containing single instrumental items, such as Maynard's and Corkine's. The bulk of the music for viols was passed on from one group of players to another by copying ; up to the present day the music for viols is preserved almost exclusively in MS. copies.

[1] More about the chest of viols and music for viols may be found in Hayes' book.

Seventeenth-century English music for viols includes some of the best compositions of one of the greatest periods of chamber music in all ages and countries. We may profitably consider this wonderful body of work in some detail.

It will be necessary to deal with this music from two angles : first, its instrumental style, which at last establishes itself, in this period, as the antithesis of that of the religious vocal motet of old ; and secondly, its great intrinsic value, for early 17th-century music for viols is the crowning achievement, the climax of the entire development of instrumental music in this country.

In the development of its formal structure, the ' music for viols ' was the field for experiment which played an important part in determining the instrumental forms we use to-day.

The *fantasia* is the chief form used in writing for viol ensemble. The fantasia, freest and most abstract species of early English instrumental music, was shown to be an offspring of the vocal motet of the 16th century. The motet consisted of a number of successive sections each of which was built up on the contrapuntal development of one thematic subject. Each of these subjects was based on whatever melody of the Gregorian Chant happened to go with the particular sentence of the biblical text that was needed in the service. The instrumental fantasia was shown to be, exactly like the vocal motet, a succession of polyphonic sections ; the only difference between the motet and the earliest instrumental fantasias was that the thematic subjects of the fantasia were never based on Gregorian melodies but invented by the composers. Morley defines the fantasia in the *Plaine and Easie Introduction* :

The most principall and chiefest kind of musicke which is made without a dittie is the fantasia, that is, when a musician taketh a point at his pleasure, and wresteth and turneth it as he list, making either much or little of it according as shall seeme best in his own conceit. In this may more art be showne then in any other musicke, because the composer is tide to nothing but that he may adde, deminish, and alter at his pleasure. And this kind will beare any allowances what-soeuer tolerable in other musicke, except changing the ayre & leaving the key, which in fantasie may neuer be suffered. Other things you may use at your pleasure, as bindings with discordes, quicke motions, slow motions, proportions, and what you list.   Likewise, this kind of musick is with them who practise instruments of parts in greatest use, but for voices it is but sildome used.[1]

Thomas Morley, we found, carried the fantasia form a step beyond the ' instrumental motet ' stage by discarding the device of overlapping the sections.   The sections became detached from each other ; thus the formal structure of the fantasia became clearer and much easier to understand.

Now the various sections in these early fantasias (those by Thomas Morley and many of his contemporaries such as Elway Bevin,[2] Thomas Bateson,[3] John Baldwyn[4] and also the famous virginalist John Bull[5]) were still based on motifs of fairly similar character throughout the piece.   Therefore the general im-pression made by most of these fantasias is one of a thematic uniformity almost as constant as in the vocal motets, even though Morley's fantasias, as we have seen, were much livelier in style than the vocal motets, and even though we have already recognised in Morley's fantasias important changes towards formal clarity such as the abolition of overlapping.

Yet bolder innovations were introduced by Morley's successors. The earlier generation of composers merely carried out a clearer *separation* of the sections from one another.   The momentous new advance of the composers of the generation that succeeded Morley was the introduction of *variety* into the fantasia form. The sections were no longer based on subjects of more or less similar character and equally moderate speed, but on definitely different types of themes.   Christopher Simpson's description of the fantasia of a somewhat later date depicts this new achieve-ment very clearly :

In this sort of Musick the composer (being not limited to words) doth imploy all his art & invention solely about the bringing in and carrying on these fuges according to the order and method formerly shewed.   When he has tried all the several ways which he thinks fit to be used therein, he takes

1 Pp. 80 ff.
2 Oxford, Bodleian, MSS. D. 212-6.
3 Christ Church.   ﹨
4 Brit. Mus. Roy. MS. RM. 24, d. 2 (dated 1595-1606).
5 Fifty short fugues or fantasias a 4, all in Cambridge, Fitzwilliam Museum ; no press mark.

some other point, and does the like with it, or else, *for variety*,[1] introduces some chromatic notes, with lighter humour like a Madrigal, or what else his own fancy shall lead him to ; but still concluding with something which hath art and excellency in it.[2]

Variety was introduced in response to the demands of the time. The changeability of the mind and temper of the new human being, his need to expand, to fit himself into new and changing situations, was one reason for the new mobility and variety in art. Another reason was that it became part of the function of early 17th-century music even more than of any 16th-century art to offer an antidote to the increasing feverishness of economic life, at any rate in London. In music the increasing restlessness of the age is reflected in the desire for variety. Monotony, anything that savoured of the uniformity of the medieval motet, had to disappear.

A fantasia by Thomas Lupo (fl. about 1605)[3], one of the most important composers of the new generation, shows this significant advance :

[1] Author's italics.

[2] *A Compendium of Practical Musick*, 1667.

[3] Englishman, of Italian descent; fl. 1605–15. This fantasia like most of Lupo's numerous fantasias a 3 are in Oxf. Bodl. MS. E. 437–42. His four, five and six part fantasias are mostly in Oxf. Christ Ch. MS. 2.

Example 37 : Fantasia for three parts by Thomas Lupo.[1]

TH. LUPO
FANTASIA

[1] Oxf. Bodl. MS. E. 437ᴸ-42.

LUPO (2)

LUPO (3)

LUPO (4)

The first section (the sections in Lupo's fantasias are numbered) is based on two subjects that appear successively. One of these starts in minims and slides into faster movement :

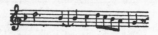

The other one is built on a quaver figure (tenor part) :

After thorough fugal exploitation especially of the second subject the following simple motif introduces the second section :

It is developed in sequences throughout the score. The third section has a theme that suggests folk-song influence, especially as it is (like the whole section) almost entirely homophonic :

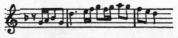

The fourth section stands on this motif:
It is carried through all parts in a very syncopated manner which veils the arsis and thesis of the bars and gives the section the air of an extremely busy polyphony, while the fifth and last section returns to straight 4/4 rhythm with clearly marked accents on the main beat of the bars :

Most of Lupo's fantasias are similar to the one just analysed, in that they introduce a variety of musical ideas.[1] The same principles of form appears in the numerous fantasias by the composer Giovanni Coperario. While most of Coperario's 5 and 6 part pieces are either transcriptions or imitations of his vocal madrigals, his 3 and 4 part fantasias are important here, especially regarding their formal structure. The number of

---

[1] Lupo wrote about 70 fantasias a 3–6, including some In Nomines. The above fantasia a 3 is No. 8 of his three-part pieces ; the numbering of this and other pieces by 17th century composers is taken over from the author's *Die mehrstimmige Spielmusik des 17 Jahrhunderts*, where a detailed list of these works is given (including all sources).

sections in the three and four part pieces even exceeds that in Lupo's fantasias. Coperario's fantasias are full of variety ; of changing musical pictures which pass by in constant succession. The idea of the ' musical kaleidoscope ' never forces itself upon the mind with greater insistency than when one listens to a fantasia a 3 by Coperario.[1]

Thomas Ravenscroft, chiefly known as a writer on music,[2] left a number of fantasias for viols which amply illustrate the same principle. In fantasia No. 3 a 5 for instance, the first section introduces a warm and singable subject and stricter counter-subject at the same time[3] :

Example 38 : from fantasia a 5 by Thomas Ravenscroft.

(*a*) first section :

The second section, based on this motif :

(*b*) second section :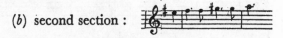

which appears numerous times in all parts of the score, produces a curious effect which suggests a man trying again and again to climb up a ladder and always falling back. The third section

[1] Coperario's real name was John Cooper ; he was a Londoner and only italianised his name as Italian music and musicians became more fashionable. He lived from 1570–1627, for a long time as musician at the royal court. Ninety-six fantasias a 3–6 are known to be by Coperario. Oxford, Christ Church, MS. 2, and Roy. Coll. of Music, MS. 1145 contain most of his fantasias.

[2] Ravenscroft's chief theoretical work is called *A brief discourse of the true* (*but neglected*) *use of Charact'ring the Degrees* . . . 1611. He lived from 1593 to 1633 as bachelor of music in Cambridge.

[3] The simultaneous introduction of two themes at the beginning of a fantasia is also one of Lupo's favourite features. Here is an example (from a Lupo fantasia) of a section based on a *couple* of themes :

Fantasia No. 6 a 5 :

Both themes are developed together or rather against each other.

of this amusing piece is homophonic and only a few bars long ;
the theme is :

(c) third section :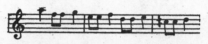

The fourth section climbs down the ladder in all parts :
(d) fourth section :

The fifth section displays long melodic lines, all in minims and
semibreves :
(e) fifth section :

The variety in all these' pieces is unlimited.   No rules or
customs seem to prescribe a definite order for all the small
movements that are piled up ; the whole production blossoms
forth unchecked, in a sort of festival of happy creation.   Many
more composers could be mentioned such as H. Bassano
(d. 1630),[1] J. Bennet (d. after 1614),[2] W. Cobbold (1560–1639),[3]
Nath. Giles (1558–1633),[4] J. Gibbs (d. about 1640),[5] J. Mundie
(d. 1630),[6] J. Milton (father of the poet, 1562–1647),[7] and others ;
all of their fantasias and In Nomines convey the same impression,
that of general joy and triumphantly creative effort.
However, in the midst of this abundance of types and characters
certain preferences are beginning to be shown, certain habits to

[1] 4 fantasias a 5 in Oxford, Christ Church MSS. 716–20.
[2] 1 fantasia a 5 in Add. 17786–91.
[3] 1 In Nomine a 5 in Add. 18936–9.
[4] 1 Miserere a 2 in Roy. MSS. RM. 24, d. 2.
[5] 1 In Nomine a 5 ih Oxford, Bodleian MSS. D. 212–16.
[6] 4 In Nomines a 5–6 in Roy. MSS. RM. 24, d. 2 ; 1 fantasia a 5 in Add. 37402–6.
[7] 5 fantasias and 1 In Nomine a 5–6 in Oxford, Christ Church 423–8.

be found : some types of sections occur again and again. For instance restful sections in minims and semibreves, like the fifth section in the piece by Ravenscroft just shown, appear in many pieces, mostly in the second half. Another very common feature is the conclusion of a fantasia with a lively polyphonic section. The fantasias by the great composer Alfonso Ferrabosco, jun. (1578–1628), excel in such striking conclusions[1] :

Example 39 : from fantasia No. 1 a 4 by Ferrabosco (conclusion).

This example shows, however, that a new element is entering the fantasia. The piece ends in a climax ; and to conclude a piece on a particularly effective and convincing note (a long pedal just before the end is another one of Ferrabosco's favourite devices) is an architectonic principle. This implies that more of the element of emotion and drama, of personal expression, is wanted in chamber music. We shall have to deal later with this new tendency ; it is symptomatic of the rapid advance of individualism in art. In its effect upon the formal structure of the fantasia, this new element leads to an extension of the previous limits of variety : very soon the connecting-up of sections of

[1] 47 fantasias a 2–6 by Ferrabosco are known ; among them 5 In Nomines. Chief MSS. containing his works are Oxford, Christ Church MS. 2 and Dublin, Marsh's Library MS. Z. 3.4.1–12 ; also Brit. Mus. Add. 29996. The composer was in the service of the Crown as was most of this widespread and famous family of musicians. See G. E. P. Arkwright, " Notes on the Ferrabosco Family " (*Musical Antiquary*, July, 1912).

varying character begins to approach *dramatic contrast*. The juxtaposition of very different, or even antagonistic types of sections is something deeper, something more emotional than the simple enumeration of little pictures which have no inner relationship with each other. It is this ' light-and-shade ' expressionism that has so often reminded people of Rembrandt's art and induced scholars to call 17th-century music ' baroque,' a term otherwise applied to painting and architecture of this and the following century.

Alfonso Ferrabosco jun.'s numerous works are among the first in which stress is laid on expression based on contrast. The evolution of greater dramatic strength is Ferrabosco's chief contribution to instrumental music in England. This is how it is done. Take, for instance, fantasia No. 17 a 4. The opening section is an extensive, gay and lively fugue :

Example 40 : from fantasia No. 17 a 4 by Ferrabosco :

(*a*) first section :

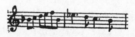

It moves about in crotchets and minims and concludes on a cadence on D. The second section hurries in with quite an exciting combination of an augmentation and a diminution of the first subject, deliberately outdoing the first section in vigour and intensity :

(*b*) second section :

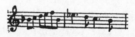

This section soon concludes in F ; another section starts, introducing a strongly ornamental duo of the alto and tenor viols, all in quavers and semiquavers :

(*c*) third section :

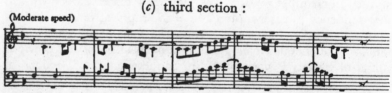

It leads into an equally lively concert of the two other parts, and finally into a complete symphony of four intricate instrumental lines. Here the architectonic conception becomes clearest, for a pedal that stretches over eight bars forms the crowning climax of the whole piece.

Another fantasia by Ferrabosco, No. 3 a 4, begins with this bright and happy theme :

Example 41 : from fantasia No. 3 a 4 by Ferrabosco.

(Moderate speed)

After a tuneful development of this cheerful subject, a contrasting section appears, all in long notes, definitely calming down the gayı excitement of the first. Yet the excitement returns : the third and concluding section takes up the thematic material as well as the general behaviour of the first section.

We give the whole fantasia.[1] It is one of the best of its kind.

It should be noted that Ferrabosco's innovations are in no sense due to the Italian origin of the Ferrabosco family, for he was born in England and grew up in the atmosphere of London's musical life, under no specifically Italian influence beyond that which may possibly have come from his father, who taught him.

Orlando Gibbons (1583–1625) in most of his fantasias, and William Byrd in at least a few of his latest instrumental compositions, go yet a step beyond Ferrabosco. The various sections have different time signatures ; the order of their arrangement is, at the same time, by no means casual : they are arranged according to a well-devised plan ; simultaneously the sections grow in extension to real miniature ' *movements*.'

Gibbons—we shall have to recognise him as the greatest master of the fantasia of the period—was singularly consistent in the application of his architectonic principles. Among, his main instrumental works are two collections of three-part fantasias, one containing seven, the other nine pieces. From the point of view of formal development his seven fantasias a 3 (and one a 4) " with the greate dooble base,"[2] and also some of the 3-part pieces in his printed collection[3] are most interesting. In

---

[1] See Appendix, Example I.

[2] 27 fantasias (among them 4 In Nomines) are known to be written by Gibbons. The 7 a 3 and 1 a 4 (all with double bass) are in the Marsh Library (Dublin) ; the one a 4 is reprinted by Fellowes (Stainer & Bell) and two a 3 in my edition of 3-pt. fantasias (Baerenreiter). See also above, p. 3 ff. The old double bass is the violone which has the contra-A as its lowest string.

[3] 9 fantasias a 3 (either 2 trebles and bass, or bass with tenor and treble viols) were printed in 1609 and reprinted in Matthysz's collection of 1648 ; later by Fellowes (Stainer & Bell, 1924)

all these pieces, some of which are of much greater length than earlier fantasias, we find at least four complete movements. They all begin with a fugato section of moderate speed :

Examples 42 and 43 :   from fantasia No. 2 a 3 and fantasia No. 1 a 4 by Orlando Gibbons :

from fantasia a 3 :   from fantasia a 4 :
    (a) first section :   (a) first section :

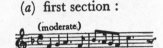

A section of the Galliard type follows :

fantasia a 3 :   fantasia a 4 :
    (b) second section :   (b) second section :

succeeded almost invariably (either immediately or after another short fugato) by a melody in common time of definite folk-dance character (the melody from the 4 part fantasia is taken from a contemporary Morris Dance) :

fantasia a 3 :

(c) third section :

fantasia a 4 :

(c) third section :

This section usually leads back to a fugato which is of the same nature as the first section and often also thematically related to it ; sometimes a finishing touch is provided by a coda in which the movement slows down considerably.

Externally this form is influenced by the dance-suite which had grown out of the ' couple ' (pavan plus galliard)[1] and was at this time (about 1610–20) mainly cultivated by German composers such as Schein, Peuerl, Groh, Otto and others.   A strong similarity between Gibbons' form and the Italian ' chain-canzona '

[1] See above, p. 73.

also exists, especially in the fantasias with the double bass. The chain-canzona consisted of 10 to 20 little sections, each only two or three bars long, rarely more ; it represented the final breaking-up of the motet form in the radical Italian way and was sponsored by most of the great composers of the period, Giovanni Gabrieli, Massaini, Grillo, Rossi and others. However, the evolution of the Gibbons fantasia seems to me to have come about chiefly as a logical development of the genuinely English fantasia form whose development we have been following from its origins in the middle of the 16th century.

Gibbons is master of the art of contrast ; the way he mixes tragic and gay often reminds us of Shakespeare. In Gibbons' instrumental works the technique of contrast is a clear expression of a desire to get away from the ' epical evenness ' of the medieval motet ; to unite the parts of the piece in a dramatic unified whole. For to connect two movements of opposite character means to *unite* them, by giving them a functional relationship to each other.

We realise that an important factor, perhaps indeed the main motive force, of this urgent development of style was the subjective desire on the part of many composers to *communicate* their indi-vidual problems and ideas to the world. In earlier centuries most music was imbued with the non-individualist spirit pre-vailing in medieval life. In the 17th century the individual imagination of the composer is allowed (and even desired) to take its free and independent course. The work of art now begins to take shape as a self-contained whole or organic unity of divers kinds. The composer submits a course of mental and emotional experiences to the public. The contents of such a course of events are more and more subordinated to the *general* trend of the *whole* work. It should be clear, however, that Ferrabosco's and even Gibbons's pieces represent but a first and modest step on the road towards real ' dramatic consistency ' ,as it was achieved, for instance, in Purcell's works. We admire in early 17th-century music many qualities in which it differs essentially from classical music. There is still much reserve in the tidy sectional structure even of the most advanced composers of the Gibbons-Ferrabosco era. Yet the development which is taken up by Purcell and finally by the great Vienna classics begins with our masters of the Jacobean age and their Italian contemporaries, and there are more indications that the music of this time points

in that direction.   In the English development they can be sum-
marised under two headings :   (1) the sections of a fantasia
become more and more independent of each other ;   at the same
time they are grouped in a way that puts them into closer relationship to each other and to the piece as a whole ;   (2) the number
of sections diminishes while the sections themselves grow in length.

The first tendency points more and more towards the sonata
form in which the sections have become independent movements,
arranged according to a definite order (allegro-adagio-allegro, or
adagio-allegro-adagio-allegro).   The second tendency points to
the ' fugue ' in the modern sense ;   the thematic material is
unified more and more until there is only one subject to a whole
movement, and the former ' sections ' of the fantasia become the
' developments ' of the fugue.

A fantasia a 6 by William Byrd offers a perfect example of the
first tendency.   It is one of the last works of the master, and
it is quite as elaborate as those of Gibbons, but it is less militant
and more amiable and ' human.'   The piece in question is in
C-minor and consists of three movements.   The first is an adagio-
like fugato that is full-of warmth and intimacy, recalling Byrd's
lovely c-minor " Lullaby " :

Example 44 :   from fantasia a 6 by William Byrd.[1]
(b)   first section :

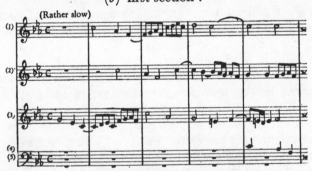

A more popular episode of the gigue type follows :
(b)   second section :

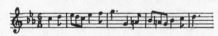

---

[1] From Psalms, Songs and Sonnets, 1611 ;   reprinted by Fellowes (Stainer & Bell).   Altogether there are 21 fantasias a 3–7 by Byrd, including In Nomines and the Browning (see E. H. Fellowes's already mentioned book on Byrd).   The " Lullaby " was re-edited by Fellowes in 1925 (Stainer & Bell).

succeeded by a 3/4 movement that resembles a minuet as well as a galliard :

(c) third section :

A short coda takes up the mood of the adagio beginning. Here the form of the later sonata is definitely prepared, especially by the introduction of the ' da-capo ' element in the concluding coda. Several fantasias (called ' Ayres ') by the composer Thomas Holmes (son of John Holmes)[1] strongly resemble those by Byrd and Gibbons. The beginning returns at the end, and in the middle the changing little movements are grouped round an imaginary centre.

The second tendency (the unification of the thematic material) is shown in several fantasias by Ferrabosco. In fantasia No. 16 a 4 the opening theme :

is quoted again and again throughout the piece. The above mentioned fantasia No. 17 a 4 keeps one subject all the way through, although it appears in several variations and the sections differ greatly in kind.[2] Some of John Bull's (1563–1628) short fantasias[3] are miniature one-theme fugues almost of the Bach-Handel type, with only this difference, that the strict division of the classical fugue into developments, transitions, episodes, coda, etc., is not yet established in all details. Fantasia No. 10 a 3 by Lupo also returns to the opening subject :

in every section. This subject is, incidentally, very common in this music, as it ' turns on ' the movement with the crotchets running into quavers. Gibbons, Ferrabosco, Coperario and others all use this subject in some form or other.

In the fantasias of several masters we see the number of sections dwindling down. Some of Tye's In Nomines indeed had only

---

[1] All in Brit. Mus. Add. 40657–61.
[2] See above, p. 152.
[3] All in Cambridge, Fitzwilliam Museum (no press mark).

two or three sections, and few-section compositions were long-section compositions. This layout was rare at his time ; but after 1600 fantasias that consist of two sections only become quite a normal occurrence. The one-section fantasia, i.e. the new ' fugue ' tentatively handled by Bull, Lupo and Ferrabosco is taken over and further perfected by John Jenkins, the chief master of the following generation. For the time being we can watch the two tendencies as described above growing rapidly : one, the establishment of a cyclical form of several more or less independent movements, and the other, the creation of single long movements based on one subject only. Both aim at the unification of the work of art.

Returning to Gibbons and his nine printed fantasias a 3, we find a similar tendency to unify their thematic material. Some of them consist of four independent and strongly contrasting section-movements. Yet in No. 7 of the set the sections are put into closer inner relationship to each other by using similar themes for all of them. The likeness of the thematic material in all the four sections is really conspicuous.

Example 45 : from fantasia No. 7 a 3 (without double bass). Section 1 is in 2/4 :

(a)

section 2 in 3/8 :

(b)

section 3 again in 2/4 :

(c)

section 4 also in 2/4 :

(d)

In addition to this tendency to unify the thematic material we notice again the attempt to balance the formal structure as a whole. The end rather recalls the beginning ; so again we approach the vital formula A–B–A which became so absolutely dominating in the 18th century, determining the sonata, arias, scherzo, minuet and all the other key-forms known to-day.

As in other fields Gibbons' advance in the field of form shows him as an independent personality gifted with greater courage and deeper understanding than most, of his contemporaries. There is a certain atmosphere of struggle in Gibbons' works. Orlando Gibbons does not evade the problems of his time ; he tackles them in a bellicose way ; he assaults them. His instrumental language—and the expressionistic formal structure of his fantasias is part of it—is proof of this. It recalls the most dramatic moments in his vocal works. It is very striking how Gibbons always becomes particularly dramatic and passionate when setting to music texts which expose the wrongs of human life. It was the wrongs of his own age which Gibbons interpreted in : " What is our Life ? ", " Oh, Lord, how do my woes increase," " O Lord, in thy wrath," " Why art thou so heavy oh my soul ? "

We also think of the emotional beauty in the composition of the concluding words of the " Silver Swan," most famous of Gibbons' madrigals :

Farewell, all joys ; o death, come close mine eyes.
More geese than swans now live, more fools than wise.

Again and again he tries subconsciously, we fancy, to achieve in his music that classical unity which made Elizabethan society appear to the 17th century ' merry England ' and the lost paradise. In this endeavour, which is at the same time heroic and tragic, Gibbons resembles Beethoven—we do not hesitate to make this comparison : it can be substantiated in detail, for instance by the analysis of Gibbons' fantasias and Beethoven's last quartets. Beethoven's age was, of course, an age of far greater

tension, owing to the far-reaching social developments of this
era of the industrial transformation and the French Revolution.
Moreover a study of Beethoven's works shows that at his time
the spiritual emancipation of the individual had progressed much
further than in the time of Gibbons. But essentially the comparison, we believe, can be made.

*   *   *   *   *

Thus we have seen how the development of the *formal* structure
in the fantasias foreshadows the final achievements of the Vienna
classics.

In *melodic* development we shall find that the progress towards
a proper instrumental style is even more striking.

The melodic material of the 16th century chiefly relied on scale
progression, step by step, rather than on characteristically-shaped
and striking themes. The proximity to the vocal age was
still very noticeable in the instrumental works of the 16th century.
But truly instrumental patterns appear with increasing frequency
in the fantasias of Elizabethan and Jacobean composers. Such
an interesting instrumental figure as Ferrabocso's :

Example 46 : from fantasia No. 3 a 4 by A. Ferrabocso.

which, as everyone will agree, is far removed from the vocal age,
is essentially a 17th-century achievement. Such figures became
indeed part of the natural instrumental language of the time.
With the increasing valuation of the subjective element in the art
as a whole, the development of marked and personally-shaped
themes progresses. Here are some more instances of such striking
melodic ideas :

Example 47 :
(*a*) William White, fantasia a 6[1]   (*b*) Wm. White, fantasia a 5.[2]

Example 48 : from fantasia No. 13 a 4 by A. Ferrabosco.

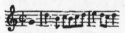

[1] Oxford, Christ Church MS. 2.
[2] Ibid.

This new individualism in the melodic element begins to per-
meate all sections of the fantasia—we say " begins," for only the
latter part of the 17th century sees its full unfolding.

The example by Ferrabosco shows that as part of the evolution
of characteristically-shaped themes a process of *metrical clarification*
was going on. Already in Morley's pieces we have seen a
division of the themes into two or four corresponding phrases
which were in the nature of question and answer. More so in
Ferrabosco's and Gibbons' themes :

Example 49 : from (*a*) fantasia a 3 (No. 3 with the double
bass)[1] by Orlando Gibbons :

(*b*) from fantasia No. 7 a 3 (1609), by Orlando Gibbons.

Melodies of this kind are obviously influenced by dance music
with its metrical clarity.

The popular element is still prominently displayed in early
Jacobean chamber music. We find that in the fantasias not only
are existing popular themes taken over and developed, but the
spirit of folk-music is embodied also in newly-composed pieces,
just as it happened earlier in the music of Henry VIII's court.
The popularity of such folk tunes as the Browning in chamber

[1] MS. in Dublin, Marsh's Library and Oxford, Christ Church MS. 419–22.
The piece is one of Gibbons' greatest works, incidentally one of his longest. In
the same series of 3-part fantasias there is a piece (No. 7) with the same subject
in opposite movement :

This theme seems to have been used by other composers of the time, too. In
the Fitzwilliam Virginal Book, new edition, Vol. II, p. 489, there is a fantasia for
harpsichord or virginal by Giles Farnaby, built on a very similar subject :

music is proof that English chamber music about 1600 and some time after had still retained its vigour and soundness. Several popular melodies in Gibbons' pieces have already been mentioned ; here are some more :

Example 50 : (*a*) from fantasia No. 7 a 3 (with double bass), by Orlando Gibbons.

(*b*) From fantasia No. 3 a 3 (with double bass), by Orlando Gibbons[1] :

They all show how the great master in particular relied on the directness of folk-melodies in order to achieve the classical forcefulness in which his works excel.

Another feature of the melodic element in chamber music of the early years of the 17th century is its increasing liveliness. It is very rich in purely instrumental features—again a comparison between an average melodic line of the 16th century with a typical one of the Jacobean fantasia will be instructive :

Example 51 : (*a*) Preston, In Nomine a 4[2] (about 1575) :
(about 1575)

(*b*) J. Ward, fantasia No. 6 a 4[3] (about 1615) :

The 3-part and 4-part pieces of most composers are of especially

[1] This episode from fantasia No. 3 (with double bass) is a Dutch tune called " de Rommelpot," popular in England at the beginning of the 17th century (as were other Dutch melodies which were probably introduced here by the English soldiers who fought for Dutch freedom and by the numerous English actors who toured Holland during that time). This melody also occurs as one of the three voices in a Quodlibet Round (No. 70) in Ravenscroft's *Pammelia* (a collection of contemporary rounds published in 1609–11) ; there it appears as a ' country dance.'

[2] Oxford, Bodleian MS. D. 212–6.

[3] Oxford, Christ Church MS. 2. Ward (d. 1640) was an ingenious composer of madrigals and instrumental works. He was partly in the service of Mr. Fanshawe, remembrancer of the exchequer of Ware Park, Herts, and Warwick Lane. Thirty-one fantasias by Ward are known.

great animation and complexity, while those a 5 and 6 mostly rely on calmer movement, although they are similarly based on polyphonic rather than on homophonic conception. Very small note values such as demi-semi-quavers are introduced. At the same time quite unvocal jumps become more and more frequent :

Example 52 : from fantasia No. 1 a 5,[1] by John Ward :

The quick note-repetitions which were so new at Tye's time[2] are now well-established. Moreover, long sequences of fast instrumental figures appear :

Example 53 : from fantasia No. 9 a 3 (1609), by Orlando Gibbons.

Generally the ' sequence ' becomes a more and more frequently employed technique for the building-up of melodic developments ; notably the fantasias by the composer Chetwoode largely depend on the employment of sequence,[3] this important feature of the music of the past 350 years.

There is one more important instance of the advance of the instrumental style. The compass of the part grows. Not only that sometimes passages run over two complete octaves :

Example 54 : from fantasia No. 2 a 3 (with the double bass), by Orlando Gibbons.

but the actual extension of the scale is widening. While in earlier instrumental music the highest notes were g″ and a″, we now find many instances of b″, c‴, and even d‴ being used in treble or descant viol parts by Gibbons, Thomas Holmes and others. In Gibbons' often-mentioned fantasia a 4 No. 1 (with the double bass) the top part even climbs as far as e-flat″ ‴ : at

[1] MS. Add. 17792-6.
[2] See above, p. 88 f.
[3] Fantasias and other instrumental pieces by Chetwoode in Brit. Mus. MS. Add. 40657-61.

the other extreme Gibbons' use of the double bass (violone) in some of his fantasias enables him to introduce contra-A ; there are many examples of the employment of this note in such fantasias.

In the music of the best composers of the period the ' freedom ' of the writing is the same in all parts of the score. The melodic material is more or less the same in all instruments. The means to achieve polyphony is *imitation*. One part introduces a motif, theme or melody which is imitated or literally repeated by the other parts that enter the score one by one. All parts achieve in this way equal mobility and equal rights. A highly instrumentalised, ' concertante ' polyphony is the result ; it is the chief characteristic of English instrumental music compared with that of other nations. Episodes like this one :

Example 55 : from fantasia No. 8 a 3 (1609), by Orlando Gibbons.

are found only in English chamber music.

If it is seen as part of the whole panorama of European musical history in the 17th century this highly-evolved polyphony (which is ultimately an offspring of the old Netherlandish polyphony) might appear backward in face of such ' futuristic ' achievements in the contemporary scene as the Italian monody, basso continuo, stilo rappresentativo[1] :

[1] The Italian ' monody ' represents the victory of expressive melody over medieval constructivism. One melodic line, either vocal or instrumental, and produced by one performer only, replaces the intricate counterpoint of earlier 16th century schools.

The ' basso continuo ' represents the victory of functional harmony over ' horizontal ' line. From 1600, a permanent harmonic background accompanies even complicated polyphonic structures : first in Italian music, later in all European music. All the contrapuntal happenings in the score are thus given a harmonic meaning. The harmonies of the basso continuo are performed on instruments capable of producing *chords* (such as organ, harpsichord, theorbo or harp). The chords to be performed by the player of the basso continuo are indicated in the form of figures and accidentals above the notes of the bass part—a kind of musical shorthand.

The ' stilo rappresentativo '. is another achievement of Italian composers about 1600. It means the expressive and dramatic recitativo which replaces the neutral flowing of the voice parts in earlier Church music.

Example 56 : from Concerti Ecclesiastici by Ludovico Grosso da Viadana, 1615.

And yet the English composers from about 1600 and after exhibited characteristic qualities of initiative and adventure as the promoters of an instrumental style, and they evolved an instrumental technique embodying these features. That is one of the enduring contributions of this country to European music of this and later times.

In a few fantasias a 5 and 6 by Ferrabosco, jun., Thomas Lupo, and also William White,[1] the compact polyphony of the fantasia seems to be broken up by the introduction of concertante solo parts which here and there come to the foreground of the ensemble. This technique anticipates indeed certain elements of the later ' concerto grosso,' if only in those few isolated examples by the composers mentioned. In the concerto grosso of the

[1] All in Oxford, Christ Church MS. 2. William White is chiefly known from three fantasias a 5, and seven a 6 ; chiefly in Oxford, Christ Church MS. 2. Little is known of his career.

Handel type, single instruments occasionally have livelier passages to perform than the orchestra. The following episode, which is taken from a fantasia a 6 by Thomas Lupo,[1] even shows some features of the later solo concerto :

Example 57 : from fantasia for a chest of viols (2 trebles, 2 tenors, 2 basses), by Thomas Lupo.

The two bass parts dominate the whole piece which sounds like a concertino for two bass viols accompanied by four higher-pitch viols.

Yet it can be stated quite definitely that not Italian influence but rather an established English practice is behind this curious development. For these virtuoso solo episodes are mostly found in the bass parts of pieces. In view of the preference that was given to the bass viol in the musical life of the time it is only natural that sometimes the bass viol took a more prominent part in the score, for the simple reason that it was often easier to find a really good player on the bass viol than on the treble or tenor viols. If we remember that many fantasias were written for

[1] Oxford, Christ Church MS. 2.

particular players we understand the varying demands on the technical skill of the executants so that certain parts emerge almost as solos.

Occasionally in pieces by Gibbons and Byrd the treble part dominates and reduces other instruments to the function of accompaniment. But for the time being such 'homophonic' episodes are rare. In general the polyphonic character of this music is little contested by homophonic arrangements. It is, as already stated, the most 'genuine' polyphony of the time throughout Europe.

Real Italian influence on English instrumental polyphony at the beginning of the 17th century is felt only in certain minor and purely external features. Arising out of the monodic style of the Florentine and Venetian schools a trio combination of two trebles and one bass became the great fashion in Italian chamber music. The two trebles were equally busy and equally important as concertante and expressive melodic instruments ; they were supported by the bass which provided, as basso continuo, a continuous harmonic background of chords all along throughout the piece. Now this arrangement of two sopranos and one bass was taken over by some English composers, in particular by Coperario, Gibbons and Lupo. But there was no question of importing, with the instrumentation, the 'vertical' harmonic conception as against the native 'horizontal' polyphonic idea. The three parts were just polyphonic lines as in all English music ; only the external form was Italian. An interesting compromise between the Italian trio-sonata and the English polyphonic style is found in a fantasia by Lupo in which three treble parts of equal pitch and importance perform a polyphonic concerto.[1]

Once again, the musical life and production of this country, especially the progressive instrumental polyphony, was so closed in itself, so healthy and independent that—at least for the time being—it could resist all the splendour and all the allurements of the new art that came from the south.

This polyphonic activity and achievement does not so occupy the composers as to prevent them from developing instrumental expressionism and emotionalism in yet another direction, the *harmonic*. On the contrary, the depth of sentiment which we found in earlier English music, reached new intensity in early Jacobean chamber music, largely owing to the exploitation in an

[1] Oxford, Christ Church MS. 2. Re-edited by the author (Baerenreiter).

intensely conscious way of the emotional possibilities of the major and minor keys.

The full and lively polyphony of the score when built up on one of those radiantly gay themes in which this music is so rich becomes a feast of optimism and brightness as in some pieces by Ferrabosco and Gibbons. A pavana a 6 by Gibbons[1] is a particularly beautiful example of such ' radiant major.' How deliberately some composers contrived their polyphonic textures with a view to utilising these qualities of major and minor is shown by the fact that chord motifs were often chosen as chief subjects in fantasias. William Cranford's first fantasia a 6[2] has such a theme :

Example 58 : from fantasia a 6 by William Cranford.

On the other hand, the emotional implications of the minor mode were no less recognised by composers. A fantasia a 4 by G. Coperario may serve as an example of the ability of some masters to create musical lyrics in an extremely tragic mood.[3]

This is the place to mention Richard Deering (d. 1630) whose fantasias[4] were well-known at their time and indeed are among the best. Deering's always moderate musical diction avoids too heavy accents yet shows most beautifully the early English sense of brightness and radiancy of colour. Again it is especially the minor (usually a-minor) which Deering employs. Here is at least one example of the simple yet masterful art of Richard Deering :

[1] Published by E. H. Fellowes (Stainer & Bell).

[2] Brit. Mus. Add. 39550–4. Bass part is missing ; here added tentatively by the author. Cranford who flourished during the first quarter of the 17th century left about 15 fantasias and In Nomines most of which are in Dublin, Marsh's Library and Brit. Mus. Add. 39550–4.

[3] Oxford, Bodleian MSS. F. 568–9 and Christ Church MS. 2 (here no name is given). See Appendix, Example II.

[4] An almaine for strings by Deering was re-edited by Sir R. R. Terry, 1925. Further instrumental works by Deering are to be found in Add. 39550–4 (8 fantasias a 5), Add. 17786–91 (2 fantasias a 6), Add. 17792–6, and Dublin, Marsh Library (1 a 6 ; the copy in Dublin is anonymous, the one in the British Museum incomplete), and Royal College of Music (many ayrs and dances a 3).

Example 59 : from fantasia a 5 in a-minor by Richard Deering.

Towards the end of the 'golden age,' that is to say, between 1615 and 1620, expressionism by harmonic and tonal means became more intense. Chromatic harmonies appear and there is a curious liking for long chains of modulations. In this respect, more than in any other, a moderate influx of Italian modernism has to be recognised at this stage. While chromatic progressions were already cautiously used by Thomas Morley and Dowland,[1] modulations such as were used now were new in English chamber music.

Thomas Simpson wrote a pavan in which one of the parts

[1] E.g. Dowland's " Forlorn Hope " (fantasias for the lute). Here as elsewhere in 17th century music, suffering and disappointment are expressed by chromatic progressions. Copy in Cambridge University library.

slowly climbs first up and then down in half-tones ; this piece
was obviously inspired by similar compositions by the Italian
madrigalist Luca Marenzio.   In Ravenscroft's fantasia No. 5 a 5,[1]
easily the master's most outstanding instrumental composition,
the third section has chromatic lines in all parts :

Example 60 : from fantasia No. 5 a 5 by Thomas Ravenscroft.

The long first section of a fantasia by Thomas Tomkins (1573–
1656),[2] also an ingenious piece, is built on a chromatic subject :

Example 61 : from fantasia a 6 by Thomas Tomkins.

While such chromatic progressions do not necessarily mean a
definite upsetting of the key, even though they bring about, by
their very nature, a quick change of chords and relationships,
some composers deliberately aim at breaking-up the tonal
uniformity of the pieces.   Thomas Tomkins, a great and daring
composer who had an unusual technical skill at his command,
wrote a fantasia a 3[3] in which he modulates from C-sharp minor
through B-minor, A-minor, G-minor, F-minor, E-flat-minor back
to C-sharp-minor, the key from which he had started, and in
steady progress on to A-minor where he stays :

Example 62 : from fantasia a 3 by Thomas Tomkins.

[1] Brit. Mus. Add. 39550–4.

[2] Oxford, Bodleian MS. c. 64–9 ; reprinted by Stainer & Bell ; ed. Fellowes.
21 fantasias are known to be by Tomkins.   Tomkins who was W. Byrd's pupil,
was organist at Worcester Cathedral and later at the Royal Chapel.   He is chiefly
known as composer of *Songs of 3, 4, 5 and 6 parts* which were printed in 1622
(re-edited by Fellowes in *The English Madrigal School*).

[3] Oxford, Bodleian MS. D. 245–7.

John Ward modulates in fantasia a 5 No. 1[1], a piece in A-minor, first to E-flat-major, then from sub-dominant to sub-dominant through A-flat, D-flat, G-flat, B, and E to A-major ; the rest of the piece is in A-major.

Here is the point where the classical unity (and security) of the old English polyphonic style was breached for the first time. Through the element of harmonic expressionism Italian influence —and with it experiments and even speculation—gained a foothold in English music. In the next chapters we shall have to inquire why this had to happen. What a wise man was Morley, who with prophetic foresight had stated quite definitely that " leaving the key in fantasie may never be suffered ! " Now, twenty years after Morley, the search for the new and startling begins ; the old rules of moderation and restraint are left. ' Newness ' is demanded for the first time ; as John Adson puts it in his work in 1621 :

> There are three Vertues (Goodnesse, Truth and Newnesse) which, as they embolden a Worke, and make it an unblushing Offspring at the Noblest Altar : So doe they also preserve from Taxation the Presenter ; and from disparagement the Protector.[2]

However, such experiments do not occur until the end of the classical age of English chamber music. Indeed, as one age grows out of the previous, they herald the next ; they are definitely outside features and do not affect the general character of the music of the period, which is best seen as something complete in itself, and quite unique. Within this unity of the whole body of production the subjective characters of the composers yet found full individual expression. There is no end to exploring all this wonderful music, to counting up all the beauties and ingenuities which are found in the works of the distinguished and aristocratic

---

[1] Brit. Mus. MS. Add. 17792–6.

[2] *Courtly Masquing Ayres*, Dedication. Morley was also the first to warn his pupils not to exaggerate such ' newness ' and that at a time when the question of Italian influence in this country was still only of secondary importance compared with the end of the 17th century : " the composers of musick who otherwise would follow the depth of their skill . . . are compelled, for lack of maecenates, to put on another humour and follow that kind wherunto they have neither beene brought up, nor yet (except so much as they can learne by seeing other mens works in an unknown tounge) doe perfectlie understand ye nature of it, *such be the newfangled opinions of our countrey men, who will highlie esteeme whatsoeuer cometh from beyond the seas, and speciallie from Italie* (author's italics), be it never so simple, contemning that which is done at home, though it be never so excellent " (*A Plaine and Easie Introduction*, p. 179).

Holborne, the witty and serene Morley, the restrained, melancholic Coperario, the vigorous Ferrabosco, the concentrated musical thinker, Gibbons, the profoundly human W. Byrd, the innovator Tomkins, and all the other men, all true masters, White, Ward, Cranford, Edward Gibbons, Ravenscroft, and many more who, like the great madrigalists Wilbye, Weelkes and Farmer can only be mentioned here as composers of fine stylised dance music.   Pavans, galliards, allemands and other dance tunes, incidentally, occupied a secondary place compared with the fantasia in the music for viols ; dance styles cannot therefore be discussed at length now, although the dance repertory contains such pearls as Ferrabosco's " Dovehouse Pavin."[1] Much must be left to the exploring initiative of the music-lover ; this review being intended but to draw public attention to these half-forgotten thirty years of glorious achievement as a whole.

[1] Collections of dance music for viols are in the great libraries of London and Oxford.   I mention the contents of Brit. Mus. MSS. Add. 15118, 17792–6, 34800, 30480–4, 37402–6 ; composers represented in these MSS. and also in the Oxford libraries and not mentioned here yet are : Cormack, Diomede, Robert Johnson, Joseph Lupo, and Sylvanus Taylor.

CHAPTER VI

THE CRISIS

THE student of early English chamber music, holding a general
review of the musical life of this country, cannot but be struck
by the ominous change which takes place between 1620 and 1642.
England fails to keep pace with other countries in the development of chamber music. The slowing-up, which we had occasion
to notice in reviewing the first 20 years of the century, becomes
exceedingly obvious after 1620. The appreciation of chamber
music is no longer universal, nor is artistic achievement maintained on the level reached in Elizabethan and early Jacobean
times.

It may well strike us as tragic that the classical unity of style
and approach that distinguished the art of the first two decades
of the century was so soon broken down. The old cleavage
reappeared—the gap between the ' music of the many ' and the
' music of the few ' which the age of Elizabeth had for a time
succeeded in bridging. From about the beginning of the second
quarter of the century the stream of production divided and
flowed in two very different directions : on one side towards
intellectualism, complexity and speculation, as represented chiefly
in the music of the Court and the Anglican Church, on the other
side towards facility, superficiality and obviousness, as shown in the
music of the public.

We must try to discover why this cleavage took place.

Once more we have to recall the spirit of the 16th century.
The culture of Elizabeth's court was the culture of the nation at
large. Close ties united the Court with most of the other sections
of higher society, for the political, economic, and cultural aspirations of the Crown expressed those of the young English society
as a whole.

Signs of a clash of interests between the Court and parts of the
new bourgeoisie had already appeared during Elizabeth's last
few years. Such signs of disagreement reappeared again and
again during James' reign and open conflict broke out under
Charles I.[1] The Crown and the royalist gentry, the representatives of absolutism and monopoly, rallied to their side all the

[1] For the whole development the reader is referred to R. H. Tawney's *Religion
and the Rise of Capitalism*, and Christopher Hill's *The English Revolution*.

forces of stagnation and retrogression, while the stand of the bourgeoisie and parliament to maintain themselves against Charles' increasingly aggressive demands, in the end united all the forces interested in breaking the feudal bonds.

The issue was one of political power. The bourgeoisie had rejected Charles I's government, not because he was a bad man, but because he represented an obsolete social system. His government tried to perpetuate a feudal social order when the conditions existed for free capitalist development, when the increase of national wealth could only come by means of free capitalist development.[1]

At the same time Charles endeavoured to bring about a new Anglican sacerdotalism, a relationship between the Church and the country's economic and political regime which to an increasing degree made the Anglican Church an instrument for appropriating to the Crown the dictatorial powers . of the pre-Reformation Catholic Church.

In the cultural life of the country the Court rapidly became isolated. A screen of glass seemed to surround it and its grandees ; they could well see what was brewing outside, but were unable to influence events. The society of the striving and blossoming new England was not represented in the life at Court. The Court itself increasingly lost touch with public life. Cultural in-breeding in the circles round Charles was the logical consequence.

Not that this close atmosphere killed art altogether. On the contrary, Charles was no less ambitious and fond of display than his father ; he took a certain Neronic interest in matters of art. The Court attracted a considerable number of artists and musicians.

The Puritan austerity drove to the King's faction all who made pleasure their business, who affected gallantry, splendour of dress or taste in the lighter arts. With these went all who live by amusing the leisure of others, from the painter and the comic poet, down to the rope-dancer and the Merry Andrew. For these artists well knew that they might thrive under a superb and luxurious despotism, but must starve under the rigid rule of the precisians.[2]

[1] Hill, p. 56.
[2] Macaulay, *History of England*, ed. 1889, I, p. 51.

The masques at the courts of James and Charles offered more than enough room for all kinds of mummeries, from the pastoral-idyllic to the piquant-obscene. A large instrumental apparatus was frequently employed to produce pretentious orchestral effects in these masques which were to a high degree imitations of Italian entertainments.[1] The melodic substance of the music in the masques was, however, usually slender, now that the great days of Ben Jonson were past. They were just two-part tunes of treble and bass conceived on the simplest possible lines.[2] There was a curious atmosphere of forced merriment and spurious simplicity about the tunes contained in the masques of Charles' court, particularly between 1630 and 1640.

This was just the trouble. Those men of art who had a deeper understanding of the trend of society under Puritan influence were the more bewildered at the character of Court life. This irresponsible flippancy must have appeared disgusting to such genuine artists and thinkers as were close enough to observe it without being too close to criticise it.

Court and Anglican Church were united like the Siamese twins in their reactionary cultural policy. Laud's very ability and success in advancing and consolidating Charles' aims in Church policy largely contributed to the deepening of the antagonism between Church-cum-Court on the one side and the main body of society on the other. The Church in particular became the more reactionary the keener the attacks on it grew. More and more elements of the cultural ' defence-system ' of the Catholic Church of the previous century were dug up by the Anglican clergy. Not only did many paintings and carvings which had escaped the zeal of the Anglican Reformation 100 years before, return to the churches, but the musical side of the service took on more and more traits of Catholic ornamental splendour. Sir Richard Terry was the first to observe that the Church composers of the first quarter of the 17th century reintroduced polyphony into religious music—that rich and complex art which was so strongly denounced by Cranmer and other Anglican reformers of the 16th century. Catholicism and Anglicanism approached one another closely. In 1641 the Anglican Church issued an

---

[1] About the Court masques, see E. J. Dent, *Opera*, 1940, p. 144.

[2] The British Museum contains a large number of masque tunes ; see Add. 10444 where there are many popular melodies used in masques. Here are some titles :—" The beares dance," " Wiches dance," " The Haymakers Masque," " The Furies," " The Gipsies Masque," etc. They date from 1603 to 1641,

official collection of Catholic tunes and polyphonic motets
(" Barnard's Collection ") which were taken over bodily into the
Anglican service, with the one alteration that English words
were written to them. No clearer proof of the retrospective
attitude of the Church need be offered.

So polyphonic music once more had the official blessing of
Crown and clergy. It was intended, just as in the middle ages,
to symbolise the continuity that the clergy wished to preserve,
and to bring back the atmosphere of mysticism that the rising
rationalism threatened.

Polyphony became a symbol of the ' good old times ' which
were to be kept alive against the rising flood of bourgeois
Puritanism. Is it surprising that during the years before the
Civil War, Church and Court and the high-society circles around
them patronised polyphonic music more than ever before, and to
an increasing degree? And not only music of the past was
performed—quite a number of composers were willing to write
new works in the required polyphonic style of the Church.

In such an atmosphere polyphony became over-intricate,
exaggerated, and finally decidedly retrogressive. Partly for this
reason, and partly because of its association with an increasingly
obsolete social tradition, the new-old idiom became discredited
in the minds of the public. It cannot be denied that many
composers at Court and Church tried to give their best in this
hopelessly muddled and confused situation. But no fresh air
blew on them from outside ; the old forms were used, with
complications and ornamentations, and left in an advanced stage
of baroque refinement. Court and Church music (if we forget
for the moment the ' le-roi-s'amuse ' style of the masques) adopted
mannerisms, even at the hands of the very best masters England
had at the time. There was little living inspiration or public
admiration for these men. They found themselves in a vacuum.
Towards 1640 Court music reached an astonishing state of
introversion and involution, like some creeping plant writhing
fantastically in a confined place.

It is true, the encouragement of an obsolete style was unable
to obscure the talents of such an eminent musician as William
Lawes ; but at the same time it was absolutely incapable of
creating as healthy a general musical life as Elizabeth's time had
called into being.

Some of the instrumental music of Thomas Ford (Foord,

1580–1648),[1] in so far as it was composed after he joined the
chapel royal in 1626,[2] reflects the state of intellectualism and
over-development which had been reached under Charles I.
Let us take, for instance, a piece a 4, presumably for viols, called
" Ayre "—in reality a hybrid, something between a fantasia
and a pavan. Its scholasticism is almost mathematical.

While the work is composed in perfect conformity with the
traditional rules of counterpoint, and conceived with admirable
technical skill, one searches in vain for anything like the life and
spirit of true musicianship that had characterised the music of
the previous generation. Ford calculates and constructs. An
elementary subject in breves :

Example 63 : (a) :

is introduced in one part, while the same subject, executed in
quavers, serves to weave an extremely difficult contrapuntal
texture in the three remaining parts :

(b)

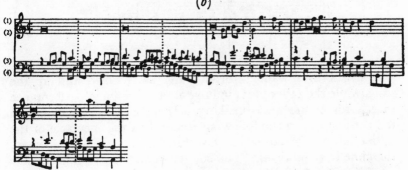

When the first part finishes its figure in breves as shown above
another part, the tenor, takes over the same subject, also in
breves, but a tone higher, while again contrapuntal lines in

---

[1] One fantasia for 2 bass viols, and 6 fantasias for 5 viols are known to have
been written by Ford at a comparatively late date, also the ayre a 4 which is discussed here. Oxford, Bodleian Library C. 59–60 contains the piece for bass
viols ; Royal College MS. 1.145 the 6 fantasias (in this MS. one part is missing
but can be added from Brit. Mus. Add. 17792–6 where the pieces are complete
though anonymous). The ayre is in Brit. Mus. 40657–61. A few dance movements for 2 viols were already published in Ford's collection of songs and madrigals
of 1607, called *Musicke of Soundry kindes* (ed. Fellowes, 1921).

[2] Before this time he was musician to Prince Henry of Wales.

quavers—based on the initial figure—circle round (these are always highly syncopated and lacking rhythmic clarity and vitality) :

(c)

The bass part follows next with the five-notes subject, another tone higher ; this time the other voices move about in minims, and the counterpoints also rely on the five notes of the chief motif which are, however, thrown about in varying order :

(d)

The five breves wander through the parts down and up the scale, while the other parts indulge in a polyphonic performance that is sometimes neck-breaking. There is a ' semi-colon ' on the dominant ; in the following second half the spectacle of the initial subject threading its way through the score is repeated, this time in semibreves. The counter-subject that builds up the polyphony is itself derived :

(e)

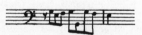

it had already occurred during the first part (in crotchets) :

(f)

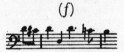

The main motif, this time in crotchets, concludes the piece, leading up to a short fugato in all parts.

The listener can but admire the intricacy of the polyphonic result—but this music makes no attempt whatsoever at popular appeal. Its essence is intellectual construction. Yet we do not by any means desire to deny to Ford's music interesting qualities. The restriction to one thematic subject is an especially noteworthy feature ; Ford really tries to plan a piece of considerable length by developing it out of one or two seminal motifs. In this way this technique is progressive. Moreover, the same Ford had proved in his earlier works that he could also write tuneful madrigals ; these bore no traces of Court style, however, and had no relation to it.

John Withy[1] and William Simmes,[2] as well as some less known composers of the chapel royal who worked chiefly during the years preceding the Civil War, can be counted as Thomas Ford's spiritual relatives, though not perhaps so given to extremist practices.

There was, however, one real genius among Charles I's composers. We must now turn to him and his work, for it is certain to outlast the music of the whole period, and to conquer the hearts of chamber music lovers whenever and wherever it is awakened from its centuries-long slumber.

William Lawes (1602–1645) was certainly one of the outstanding musical personalities of the whole century. Being a pupil of Coperario's, one of the best composers and teachers of the time, he was able to join the chapel royal as a boy and remained in the royal service until 1645 when he fell at the siege of Chester. Out of sheer loyalty to his master William Lawes supported the Royalist cause and died fighting a losing battle. Lawes was an unusually alert and ingenious musical thinker. He was adored by his friends and admired by those few musical amateurs who could grasp the spirit of his art. When his colleagues wrote elegies mourning his death (among them were his famous brother Henry, Simon Ives, D. Cobb, Capt. Edmund Foster, John Hilton

---

[1] Fantasia and In Nomine by Withy in Oxford, Christ Church MSS. 473–8 ; 24 fantasias for 2 bass viols in Oxford, Bodleian C. 59–60 and 127–30. A number of dance tunes a 3, also in the sophisticated Court style without being anything but average art are in Brit. Mus. MSS. Add. 29283–85 and 31423.

[2] Simmes wrote 7 fantasias a 5 (Oxford, Christ Church MSS. 716–20).

and others) his keenness and versatility of mind were repeatedly referred to. As Cobb put it[1] :

> Dear Will is dead. Will Lawes whose active brains
> Gave life to many sweet harmonious strains,
> Whose boundless skill made music speak such sense
> As if't had sprung from an intelligence.
> In his just proportioned songs there might you find
> His soul convers'd with heav'n with his mind,
> And in such language that rhetorick never knew. . . . .

We have seen how some composers of late Jacobean time, such as Tomkins, Ward and Holmes, began to affect mannerisms. We found the beginnings of a search for the uncommon, for the out-of-the-way, which always appears where the healthy social impulse is fading. There were also certain signs that some products of Italian modernism were employed which were foreign to the original character of English chamber music. We further had to recognise that polyphony which in the last analysis is derived from the old Netherlandish masses and motets, still dominated instrumental music in this country, if in a very refined style.

These tendencies are manifest in Lawes' works. It was only owing to Lawes' great capacity and daring that something quite extraordinary blossomed in spite of such contradictory tendencies. Lawes' music is the most personal of the whole century. Many features of his music are hard to explain and place by any critical standard, and in the development of 17th-century music this peculiar art of Lawes' led nowhere. In spite of numerous progressive and even experimental elements contained in it, it is the termination of a development, an end, not a beginning. Posterity, however, must recognise in his work a singular combination of such conflicting qualities as Court splendour, hyperculture, profound sentiment, a kind of waywardness and a prevailing amplitude of style, a breadth which is part of the grand tradition of a grand time.

Lawes' compositions are very numerous, and instrumental fancies and airs form the greater part of his life-work. His most widely known work, the *Royal Consort*, is at the same time his least sophisticated composition. This collection comprises 66

[1] Poem and composition in MS. Add. 34071 ; here the other elegies are also found, except the one by Hilton which is in Add. 11608.

dance movements—almands, corants, sarabands, pavans and airs
(one is called ' echo ')—organised in six suites, the first two in
D-minor and D-major containing not less than 20 items each.
The instruments required are two treble viols, a theorbo, and a
' dividing bass ' (these two mostly in unison) ; in one copy there
is one more part at tenor level called ' breaking base.'[1] The
theorbo part is obviously supposed to play chords on top of the
bass which is merely given as a line—it is not figured.   In this,
signs of the influence of the continental basso continuo technique
appear.   It is making headway at this period.   The omission
of the figures means that the realisation in chords in the accompaniment is left to the player whose ability to build up triads on
each bass note is taken for granted.   The two trebles are
'concertante,' which is to say that both are equally lively at equal
pitch crossing and recrossing each other.   These two parts are
melodically already rather erratic and out of the old English
tradition ; they often make sense only when heard together with
the whole score and seem quite odd when played alone :

Example 64 : (For two treble viols, theorbo, dividing bass
and breaking bass ; about 1640).

WILLIAM LAWES

ALMAND FROM " ROYAL CONSORT "

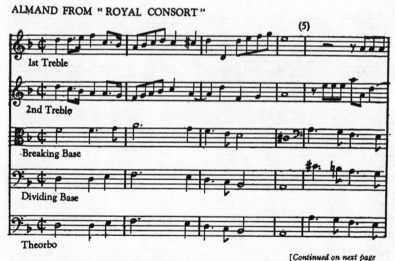

[Continued on next page

[1] The two trebles are in Brit. Mus. Add. 31431 ; the dividing base and theorbo
in 31433.   The breaking base is in Add. 10445.

Continued from previous page]

The parts are sometimes bizarre ; but the bass is usually fairly simple, relying on easily comprehensible scale progressions, or on fourths and fifths up and down. It obviously holds the composition together, countering the extravagance of the other parts and of the harmonic structure as a whole. Most of the pieces keep to the traditional metrical dance scheme of two or three independent strains, each consisting of eight, twelve or sixteen bars. These two features—the harmonic base and the conventional dance form—explain the comparatively wide popularity of the *Royal Consort*.

There are true high-lights in the *Royal Consort* which is altogether well worth reviving, as is his *Great Consort*, a similar collection.[1]

A second group of instrumental pieces, consisting of about 28 fantasias, pavanas and In Nomines a 5–6[2] and also a very large number of three and four part ' Ayres,'[3] displays many more unusual features. Here we miss the restraining influence which the familiar dance rhythms and simply conceived bass lines exercised in the *Royal Consort*. The *Royal Consort* was at least semi-homophonic, being based on the two melodic parts and a more or less harmonic bass. But the second group of Lawes' pieces is very polyphonic indeed.

In these pieces (all of them for viols) we find a great variety of impressive and individual themes. Some are nostalgic in character :

Example 65 : from fantasia No. 1 a 5, by William Lawes.

Others display a manly vigour :

Example 66 : from fantasia No. 2 a 6, by William Lawes.

All show Lawes as a genuine artist, capable of giving convincing artistic realisation to the most contrasting emotions. But even more remarkable than this talent in the invention of

[1] Oxford Bodleian Library.   [2] Add. 29410–5.
[3] MSS. Add. 40657–61 and 18940–4.

new and interesting themes (which after all he had in common
with men like Gibbons and Ferrabosco) is the adventurous spirit
that characterises the *developments* in these pieces. Lawes builds
up developments and climaxes out of very unusual, even eccentric
figures. The folksong themes of the 'golden age' have disappeared. Concessions to popular taste will be sought in vain in
this music. Lawes is far too isolated, too much occupied with
his own personal problems—cut off from the living outside world
as he was in his position at the Court—to be able or even willing
to speak to the people in their own musical language.

The   motif ♪♪♪ in the just quoted fantasia

a 6 is later changed to ♪♪♪

This is what happens when this queer new figure is developed
polyphonically :

Example 67 : from fantasia No. 2 a 6, by William Lawes.

(*a*)

And yet such difficult contrapuntal combinations appear
quite normal if compared with what comes after :

(*b*)

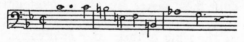

Here the language becomes very strange ; certain bars seem really daring, such as bars 48, 49, and 50. Quite often it happens that a new voice comes in on a violently dissonant note (bar 48 and others). At the same time we see that Lawes has taken a curious liking to chords of the seventh, even unprepared ones, and for the first time the vital dominant-seventh appears (bars 45 and 51), if not yet used to strengthen the tension of the dominant leading to the solution in the tonic.

In his harmonic adventures Lawes goes very far, considering how early the date (about 1635). Another fantasia a 6 contains the element of harmonic extravagance already in its initial subject:

Example 68 : from fantasia No. 7 a 6, by William Lawes.

This is great music. The complete fantasia may serve as an example of Lawes' art.[1] In the last years before the Civil War Court life was still brightened by such fantasias and pavanas for viols. But the golden age is hastening to its close. Lawes and his fellows write not as a glorious company, but as individuals, as isolated experimentalists. Their music is introspective, personal, subjective.

[1] See Appendix, Example III.

The noon-day of spontaneous and happy creation is well past. A sun is setting, and just as long, eccentric shadows invade the countryside at sunset, so now strange beauties, mysterious and otherworldly, invest the art of the English Court.

The third and last group of Lawes' works—obviously written during the last years of his life—is even more personal than the other two. It comprises works for three to seven instruments (violins, theorbos, viols and harps or organ in various combinations). The peculiar feature of these pieces is that the harp or organ parts are mostly neither basso continuo parts nor ordinary polyphonic single lines, but very elaborate scores in themselves.[1] These pieces are the only examples of early chamber music (apart from one single piece by the Italian Frescobaldi[2]) which have independent and completely worked-out keyboard or harp parts. Not till Bach's violin and piano sonatas does this technique reappear. In the interval between Lawes and Bach, the making up of the continuo parts is left to the mercy of the continuo player.

The fact that violins are used in these fantasias by Lawes needs explanation, too. In their external appearance these pieces follow the tradition of the consort, mixing tone colours of various classes of instruments. But the spirit of the old ' quiet ' chamber music has gone. Here is music that was intended for an unusually ambitious court, not for the private home of the wealthy citizen as at the beginning of the century. The old, quiet viols will not do any longer. Lawes needs the strength of the violins which at the same time are more in agreement with the rapidly spreading Italian fashion, and he needs also their greater compass, for he employs all means and all instrumental ranges to achieve his ends.[3]

Without doubt these pieces are Lawes' most interesting compositions. Some of them are magnificent in their structural proportions, and moving in their emotional content. It is true

[1] The whole group of pieces is contained in Oxford, Bodleian MS. Mus. Sch. B 1 and B 2 ; there are many fantasias, pavanas, corants, sarabands and ayres, existing either singly or in suites.

[2] Brit. Mus. MS. Add. 34003. Some fantasias by Jenkins, Coperario, Ferrabosco and Locke have also organ parts ; but these are only short scores, extracts from the viol parts and intended for performance ad libitum, without being necessary to the score. They add no new counterpoint to the string parts.

[3] Only a few examples of the use of violins in England before 1620 can be found (for instance, Holborne's collection ; see Chapter IV). See also Scholes, *Oxford Companion*, and Hayes, *Musical Instruments*.

that the extravagance and oddness of Lawes' melodic lines
nowhere else in his work appears more conspicuous. The parts
move violently as though the old rules of counterpoint as exemplified by Morley had never existed. But in the polyphonic result
they always add up to a convincing whole.

A fantasia for two violins, viola da gamba (bass viol) and harp
will probably give a better idea of Lawes' art than any description.[1]

It seems natural to compare Lawes' twisted melodies and
unusual harmonies with the stylised, long-shaped figures of El
Greco, the painter. El Greco's life-work also represents the
last stage of a great tradition. Notwithstanding the greatness of
these men, their art sometimes came dangerously near to
preciosity. But their works express both the exclusiveness of
unpopular artistocratic surroundings and the loneliness of great
artists trapped in them.[2]

A number of compositions by another great composer-member
of Charles' court, John Jenkins (1592–1678), are in the same
spirit as those of Lawes. But as the real importance of this
master lies in the output of his last 15 years of life his works
will be discussed in a later chapter.

*   *   *   *   *

So much for the state of such chamber music as was sponsored
by Court and High Church. In the meantime the music of the
general mass of the population also underwent a crisis—a crisis
that proved even more serious for the future of English music.

The cavaliers, among them many highly cultured, somewhat
morbidly refined noblemen whose scions Peacham still calls
" plants from Heaven."[3] were the main support of the Court and
particularly the Church. On the Court side also were the

---

[1] See Example IV in Appendix.
[2] How far ahead of his time Lawes' discordant harmonies were is shown by
the fact that theorists who were considered progressive remained reserved and
sceptical whenever dissonances were under discussion. " A Discord," says
Charles Butler in his *Principles of Musick* of 1636, " is a jarry noiz of two permixed
sounds offending the ear " (p. 48). Later on he goes into details :—
      " Discords are the Perfect and Imperfect Second,
            the Perfect and Imperfect Seventh,
            the Tritonum and Semidiapente . . ."
      " Yet a discord, as in Œconomi, so in Musick, is sometimes allowable, as making
the Concord following the sweeter : but neither in that nor in this is it too bee
held too long . . ." (p. 51).
William Lawes is omitted in Butler's list of noted contemporary composers
(p. 48).
[3] *Compleat Gentleman*, 2nd edition, 1634, p. 1.

greatest of the landowners with many of their tenants, and the
conservative, clumsy, and uneducated country gentlemen of
remoter parts of the country. The vast mass of Englishmen were
against the outmoded order which Charles was bringing back.
Their common resentment drew close together citizens of all
classes, from the wealthy merchants, empire-builders, and
navigators, to intellectuals, members of the growing middle-class
professions, and above all, the small producers, and those independent yeomen who formed the backbone of Cromwell's army.
In spite of their separate interests, which found expression in the
formation of all their party movements, Presbyterians, Independents, Levellers, Diggers and others, they were united in the
desire to check the encroachments of the Crown, and in the
hope that after victory was won, each would find the way clear
to achieve its own ends. It is true, this union did not last for
ever. It lasted, however, as long as was necessary.

What united the bulk of the population was their opposition
to the fetters on *economic expansion*.

The religion of economic expansion was Puritanism, and Puritanism was the guiding spirit in matters of culture and philosophy
during the age which now began. Puritanism was more than a
philosophy—it was a social discipline. Under the constant and
growing enforcement of royal-ecclesiastical privileges Puritan
determination and self-discipline grew in strength.

The middle classes of the first half of the 17th century moulded
themselves and their children to this pattern :

> a picture grave to sternness, yet not untouched with a sober
> exaltation—an earnest, zealous, godly generation, scorning
> delights, punctual in labour, constant in prayer, thrifty and
> thriving, filled with a decent pride in themselves and their
> calling, assured that strenuous toil is acceptable to Heaven. . . .[1]
> . . . thinking, sober and patient men, and such as believe
> that labour and industry is their duty towards God.[2]

From gradual beginnings the demand for economic freedom
permeated English cultural life. Under the influence of Puritanism the attitude of a great number of citizens towards philosophy,
science and art became *utilitarian ;* 17th-century English
philosophy began to despise ' vague ' utopianism and ' hot-

---

[1] R. H. Tawney, *Religion and the Rise of Capitalism*, 1926, p. 211.
[2] Petty, quoted by Tawney, ibid.

headed ' speculation. Instead, the ideal of pious sobriety and divinely ordered commercial realism was advanced more and more consciously by the philosophers.

The beginning of this process in the philosophy of art is to be seen in the writings of Francis Bacon. To him art is useful. Gone the magic beauty, the profound emotionalism that Elizabethans adored in music and poetry. Now the " Muses . . . ought to be the leaders and conductors of human life, and not the handmaids of the passions."[1] Art is useful, as useful to state and commerce as science. Bacon found " no work so meritorious as the discovery of arts and sciences that tend to civilise the life of men." This is the attitude of a political scientist, and a new phenomenon in the development of æsthetics.

The philosophy of music in particular undergoes an amazing change within a decade or two. Music begins to be analysed with regard to its potential value in relation to daily work and the development of industries and state institutions. Ardour gives way to cool, scientific detachment in the references to music in contemporary writing. Less and less is heard of the element of beauty, the imponderables of music ; more and more of its usefulness as a means of providing recreation after work. For in this part of its function it helps to make man fit and disposed to resume his civil duties. He is stronger and more useful after having had a half-hour's dose of music. A *Treatise against Stage Playes* of 1625 is full of the utilitarian spirit.

Recreation . . . signifieth to renew, to repair, to recover, to restore, or to refresh eyther the body or the minde, or both, when they are impaired, overworne, wearied, or spent in the imployments of mens lawfull callings . . . and refreshed may chearefully returne to their lawfull callings againe and therein serue Got faythfully.

Different kinds of recreation are permissible :

First some little rest from labour as, if the reapers in harvest time may but sit downe and rest themselves for one quarter of an hour, they will return more freshly to their worke againe. . . . . Secondly, foode, meate and drinke which refresheth man comfortably and maketh him fitter and more able to performe the duties of his calling. Thirdly, Sleepe reneweth man and refresheth him greatly that he is thereby as if he had

[1] *Advancement of Learning*, p. 114.

not beene wearied before. Fourthly, some change of labour quickeneth man that his former weariness is forgotten. Fiftly, Musick is a chearfull recreation to the minde that hath beene blunted with serious meditations. These and such like are holy and good recreations, both comfortable and profitable.[1]

Charles Butler, too, thinks of non-Church music as something that is " most seasonable in the time of Feastings : wen men meete together to be merry, and to enjoy the fruit of their labours."[2] Thomas Mace, author of the quaint *Musick's Monument* of a somewhat later date (1676), has music laid out in his mind in two categories and two categories only : " sober-civil Musick " and " solid-divine Musick," the art of the Church.[3]

Less and less is said of music being a " ladder to the intelligence of higher things."[4] More and more frequently music appears in company with such useful inventions as food or exercise. W. Perkins, in his *Cases of Conscience* (1631), says that athletics, fencing, music, chess, " and all of this kind, wherein the industry of the mind and body hath the chiefest stroke, are very commendable."[5] In *Salomon's House* Bacon grants a statue to " the inventor of music " ; he grants another one to the inventor of gun-powder.[6]

Music is recommended to doctors as an excellent medicine for various kinds of patients. " Musica mentis medicina," written by an early 17th-century copyist as postscript to an instrumental air a 3[7] becomes the motto of many a writer on music. Even such humanists as Peacham look at music from a sober and practical point of view : Music

> . . . is a principall meanes of glorifying our mercifull Creator, it heightens our devotion, it gives delight and ease to our travailes, it expelleth sadnesse and heavinesse of Spirit, preserveth people in concord and amity, allayeth fiercenesse and anger.

The passage ends with the familiar recipe for the pathologist :

[1] Roxburghe Library, 1869, p. 241.
[2] *Principles of Musick*, p. 124. It should be noted that Butler is anti-Puritan, despite his theories on music.
[3] *The Highways of England*, 1675, p. 25 (advertisement for a new book of Mace's).
[4] See above, p. 117.
[5] H. Davey, *History of English Music*, 1921, p. 244.
[6] *New Atlantis*, ed. H. Osborne, 1937, p. 43.
[7] Brit. Mus. MS. Add. 36484.

" . . . and lastly, it is the best Phisicke for many melancholy diseases."[1] Charles Butler, too, expresses the view that " music is a medicine for those complaints which arise out of hard labour."[2] Herrick's " To Music, to becalm his Fever " reflects this conception of the art :

> Charm me asleep, and melt me so
>   With thy delicious numbers,
> That being ravished, hence I go
>   Away in easy slumbers.
>   Ease my sick head,
>   And make my bed
>   Thou power that canst sever
>   From me this ill ;
>   And quickly still,
>   Though thou not kill
>   My fever.
>
> Thou sweetly canst convert the same
>   From a consuming fire,
> Into a gentle-licking flame,
>   And make it thus expire.
>   Then make me weep
>   My pains asleep ;
>   And give me such reposes,
>   That I, poor I,
>   May think thereby,
>   I live and die
>   'Mongst roses.
>
> Fall on me like a silent dew,
>   Or like those maiden showers,
> Which, by the peep of the day, do strew
>   A baptism o'er the flowers.
>   Melt, melt my pains,
>   With thy soft strain ;
>   That having ease me given,
>   With full delight
>   I leave this light,
>   And take my flight
>   For Heaven.

[1] *Compleat Gentleman*, ed. 1634, p. 104.
[2] *Principles of Music*, 1636, p. 123.

Music is thought of as an excellent means to find husbands for young girls :

A thing . . . frequently used, and part of a gentlewoman's bringing up, to sing, dance, and play on the Lute, or some such instrument, before she can say her Pater Noster, or Ten Commandments. 'Tis the next way their parents think, to get them husbands, they are compelled to learn.

However, the very same gentlewomen, " now being married, will scarce touch an instrument, they care not for it."[1]

Some Puritans, even the most militant, are very eloquent in the recommendation of " sober-civil " music, as an ally in the dissemination of utilitarian doctrines. Of all writers on music John Milton subscribes to this view most frankly and radically :

Sometimes the lute or soft organ stop waiting on elegant voices either to religious, martial or civil ditties, which, if wise men and prophets be not extremely out, have a great power over dispositions and manners to smoothe and make (them) gentle from rustic harshness and distempered passions. The like would also not be unexpedient after meat, to assist and cherish nature in her first concoction, and send (their) minds back to study in good tune and satisfaction.[2]

Did such an attitude assist the continuation and further evolution of great music ? The answer is in the negative. As England slowly took over the political and economic hegemony in the world, she lost *pari passu* her musical leadership. A new spirit had invaded the cultural life of the nation. It worked like yeast in the minds of the thinkers of the day. Many were perplexed, and many undecided ; doubtfully groping theories were put forward in the first half of the 17th century. The Puritans themselves were not quite sure which secular music ought to perform what secular function. But they were in agreement that somehow or other music ought to fit into their own pattern of social life.

The question of polyphony must have divided the musical world of England as Moses' sword divided the Red Sea. It was associated with ornament, luxury, distraction of the mind, and

[1] Robert Burton in *The Anatomy of Melancholy*, 1621, III, pp. 135 and 204. See also Westrup, *Domestic Music*, for more examples (pp. 28 ff. and 32).

[2] From a letter to Master Sam Hartlib. Complete collection, Vol. I, 1739, p. 139.

High Church. We have already seen that by about 1640 polyphony was becoming intellectualised and in danger of losing its original purposiveness. The chief anger of the Puritans must have been directed against such ornamental polyphony as was practised in the Church service.

Not that this aspect of Puritan ideology could be condemned as deliberately destructive. Puritanism in every sphere combated obscurantism' and absolutism, it struggled for the independent relation to God, against the revived mysticism of the Anglican Church. No longer does the responsibility for God and man lie with priest and king. In the case of the Puritans this positive side of man's increased sense of power is, however, doomed by its character to be unfriendly to profound music.

Inevitably these tendencies of the Puritans, it is true, were to lead to rationalism.

They accelerated a process which the public at large had felt long ago. It has already been pointed out that only a few polyphonic fantasias found their way to the printing-press. This points to the fact that they were in demand by a somewhat limited number of people. Towards 1640 it was, indeed, only a small circle in London and Oxford who practised them, and these people were usually associated with the hated Anglican outlook.

As we noticed earlier, the polyphony that was used by the composers of Court and Church was of a kind that placed all parts of the score on an equal footing. There was no 'chief melody' which the ear of the listener could catch easily. The complex polyphonic results of the combination of a multitude of parts demanded a far more attentive, intellectually alert and emotionally subtle attitude on the side of the listener than the new era would allow.

Puritanism fought Anglican polyphony, especially when it became excessive and hyper-complex, just as the Anglican Reform 100 years before had fought Catholic polyphony. Not only outspoken Puritans did so, for as early as 1613 the madrigalist Thomas Campion spoke for the general public :

> In music we yield the chief place not to every harsh and dull confused Fantasy, where, in a multitude of points, the harmony is quite drowned.[1]

[1] Preface to his *Ayres*.

Instead the melodic ideal of the " charming air " was advanced, as William Strode expressed it in one of his most beautiful poems, one which reflects the beginning of this change from the old to the new attitude towards music :

THE COMMENDATION OF MUSIC

Oh lull me, lull me, charming air,
   My senses rock with wonder sweet ;
Like snow on wool thy fallings are,
   Soft as a spirit's are thy feet :
     Grief who need fear
     That hath an ear ?
     Down let him lie
     And slumbering die,
And change his soul for harmony.

                     (WILLIAM STRODE, 1602–1645).

The end of the development is shown in a statement by Christopher Simpson :

   . . . this kind of music (fantasias of the polyphonic kind) is now much neglected, by reason of the scarcity of auditors that understand it ; their ears being better acquainted and more delighted with *light and airy music*.[1]

Light and airy music. This was indeed what was asked of the composers ; moreover the demand was for light and airy instrumental music rather than vocal. In 1659 Anthony à Wood testified that " Puritans used to love and encourage instrumental musick ; but did not care for vocall . . ."[2] " Man may play a Lesson on a Lute or other Instrument to refresh his Spirits."[3]

The earlier stages of the development of such light instrumental compositions have already been studied in reviewing consort dances and suites. A large corpus of such music was produced even in the critical period before the Civil War. Apart from the works of the already mentioned John Adson and Walter Porter many tunes and suites were composed by men like Thomas Mudd[4] (dates unknown), Davis Mell (1604–1662),[5] Nicholas

[1] *Compendium*, 1667, § 15.
[2] *Life and Times of Anthony à Wood*, ed. Llewellyn Powys, London, 1932, p. 70.
[3] T. F. Minister of Exon., 1653, quoted by Davey, p. 252.
[4] Pieces in Add. 18940-4 and other MSS.
[5] 12 suites in Christ Church, Oxford (treble part only).

Laniere (1588-1666),[1] and Maurice Webster (d. 1635),[2] to mention only some of the better-known among this group of musicians. Their compositions may be characterised as pleasant but unimportant.

A whole school of composers tried to adjust the polyphonic fantasia—with which they had been educated and had grown up—to the new ideal. No doubt a strange compromise ; but the composers who chose such a course are no more to blame than their ancestors of 100 years before who having been brought up in the tradition of the Catholic polyphonic motet, turned to the In Nomine in order to reconcile the opposing demands of the Anglican Reform with the polyphony that was their proper sphere.

The result of this compromise which was arrived at during the era of rising Puritanism might be named the ' pseudo-polyphonic fantasia.' The influence of the more popular and homophonic dance consorts was very obvious in this kind of music, of which the already mentioned fantasias a 5 by Michael East of 1610 were the first examples.[3] A later publication of fantasias by East (1638) includes items for 2 bass viols, and for 3 and 4 viols. While the interesting pieces for 2 bass viols are more deeply rooted in the old polyphonic traditions of the Morley type,[4] the 3 and 4 part fantasias are definitely of the new ' compromise ' type. All these pieces have characteristic titles, some of them religious, others madrigalesque and sometimes slightly perfumed (" Love cannot dissemble "—" Name right your notes "— " Desperavi," " Peccavi," " Vidi," etc. ; the 9 fantasias a 3 bear the names of the nine Muses).

These ' literary ' titles indicate a desire on the part of the composer to appeal to a wider public than, for instance, Gibbons' more abstract and complex art aspired to reach. In East's fantasias we find no genuine polyphony built on the simultaneous sounding of several independent parts. There is always one chief part which attracts the attention of the listener, while the other parts form a semi-homophonic accompaniment. This ' melodic thread ' travels from part to part, yet most of the time it stays in the descant.

[1] 2 short symphonies for 2 trebles and bass in Christ Church, Oxford. He was " a very ingenious vertuoso " on the violin (Roger North).

[2] *Ayrs* in Add. 18940-4 and in various MSS. in Christ Church, Oxford.

[3] East published 37 fantasias in these collections. Brit. Mus. and Royal College of Music.

[4] See also above, p. 104 ff.

A fancy for 4 parts, 1638 ("Name right your notes"), by Michael East, appears in the Appendix (No. V).

The whole character of such pieces is homophonic and 'airy' (East himself calls his 4-part fantasias in particular "ayerie fancies"). There is no pretence of any great degree of intellectual vigour. One seeks in vain in them for anything which recalls the art of Lawes.

John Okeover (d. about 1664),[1] Martin Peerson (d. 1651),[2] Henry Loosemore (d. 1670),[3] Richard Mico (d. about 1650),[4] Thomas Brewer (1611-?),[5] and other composers, most of whom were not Court musicians but in private service or independent, contributed simplified fantasias of the Michael East type. John Hilton (1599-1657)[6] provided a more personal note by the use of interesting and lively forms and by the introduction of popular and striking themes, such as :

Example 69 : from fantasia a 3, by John Hilton :

This is agreeable and easy-going art, but less inspired than the production of the Gibbons-Ferrabosco-Tomkins era. Only one master had enough vitality to contrive within the lighter fantasia style, a chamber music of a more profound character and of deeper and more radiant colours : Simon Ives (1600-60). Ives is too personal a musician to be called an eclectic or revivalist, although he did not contribute any vitally new elements of style to the period. Among his numerous fantasias and In Nomines[7] are to be found real gems that sparkled once more

---

[1] Fantasias and pavanas in Add. 17786-91, 17792-6 and Bodleian, Oxford, D. 245-7.

[2] Fantasias, almains, etc., in Add. 17786-91, Christ Church, Oxford, 423-8 and 716-20.

[3] Add. 34800.

[4] 30 fantasias and some dances in Christ Church, Oxford, MS. 2, 353-6, 403-8, 436, 473-8 and others.

[5] 6 fantasias a 4 and dance movements in Bodleian, Oxford, C. 100, F. 568-9 and others.

[6] Fantasias and præludium a 3 on Christ Church, Oxford, 744-6.

[7] 16 fantasias a 2-6, one In Nomine a 5 and innumerable dance movements in Add. 31424, Bodleian, Oxford, C. 64-9, Christ Church, Oxford, 716-20 and others.

with the old melodic optimism and originality of the golden age. Ives worked for the Court as well as for the wider public. He displayed in his works a certain nobleness of spirit combined with simplicity of means. His finest instrumental composition is a fantasia a 4, a gay piece in D-major.[1]

But while some composers were thus trying to reconcile Court style with popular demands, the real popular art was going through a crisis of its own. It is true that by no means the least important or the least valuable part of the output of the period is the ' home-made ' airs and tunes of the people themselves : 17th-century folk songs and dance tunes, some of which are today still just as familiar as they were at the time of their origin. A considerable number of popular instrumental dance tunes appeared in John Playford's collections, such as *The English Dancing Master* (1650, 1652, 1657, etc.). Here are a few of them :

Example 70 : Tunes from " The English Dancing Master. "

(*a*) Parson's Farewell :

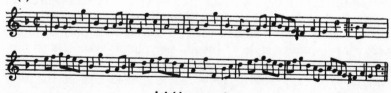

(*b*) Scotch Cap :

(*c*) Pell Mell :

[1] Add. 17792–6.

(*d*) The Fit's Come on Me now :

(*e*) The Merry Merry Milk Maids :

And yet popular music-making diminished. The rapid development of capitalism and wealth meant also the rapid development of class differentiation and division both among townspeople and peasantry.

There was no longer the same active interest and intensity ; and all the genuine, unrestrained production of the English people, amusing and colourful though it was, could not come to the rescue in this hour of crisis of English music as a powerful rejuvenating factor. And whatever productive energy remained in this kind of unsophisticated music-making, it certainly was not made use of or developed into a great new musical life by the cultural initiators of the upper classes who disputed the key positions, ideological and material. The rival authoritarians— the reactionary Court and High Church on the one hand, and the sober Puritan leaders on the other—aimed alike at the rigid control of the individual.

This, then, was the situation : English chamber music, that was universally acknowledged and magnificently homogeneous during the golden age, was split into halves. Here, appeared an inbreeding of hyper-delicate and non-popular chamber art at Court and in related circles, there, a simple tune-playing, or at best a compromise style of pseudo-polyphonic dances and fan-tasias. And when in 1649 the last remnants of Court and High Church were suppressed, only the simplified art of the new middle classes was left. A fresh impetus that might have brought new life by developing the vital productive powers of the people themselves disappeared among the social changes that took place during the following periods.

Although it would be wrong (for reasons that will be discussed presently) to put all the blame for the degeneration of English music on the shoulders of the Puritans, we cannot absolve them from heavy responsibilities. There was first the question of the deeds of Cromwell's soldiers. Direct orders for the destruction of the organs, it is true, may not have been issued, but the Puritan statesmen tolerated the atrocities of their men, who burnt instruments and music alike.[1] The behaviour of the soldiers was, however, not the really important issue ; we may say " c'est la guerre."

The matter went further. Composers, organists, and singers, representing the old era, were turned adrift and had to " seek precarious livelihoods by teaching music to the few who cared,"[2] or else escape starvation by adopting some occupation other than that for which they were fitted by talent and education. Others had to emigrate to other countries, or to retire to the countryside. William Child devoted his time and talent more to farming than to composing. Thomas Tomkins retired to the country, John Jenkins, Henry Lawes, Charles Coleman, Christopher Gibbons, Simon Ives, all former members of the Chapel Royal, became private teachers, some of them in places that were rather out of touch with the general life of the nation. Only a few composers kept their church positions (at least nominally) such as Benjamin Rogers, who spent, however, much of his time abroad (as did also William Youngh). Many composers were lost sight of completely, and of the more important masters only Walter Porter, W. Howes, John Wilson, Davis Mell, and John Hingeston were really active in the cause of Puritanism.

The average level of musical activities had already gone down during the second quarter of the 17th century and this decline was still further accelerated by the musical policy of the Puritans who kept the deeper problems of music from the masses and destroyed the main basis of the ' grand old time ' by abolishing

[1] The old Mercurius Rusticus gives an account of what was done. At Chichester Cathedral as elsewhere in other reports : the officers, having sacked the plates and the vestments, left the destructive part to the common soldiery, who broke down the organs, and dashing the pipes with their pole-axes, scoffingly said : " Hark, how the organs go ! " See W. H. Cummings, *Henry Purcell*, 1881.

[2] W. H. Cummings, *Henry Purcell*, 1881.

Church music, that great nursery of talent, in which more than eighty per cent. of the good composers before Puritanism came to power, were nurtured. During the Commonwealth musical education was neglected. When in 1660 the Royalists restored Church music, the result of this neglect was immediately manifest in a great dearth of boys' voices. Matthew Locke complains :

> . . . after the opening of His Majestie's Chappel the orderers of musick were necessitated to supply superior parts of music with cornets and men's feigned voices, there being not one lad for all that time capable of singing his part readily.

At the beginning of the Civil War " The Actors Remonstrance or complaint : for the silencing of their Profession " (1643) was particularly bitter :

> Our Musike that was held so delectable and precious that they scorned to come to a Taverne· under twentie shillings salary for two houres, now wander with their Instruments under their cloaks, I meane such as haue any, into all houses of good fellowship, saluting euery roome where there is company with ' Will you haue any musike Gentlemen ' ?

And anthems composed during Charles II's reign were nearly all for male choirs throughout the kingdom ; only the older men were available, those who had their musical education before the Commonwealth. Samuel Pepys had a difficult time when he tried to keep faithful to his principle " to hear a waiting-maid play and sing before engaging her."[1] In 1657 John Hingeston, Cromwell's house musician, issued a petition together with other composers for the establishment of public and state music schools. He prophesised the end of English music unless help came from the state. A committee was nominated by the Council of State to deal with the question, but nothing further was heard about the matter.

Once again, we do not want to give the impression that the Puritans were, as they are sometimes said to have been, wilful destroyers of English music. They were not against all music, but only against Church music, and even in this question there were exceptions. Cromwell and Milton both cared for Church

---

[1] Diary of 1662. See also H. Davey, p. 293. Yet Pepys gives a very unkind picture of the musical achievements of female amateurs in general ; see Westrup, *Domestic Music*, p. 51 f.

music, as also did other prominent Puritans. Something like a
secret remorse for their party's misdeeds may have induced both
men to cultivate musical activities, in secret if they were in
contradiction with Puritan theories as professed in public. And
in spite of the strong words of several Puritans, and in spite of
the fact that the general trend of Puritan musical policy was
fairly clear, the movement as a whole was not always completely
sure of itself. Light and pleasing music, for instance, was recommended very warmly by many Puritans, though others, such as
Prynne, came down heavily upon this type of art.[1]

An atmosphere of indecision lay heavy over many regions of
English thinking in the first half of the 17th century. The age
of Newton and John Locke had not yet arrived ; the musical
profession itself was largely composed of passionate, irritable,
pedantic, cranky, moody, and fanatical men. There were even
such types of composers as Solomon Eccles (1618–83) who became
a Quaker, and after having shown himself an excellent musician,

> publicly burned his instruments and music on Tower Hill
> and took to shoemaking. To show his contempt for ' steeple-
> houses ' he for two Sundays running insisted on making shoes
> in the pulpit of a London church during service, and had to
> be removed by the constable.[2]

The wavering of Puritanism—after all the most determined
spiritual force of the time—in the question of music is another
clear proof of this generally unstable and confused state of
spiritual life during the Commonwealth.

Milton, whose father was one of the best composers of his
generation, spoke enthusiastically as a poet about music, even

[1] It is interesting to note that in the early days of Puritanism its theoreticians
objected to instrumental music in general, wherever it appeared. They were
against any waste of time, and instrumental music was considered to be only one
form of time-wasting. That was a time when there was much unemployment and
much wayfaring, when the " sturdy beggars " swarmed over town and countryside
alike—when, on the other hand, every ablebodied human being was needed for
work by the rising small producer and capitalist classes, the main forces that were
promoting Puritanism. At such a time any form of instrumental music was
denounced as representing both paganism and catholicism, and this is what Philip
Stubbs, famous pamphleteer and theologian, had to say on the matter : " Every
towne, citie, and countrey is full of these minstrelles to pype up a dance to the
devill : but of dyvines, so few there be as they may hardly be seene. . . . May you
as rogues extravagantes, and straglers from the heavenlye country be arrested of
the high justice of peace, Christ Jesus, and be punished with eternall death, notwithstanding your pretensed licenses of earthly men." *Anatomy of Abuses*, 1583,
see New Shakespeare Society, 1877–9, p. 672.

[2] Scholes, *Oxford Compendium*, 1939.

though he gave purely utilitarian views when appearing as a politician or philosopher. In his early *At a solemn Music* he even proclaimed himself a great admirer of religious music :

> Oh may we soon again renew that song
> And keep in tune with Heaven, till God ere long
> To his celestial consort us unite,
> To live with him, and sing in endless morn of light !

In his *Areopagitica* Milton protested that there should be no question of a dictatorship over music as long as it was practised in private (apparently he was trying to lessen a control which did in fact approximate to a dictatorship over music in the home of the citizen).

Cromwell was no less inconsistent. He promoted John Wilson, royalist organist and composer, made him professor at Oxford (1650) and permitted the publication of his *Psalterium Carolinum* : *The Devotions of His Sacred Majestie in His Solitudes and Sufferings* (1657). In 1649 Cromwell removed the beautiful organ from Magdalen College, Oxford, thus saving it from destruction, and had it established at Hampton Court, in order to have the opportunity of hearing it there frequently. The same Cromwell whose soldiery demolished organs all over the country secretly secured an organ for his private use ! And he appointed John Hingeston (1683), one of the best musicians of Charles I, as his organist and music master at an excellent salary. Cromwell even liked to listen to Latin motets by such outspokenly Anglican composers as Richard Deering, and these motets were performed on the organ and other instruments by Hingeston assisted by his pupils and by Milton.

Furthermore there is no doubt that there really was much publication of music during the Commonwealth, if of " light and airy " character and of no outstanding value. The Puritans may have done harm to the development of music by refusing to admit the art to the serious thoughts of a serious age. But it cannot be said that they suppressed the art or even tried to.[1] The time between 1648 and 1660 was a musically active time. The only question is what kind of music was played, written and encouraged. That is all that matters.

In view of all this evidence it is surely an over-simplification

---

[1] Dr. Percy Scholes gives more details about the problem in his book *Puritans and Music*, 1934, and one must say that he builds up a strong case for Puritanism.

of the case to assert that English music was destroyed by the Puritans. Such indeed is the power of a title (especially a political nickname such as this one), that one is apt to forget that Puritans were no more and no less than ordinary men in peculiar circumstances. It is these circumstances which made them Puritans, and it is these circumstances which destroyed English music. Chief of the dominating conditions of the time was the way in which economic expansion, in permeating the inner life of the country, produced increasing class divisions and developed, among the decisive sections of society, the general attitude of mind which was discussed and illustrated in the earlier part of this chapter. It was this spirit which degraded music to the level of a toy, a plaything, a restorative to be applied to men to make them fit for labour. At the same time it glorified all arts and all qualities in art which make for steady application to duty, whereby money may be made.

The wordly rewards of this cultural policy were immense. The second great forward surge in the history of the economic and political advance of England took place in the Commonwealth.

But in the same period, and by the same process, the fate of English music was sealed.

CHAPTER VII

LAST RISE—ECLIPSE

AND yet, once again before the great ebb the creative power of English music was to show itself in full force.

It was the unusually happy combination of several peculiar circumstances that restored to English chamber music once more, if only for a short time, its lost greatness.

The immediate external reason for this remarkable recovery was the Restoration itself, which set up again the old Court and High Church that had been the cultivators of chamber-music life before the Civil War started.

The restoration of the Court was by no means altogether a restoration of the pre-Commonwealth order. On the contrary, on the basis laid by the revolution of 1640–1660, industry and trade could expand rapidly. The independent power of the crown as an executive authority had gone. The king was a " king by the grace of merchants and squires."[1]

But, at the same time, reactionary forces *were* strengthened, and they were conspicuously represented at Charles II's court. On the one hand the most democratic elements of the Commonwealth period (Levellers) had been defeated (the Dissenters, for instance, were forthwith excluded from municipal government and the universities). Yet the compromise of the Restoration had brought back to power, on the other hand, a clique of courtiers and landowners with a semi-feudal mentality, an essentially static and conservative outlook. While the bourgeoisie was developing strongly and economic prosperity progressed considerably, the restored Court, with the advancing years, pursued a new and cleverly camouflaged policy of reaction.

Charles II's policy in matters of art reflects quite clearly the narrow selfishness of his ambitions.

He was only concerned with the cultivation of art at the Court. He did not care one iota about what happened to musicians outside the Court. There was no question of improving their lot ; many of them died in bitter poverty. In general cultural life at the Court did not strike impartial observers as particularly sympathetic. There were many silly fashions and much empty

[1] Hill.

showing-off. Typical of the time were the dress fashions—costumes " burst into a wild efflorescence after the ' close time ' of the Commonwealth " ; " men's gloves were fringed, scented with jasmine or orange," and " both men and women used muffs."[1] The people at the Court are described by the famous Anthony à Wood as " rude, rough, whoremongers ; vaine, empty, carelesse."[2] Roger North (1650–1733) speaks similarly of their musical incompetence, if more politely : " Nothing advanced musick more in this age than the patronage of nobility, and of men of fòrtunes," but " . . . the Lords and the rest that subscribed (as the good King Charles II) had ears, but not artificiall ones, and those were necessary to warrant the authority of such a court of justice."[3]

However, as Court life differed so much from the busy capitalist working day of commercial and early industrial England, there was at least plenty of time to spend in the pleasures of the mind.

Charles himself was not disinclined to play the musical Mæcenas. It was his ambition to surround himself with the splendours of a great chapel. In addition, the patronage of a few of the more cultured men of ' nobility and fortune ' around the Court advanced and intensified musical activity on a wider scale.

The masters who were patronised included most of the great musical talents in the country. Some of the former coryphæi of Charles I's chapel had managed to survive the upheaval of the Commonwealth. Luckiest among them, from the point of view of maintaining their tradition, were those few who had found temporary refuge in and around Oxford, the asylum of Anglicanism during the critical years.[4] They were recalled and once more given an opportunity to employ their great skill and learning with official recognition.

At the beginning of the Restoration the most important among these men were Jenkins, Coleman, Christopher Gibbons, Christopher Simpson, Banister, Cooke, Humfreys, Jeffreys, Locke, Brewer and Rogers : later, only two more great names appeared, Blow and Purcell. Of all these man only Humfreys, Blow and

[1] A. C. A. Brett, *Charles II and his Court*, 1910, pp. 198 ff.

[2] *Life and Times of Anthony à Wood*, ed. Llewellyn Powys, London, 1932.

[3] Roger North, *Memoirs*, 1728 ; ed. E. F. Rimbault, 1846.

[4] Anthony à Wood wrote in 1656 : " The Musick masters who were now in Oxon and frequented the said (weekly musical) meetings were William Ellis, Proctor, Wilson and others " (ed. L. Powys, p. 51).

Purcell were born after 1630 : the other men belonged to the old school. Their musical education was deeply-rooted in the tradition of polyphonic music in which England had excelled during the first decades of the century. But Humfreys, Blow and Purcell also belonged indirectly to the older school, since their teachers were formerly active members of the commercial establishment attached to the pre-Commonwealth Church and Court.

So the restored Court commended the services of men schooled in the technique of their craft. Composers were neither forced to continue in their polyphonic tradition nor prevented from so doing ; though Charles personally tried to divert the attention of the musicians from the particular form of the old-style fantasia and especially from the use of viols, which he considered old-fashioned, to less intimate and more showy forms of art (and to the use of instruments that better suited his Court ambitions). Wood testified that " Charles did not like the viols ; preferring the violins as being more airie and brisk than viols."[1] Roger North reported that " Charles II had an utter detestation of fancys."[2]

At the same time, the Court composers themselves, although they had been brought up in the tradition of the past, were not by any means untouched by the progress of social life outside the Court, fortunately for their work. The stiffness of Court etiquette (which brought the Court increasing unpopularity) would not have been any inspiration, once the first intoxications of royalist enthusiasm had passed away. The Court was, after all, an island of old-time aristocratic mentality in a wide and fast-flowing current of commercial realism. But the combination of Court patronage with certain modern forms of practice arising from life outside the Court offered new scope for the composers and proved a healthy influence. And is it not a fact that the very nastiness and soullessness of his surroundings sometimes causes the artist to create the more soulful and passionate works of art ? just as Charles' xenophilism helped to strengthen the new nationalism among great composers as the examples of Matthew Locke and John Blow show.

The first years of Charles II's absolutism were based on a compromise, as neither the commercial-capitalist nor the aristocratic forces could do entirely without one another. There was

[1] ed. L. Powys, p. 212.   [2] Ed. Rimbault, p. 103.

a state of dispute in cultural life, too. A lively interest in topical problems and ideas was taking place, such as is always a healthy sign in cultural life—and indeed the Restoration age was not only characterised by the noble rogues of Charles II's court, but also by Newton and the Royal Society.

How actively musicians of the period in particular were searching for a way out of the spiritual crisis can be judged from the flood of theoretical treatises that appeared between 1660 and 1680. Locke, Mace, Pepys, Wood, Simpson, John Philips, Th. Salmon, J. Playford and others all discussed burning problems of musical practice and theory, tending to consider music in its philosophical aspects and often displaying a vivacity and fighting spirit that reminds one of France as it was during the second half of the 18th century.

So Restoration musicians proved to be (to use a hackneyed phrase) as much children of their time as any before them.

Of all the new forms of practice that were developing outside the Court the evolution of the *public concert* was the most momentous.

We have seen that even in early 16th-century chamber music performances there existed a much more subjective attitude on the part of the player or listener towards the art than had been the case in any previous musical practice. The public concert represented a further penetration of the individualist spirit into musical life. It became one of the most important cultural manifestations of the advance of capitalism. The consequences of the arrival of this new way of performing music and listening to it were enormous.

It was no more a closed society,[1] but an anonymous and practically limitless public that heard the performances. This concert public had few forerunners in English history. The aristocratic visitors who attended the performances of plays and masques during the earlier years of the 17th century may have helped to pave the way for gatherings of the new kind. The Music Acts in Cambridge and Oxford during the Commonwealth (musical celebrations of examina and other prominent occasions) attracted a large public though the audiences were

[1] Private chamber music circles and other closed musical societies continued to exist throughout the century. Only one example of many : Roger North mentions that after 1660 " shopkeepers and foremen came weekly to sing in consort " in London taverns (*Memoirs of Musick*).

mainly academic.[1] Cromwell introduced "state concerts" in Whitehall.[2]

The concert-going public proper evolved as the logical result of the increase in the habit of passive listening.. The public went to music-meetings in the hope of finding " much pleasure, consolation and recreation," as Charles Butler had expressed it thirty years before. Each member of the audience would sit in his chair, imbibing harmony and happiness, and relate all the happenings in the music to the memory of his own emotional experiences, or his current state of mind. And he would pay for this hour of pleasure in coin of the realm.

Here is the second important novelty. *Music became a commodity*. As such it was sold in the market and obeyed all those laws of supply and demand to which every product of capitalism was subjected. It became available to whoever cared and could pay—and dating from the economic revival about the middle of the Restoration period quite a number of citizens could afford to attend concerts. Musical life became, to an increasing degree, dependent on the commercial initiative of those who ran concert and operatic enterprises, and who often had only the commercial interest in mind.

The bigger the demand for music in concert halls grew, the larger became the halls. After d'Avenant's still modest attempts in 1656, the first concerts of John Banister and Thomas Britton, dating from 1672, drew more and more numerous audiences.[3]

The new attitude of the public led to the development of styles and forms in music acquiring more and more the unified character of complete emotional entities. Some form of dramatic consistency was now absolutely essential in the new work of art. In it there was indeed variety, but, to an increasing degree, variety of musical characters acting in the same drama. It was already Milton's opinion that " Variety (as both music and rhetoric teacheth us) erects and rouses an auditory like the masterful running over many chords and divisions. . . ." At the same time the polyphony of the old age changed. Old English

---

[1] See Scholes, *Compendium*, p. 206.

[2] Samuel Pepys reports on one of these meetings (" with trumpets and kettle-drums ") where there was " dull vulgar musique " (*Diary*, 1656).

[3] It is interesting to note how Banister's concert meetings came about. Banister repeatedly had trouble at the Court ; he finally had to leave the chapel royal because of his opposition to the Romanisation of English musical life. Then he started his weekly musical meetings. He turned to commercial and public music, the very antithesis of that at the Court.

chamber music had been, after all, music for the players rather than music for the listeners. In the ' golden age ' each performer (and each achieved an equally high standard of musical proficiency) took equal delight in playing his independent melodic line inside the contrapuntal whole. In the new concert the work of art had to adjust itself to the wishes of a non-playing public. The new patterns of musical form, for the most part, consisted of a subjective and emotional melody, accompanied by subservient parts, easy to understand, easy to ' put over.'

Thus the ' *gestic* ' (i.e., emotionally-rhetorical) ideal of music was gaining ground. All that has been said about Italian music at the beginning of the century as opposed to English chamber art now began to apply to this country. No wonder the instruments of modern subjective expression replaced the viols and recorders. After a period of opposition on the part of the representatives of the old chamber music, the violin family rose in triumph. In 1631 Owen Feltham had shown his disgust with the instrument :

> It is a kind of disparagement to be a cunning fiddler. It argues his neglect of better employment, and that he hath spent much time on a thing unnecessarie.[1]

In 1657 Anthony à Wood of Oxford wrote in his diary that gentlemen in private musical meetings

> esteemed a violin to be an instrument only belonging to a common fiddler, for feare of making these meetings to be vaine and fiddling.

But soon things changed, and the special ability of the violin to respond to subjective and expressive interpretation of music was found to be completely in accordance with the *new* attitude of the listener. And so, very shortly afterwards, the same Anthony à Wood reported excitedly :

> I saw Thomas Baltzar (the German violinist) run up his fingers to the end of the finger-board of the violin, and run them back insensibly, and all with great alacrity and very good time, which I nor any in England saw the like before.[2]

The king's preference for violins had a somewhat different origin : it was not so much the emotional quality of the violin as its greater fitness for pomp and display that caused him to

[1] *Resolves*, 1631.   [2] *Diary*, 1657 and 1659.

recommend it so strongly.[1]   The patronage of the king himself
very much helped to popularise the instrument.   Roger North
also alludes to the violoncello (bass violin) which began to be
used at that time :

> There was a set of gentlemen at that time in towne who fre-
> quently mett for pure private diversion.   And their musick
> was, of ye Babtist (Lully) way, very Good.   They were most
> violinists, and often hired base-violinns (which instrument as
> then used was a very hard & harsh sounded Base & nothing
> so soft & sweet as now) to attend them.[2]

How quickly and completely the violin finally conquered is
shown in a passage of Thomas Mace who deplores bitterly the
disappearance of the true spirit of old English chamber music :

> Very little of This so eminent Musick (for viols) do we hear
> of in These Times, the Lesz the Greater Pity.   Then again,
> we had all Those Choice Consorts, to Equally-Seized Instru-
> ments (Rare Chest of Viols) and as Equally Performed : For
> we would never allow Any Performer to Over-top, or Out-cry
> another by loud Play ; but our Great Care was, to have All
> the Parts Equally Heard ; by which means, though we had
> but sometimes indifferent, or mean Hands to Perform with ;
> yet This Caution made the Musick Lovely, and Very Conten-
> tive.   But now the Modes and Fashions have cry'd These
> Things down, and set up a Great Idol in Their Room ; observe
> with what a Wonderful Swiftnesz They now run over Their
> Brave New Ayres ; and with what High-Prized Noise ; viz. 10,
> or 20 Violins, &ct., as I said before, to a Some-Single Soul'd
> Ayre ; it may be of two or three Parts, or Some Coranto,
> Serebrand, or Brael, (as the New-Fashioned Word is) and such
> like Stuff ; seldom any other ; which is rather fit to make a
> Man's Ear Glow, and Fill his Brain full of Frisks, &ct. than to
> Season, and Sober his Mind, or Elevate his Affection to Good-
> nesz.[3]

Thomas Mace alludes to another innovation which belongs to
this short and yet portentous period, the *orchestra*.   Together,

---

[1] The use of violins at Court was not altogether new.   In 1620 Thomas Lupo
was made Court composer for violins ; see Hayes, *King's Music*, p. 64.   We also
come across violins in Charles I's Masques and in some works by William Lawes.
But it was not until 1660 and after, that violins actually prevailed.

[2] *Musicall Grammarian*, ed. H. Andrews, 1925, p. 31.

[3] *Musick's Monument*, 1676.

the large public and the new ' gestic ' function of instrumental music greatly accelerated the evolution of orchestral music as opposed to private chamber music. It is true that there are examples of almost orchestral performances before this time ; again, especially in the masques. In Ben Jonson's and Ferrabosco's *Masque of the Queens* for instance (1610) payment was given to the following musicians : [1]

To 12 musicians that were Preestes, made songs and played £24
To 12 other Lutes . . . with Flutes „ 12
To 10 Violencas that continually practized to the Queen „ 20
To 4 more that were added at the Maske „ 4
To 15 musitions that played the pages and fooles „ 20
To 13 Hoboys and Sackbutts „ 10

and there are plenty of instances of the contrivance, at almost every Tudor and Stuart court, of instrumental mass effects which played no small part in the founding of the modern orchestra. But such performances were based on the demand of kings for splendid display rather than on the demand of subjects for entertainment. Only with the evolution of the general public did the orchestra secure widely-based economic support and become an established institution. Roger North insisted strongly on the establishment of the orchestral ideals which indeed had been anticipated in the Masques of James I : " Magnitude and force of sound is among the chief excellencys of music."[2]

These developments were not without effect on the performers' attitude. The concert artist was in a position entirely different from that of the organist in the church or the minstrel in the dancing-hall. In him the individualistic ambitions of every member of the public were personified. He became so much the centre of interest that a certain exaltation of his personality was the natural consequence. It is in Wood's description that first mention is made of the *virtuoso*.[3] An artist who finds himself in

---

[1] Duncan & Crowest, *Minstrelsy*, 1907, p. 198.

[2] *Memoirs*, p. 83. The reader may be referred to Lafontaine's book, *King's Musick*, for more facts on orchestras at Stuart courts.

[3] Apart from Baltzar, Nicola Matteis is an important figure. He lived in England for many years as a virtuoso and composer of violin music, and his influence in the direction of a more brilliant style was great. North also mentions " Scheiffare " (Scheiffler), Voglesang, " and other names to fright one " (*Grammarian*, p. 30), to whom we may add Godfrey Keller, Godfrey Finger, and Gerhard Diessener (Disineer), all three German by birth. Wood further reports that the violinist Mell " was not so admired, yet he played sweeter, was a well-bred gentleman, and not given to excessive drinking, as Baltzar was."

the position of an idol soon tends to increase idolatry by startling
the public with double-stoppings, passages and ornaments played
at lightning speed.   Though sober standards of true musicianship
were still upheld by many of the numerous English and foreign
virtuosos who entered the musical life of the country during the
last decades of the century, the showing-off spirit of the concert
virtuoso had appeared.   The public, responding, soon began to
show such curious predilections as an enthusiasm for male
sopranists and contraltists.

The influence of *foreign music* began to be of decisive importance
during this time.   At first it seemed as though its influence would
be productive of a permanent reconstruction of English music.
So, alas, it was.   But not as one might have hoped.

We have repeatedly drawn attention to certain Italian elements
of style.   Such influences developed up to about 1635 only on
very general lines.   Wherever details of Italian music were taken
over they were kept within the limits of experiment.   On the
whole English chamber music (as distinct from vocal music) had
kept remarkably independent of continental influence for a long
time, compared for instance with German music which was
deeply affected by Italian art.   English composers were very
conscious of their originality and of the purity of their style,
and whenever Italian influence threatened to grow they raised,
like Morley, their warning voices.[1]   Yet the powerful subversive
element of Italian music—so full of that " fire and fury " which
Roger North admired[2]—could not be checked for ever.   More
and more features of Italian music were utilised.   Italian
instrumental music itself became popular.[3]

During the Commonwealth the infiltration of continental
elements into English chamber music made rapid progress.   In
1656 Matthew Locke had protested : " I never saw any foreign
instrumental music (a few French Corantos excepted) worthy an
Englishman's transcribing."   But during this time, the harmonic
basso continuo, a definitely foreign element in British art, was
gaining ground.   In 1639 William Child issued a psalm work
for choir " with a continental (sic) base either for the Organ
or Theorbo, newly composed after the Italian way."   This, it is

---

[1] See above, p. 171 (footnote).
[2] *Musicall Grammarian*, p. 24.
[3] In 1622 Peacham made a list of great composers of his time (*Compleat Gentleman*, p. 100) which includes 16 continental masters of whom 12 were Italians.

true, was vocal music ; and about the same time Deering composed madrigals with basso continuo. But in the instrumental field William Lawes was already compromising with the continuo, and about 1655 several composers of instrumental music used it. Even if the basso continuo in some works written during the Commonwealth by composers like Jenkins, Locke and Jeffreys was no more than a kind of short score of the polyphonic parts in the Dowland way,[1] the ' vertical ' harmonic attitude slowly won through—entirely in accordance with the new spirit that began to dominate cultural and social life in general.

The influence of Italian emotionalism is felt in the appearance for the first time in musical history of *dynamic* and *tempo* indications. In a MS. by George Jeffreys both kinds of directions are found.[2] In a fantasia a 3 by John Hilton we are told to play ' softly ' (piano), ' away ' (faster) and ' long tyme ' (slower).[3] Effects based on the change from piano to forte are exploited in ' echoes ' such as were written by Thomas Mudd, William Lawes, Maurice Webster and others.[4]

French and German influences had been operative before the Restoration—chiefly expressed in the appearance in this country of certain forms of French dances and German sonatas.[5] Yet such elements played an insignificant part in the development of English chamber music before the Restoration.

But with the restoration of Charles II to the throne, the whole ' foreign policy ' in matters of musical practice and production entered an entirely new phase. Just as Charles' political aims were more and more closely linked up with those of other powers, so he pursued to an increasing degree a musical policy which

[1] See above, p. 136.

[2] Add. 10338.

[3] See above, p. 196.

[4] MSS. in the British Museum and in Christ Church, Oxford.

[5] French ' fantasies ' written during the first half of the 17th century were themselves derived from the fancies of this country, as we can see by studying the works of Claude Lejeune, Eustache Du Caurroy, and Nicolaus Metru. Certain types of dances from France became familiar over here, but the forms were used as a mere mould for the English idiom. The introduction of the sonata form into this country from Italy *via* Germany dates from the middle of the century. Sonatas imitating the ' Baroque,' German, rather than the expressive and emotional Italian style were composed by William Youngh (printed collection, 1653 ; also single sonatas in Durham Cathedral Library), Henry Butler (ibid.), and also John Jenkins (ibid.). Youngh's edition of sonatas a 2–5 with basso continuo appeared in Innsbruck and cannot be discussed here, being really part of the German production. The rest of his sonatas, also most of those by Butler and Jenkins, are virtuoso compositions for 1–3 bass viols, and will be treated later on in this book.

favoured foreign elements of style. Italian, German and now especially French musicians, were invited to take positions at the Court at high salaries. For a period of great splendour had started in French music. Opera, under the patronage of the Roi Soleil, received an impetus hitherto unknown. It became a centre round which French music developed into an imposing art radiating the whole grandeur of Louis' absolutism. It was Charles' ambition to appear in a similar halo of artistic glorification. He could not be behind his colleague on the other side of the Channel. Opera in England, which was of only small significance about the middle of the century entered a phase of considerable success, largely owing to French influence. At his Court Charles established a band of 24 violins on the lines of the model at Paris where Charles had spent his years of exile. Louis Grabu, French violinist (d. about 1694) replaced the English Nicholas Laniere (1588–1666) as master of the Chapel Royal in 1665. The number of French composers and performers employed henceforth at the Court was high.

Ballet, dances and other instrumental forms of the French Court, such as the Overture Suite, were adopted. The works of master Lully were soon hailed almost as enthusiastically here as in Paris. Scores of arrangements of his works for all kinds of instrumental combinations are in the British Museum.[1] French influence had come to stay in English musical life. This conquest was, however, at first confined to the Court, where it amounted to a 'veni-vidi-vici.' Amateurs, teachers and the general public were slower in submitting to the startling new French style.

The French manner of Instrumentall musick did not gather so fast as to make a revolution all at once, but during the greatest part of that king's [Charles II] reigne, the old musick was used in the countrys, and in many meetings and societys in London,

says Roger North who adds, however : "But the treble-violl was disregarded and the violin took its place."[2]

The fusion of the old English tradition of polyphonic mastery and the new continental achievements proved exceedingly healthy for English music for a time, as we shall see.

[1] MSS. Add. 29283–5, 31429, 33236, 10445 and others.
[2] *Memoirs*, p. 105.

It was indeed a happy combination of circumstances which made possible the brief renaissance of English chamber music.

For, at a time when its absolutist ambitions kept the Court in constant conflict with the great and growing commercial classes outside it, chamber music was able to derive benefit from both sets of antagonists : the Court granted lavish patronage, gave composers places and pensions, work to do and bread to eat ; while the greater world provided the audiences for public concerts, a development that greatly enhanced our composers' financial chances. There was another lucky coincidence in the fact that foreign music, which for a time did English music so much good, happened to be favoured both in the small world of privilege and in the great world of enterprise, the Court cultivating it for the sake of its elegance and its association with a more successful despotism abroad, the city liking it for its eloquent, showy, emotional qualities. But these propitious circumstances, even in their fortunate combination, would have availed English chamber music nothing, if there had not been a vigorous remnant of high musical culture surviving the Civil War and the Commonwealth —a body of men skilled in its practice, to whom chamber music still meant all that is best in the art. And again it must be emphasised that the chief centre of musical activity was the Court —whatever was its moral and political outlook.

*　*　*　*　*

The main stylistic developments of chamber music from Jenkins to Purcell are the slow evolution from polyphony to homophony, and the final victory of dramatic and lyrical, of subjectively emotional elements. Although all composers of the period reflect this change in some degree, they can be divided into two groups : those whose art is still essentially rooted in the English polyphonic tradition, and those who turn more and more energetically to modern elements, whether these elements arise out of English conditions or come from abroad. The chief masters of the former group are Jenkins, Jeffreys and Coleman, those of the latter group are Christopher Gibbons, Matthew Locke, John Blow and Henry Purcell. These two categories are, however, by no means rigid ; a considerable number of composers of lighter music, among them Banister and Christopher Simpson (two composers who worked chiefly outside the Court), show characteristics of both groups.

Let us now turn to John Jenkins (1592–1678), one of the most important and most amiable musical figures of the whole century His career is a study in itself. Jenkins is essentially a polyphonist, but at the same time his immense output includes pieces in all styles current during his long life, from the most backward to the most advanced. In his early childhood right up to ripe middle age he served at the royal Court, and when the Chapel Royal was restored he was recalled with other great musicians, although he was then already 68 years old.[1] He was an excellent virtuoso on various instruments as Roger North tells us in his biographical notes on the composer.[2] A curious feature is that of the enormous number of his works none (except a few odd items that were published in contemporary collections) is definitely known to have been printed.[3]

But Jenkins' music was very well known in its time. Wood writes in 1676, two years before the composer's death : " John Jenkyns . . . most famous ; for his compositions enter into the hands of all men."[4] Roger North who was an amateur pupil of Jenkins (his actual profession was the law—he was Attorney-General) refers both to the number and to the quality of the composer's works which were " more voluminous, and in the time more esteemed than all the rest, and now lye in the utmost contempt."[5] He also calls him " the mirrour and wonder of his

[1] He was honoured by an unusual act of generosity on the part of his colleagues ; he was allowed to draw his fees without actually performing, in recognition of his great reputation as the doyen of English music.

[2] *Musicall Gramarian*, pp. 21–26.

[3] There are vague references to a publication of " 12 Sonatas for 2 Violins and a Base with a Thorough Base for the Organ and Theorbo," which he is said to have edited in 1660. Cf. J. Pulver, *Biographical Dictionary*, 1927. The work is probably in Brit. Mus. MS. Add. 31430 (contemporary handwritten copy) ; each of these sonatas consists of three or four movements. Percy Scholes (*Oxford Companion*) believes the work to be identical with a MS. in Oxford (which MS. ?). A publication more likely to be by Jenkins is a printed work mentioned in a catalogue of musical publications offered at the Frankfurt fair in 1667, as " Joan. Jenickens 5–stimmige Balletten und Sarabanden mit 2 Violinen, 2 Viola da Braccio und 1 Violon mit Basso Continuo ; Magdeburg, 1667 " (see K. A. Goehler, *Verzeichnis der in den Leipziger und Frankfurter Messkatalogen angezeigten Musikalien*, 1901–2). This rather looks like a German edition of some of his sarabands and ballets with basso continuo, possibly arranged for 5 parts by a German in accordance with the German practice which at that time preferred 5- and 6-part music to the Italian solos and trios. There is, however, no further proof that " Joan. Jenickens's " work is really by our composer ; no copy of this publication is known to be available. H. Davey, *History of English Music*, p. 271, draws attention to the article on Jenkins in Eitner's *Bibliographie* which mentions a collection of 200 pieces by English violists, edited by Jenkins in Amsterdam (1664), with 67 arias of his own. Unfortunately Eitner gives no further details.

[4] II, 335.   [5] *Memoirs*, 1728, ed. Rimbault, 1846, p. 85.

age for music."[1] Like the old In Nomines, Jenkins' works were passed from hand to hand by copying (what an indication of the narrowing-down of public interest in polyphonic fantasias in that time of printed music !) ; and indeed many copies of Jenkins' MSS. still exist in various libraries in this country. Of several pieces, e.g., certain four-part fantasias, we can still count·seven or eight handwritten copies.[2]

The number of Jenkins' instrumental compositions is exceptionally large. Like Lawes, he wrote almost exclusively chamber music. Among his works are 110 independent fantasias a 2–6, two In Nomines a 6,[3] and several hundred suites a 2–4, each of them consisting of from 2 to 15 movements (mostly starting with ayr, pavan or fantasia and containing almands, corants, sarabands, gigues, ballets, ' rants ' and unnamed movements),[4] and many individual dance movements such as the famous " Bell Pavin." His suites for two trebles and bass (mostly violins and bass viol with or without basso continuo) are exceedingly numerous, even for him ; they contain among other things the " Little Consort "[5] and the " Lira Consort harpe way flat, for 3 parts, viz. 1 lira, 1 treble, 1 Bas."[6] Special mention must also be made of his several sets of ayrs for " one treble, one base, one lyra and harpsichord " which continues the tradition of the ' broken consort ' of the ' golden age.'

Apart from its abundance the most surprising feature of Jenkins' work is its variety. Almost every style of the whole 17th century is represented. Studying this vast production one seems to be regarding a complete panorama of the development of chamber music from Elizabethan times to the ' Glorious Revolution.' There are fantasias of the Ferrabosco type and melodies that seem tó anticipate Handel.

It is difficult, if not impossible, to consider all of Jenkins' musical works in chronological order. Most MSS. are undated, and even those which are dated often contain stylistic elements

---

[1] *Memoirs*, p. 87.

[2] See E. H. Meyer, *Spielmusik*, p. 141.

[3] Chief MSS. : Brit. Mus. Add. 27550–4 for the 2-part pieces, Bodleian, Oxford, c. 86–7 and Durham Cath. (various MSS.) for the 3 part ones, Bodleian, Oxford, c. 64–9 and 98–9 for those a 4, Add. 30487 for those a 5 and Bodleian, Oxford, c. 86 for those a 6 parts.

[4] Chief MSS. : Bodleian, Oxford, c. 84–5, c. 88, f. 564–7, Brit. Mus. Add. 10445, 18940–4, 27550–4, 31423, 31426–7, 31430–1.

[5] Add. 31427.   [6] Add. 31431.

proper to much earlier or much later periods. Jenkins recurred
to certain habits of expression again and again throughout his
career.

However, it can be said that some groups of works definitely
belong to certain periods of his life. There are first of all 22
fantasias for four viols. They must have been written between
1625 and 1640 when Jenkins took an active part in Charles
I's chamber music.[1] They breathe the same spirit as many of
William Lawes' works. All these lively and highly elaborate
pieces are based on polyphony in an extreme form. Their
counterpoints are just as intricate and just as difficult as Lawes'
fantasias. This polyphony is even harder to disentangle because
the melodic lines in all parts are even longer. If the intervals
and figures in Jenkins' pieces are not quite as wild and jumpy as
those of the older master, their structure is even more personal.
There are hardly any ' full stops.' Whenever a cadence seems
to prepare to settle down, one may be sure that it will turn back
at the last moment and run into some new contrapuntal development. Rhythmically these pieces are incredibly complex. Syncopes veil the change-over from bar to bar ; accents are more
often against the beats than on them.

These fantasias by Jenkins have already been mentioned as
belonging to that era of delicate, non-popular Court music in the
production of which Lawes was the most important figure. The
main difference between Jenkins' noble and distinguished art and
Lawes' music lies not in its intricacy and elaborateness but in the
fact that his music is usually less ' showy ' than than of Lawes.
Jenkins is the more typical chamber-music composer. His art is
not based on stormy, extravagant or even particularly expressive
thematic ideas. It is as intimate, objective and detached as
chamber music can possibly be. In fact, it is the ideal chamber
music, as exemplified in a fantasia a 4[2] ; see Appendix No. VI.

It is particularly in this group of works that styles and periods
seem confused and are difficult to place. For there are 27
fantasias for treble, tenor and bass[3] which are in exactly the
same extremely polyphonic idiom as the four-part pieces, yet
bear the date 1654 quite plainly—which means they were com-

[1] Some of them are in Christ Church, Oxford, MS. 2, which contains exclusively
pre-Commonwealth music (date about 1635).

[2] Christ Church, Oxford, MS. 2.

[3] Bodleian, Oxford, E. 406–9.

posed 20 to 25 years later, at a time when this style was quite out of fashion. Jenkins was at that time rather out of touch with life and the public (even more so than during his sojourn at Charles I's court), being private musician and teacher to squires in far-off country places, such as Sir Hamon Lestrange, and later Sir P. Woodhouse of Kimberley (Norfolk). So he was bound to develop even further this brooding, ' ruminant ' style of his four-part fantasias.

Seen as a whole, this exceedingly contrapuntal music of Jenkins appears as the last island of genuine polyphony at a time when all over Europe composers were rapidly moving away from it. In spite of many progressive details this type of Jenkins' fantasia marks the conclusion of a style ; it does not contain any vitally new elements.

Jenkins' uncertain position between the styles is conspicuously shown in a second group of fantasias, those for five and six viols. In Chapter VI stress was laid on the dualism in the production of chamber music during the years before the republican period. There was the hyper-complex Court art, as represented by Lawes, and there was, on the other hand, the simplified and popularised fantasia of the East-Okeover-Brewer era. Now Jenkins wrote music in both styles. The five- and 6-part fantasias, pavanas and In Nomines of this curious composer bear definitely many traces of the latter style. The historical dualism in English chamber music during its period of crisis is now illustrated in the production of one and the same man.

It is true that most composers since the days of Morley differentiated between two-, three- and four-part fantasias on one hand and five- and six-part ones on the other. The former were much livelier and more richly figured than the latter. But Jenkins goes further. His five- and six-part works are (with the exception of a few pieces such as the two In Nomines which are more vividly polyphonic) far more homophonic and melodious than his other fantasias. There are shorter and easily comprehensible phrases. The melodies are based on slow folk-song types ; they are often ' telling,' and very charming.

Example 71 : from fantasia No. 2 in C-minor for 5 viols,[1] John Jenkins (circa 1635).

The " Bell Pavin " for six viols enjoyed great fame in its time, as Roger North, among others, confirms.[2] It imitates the 'symphony' which has been performed by the great variety of bells in Oxford churches every evening ever since the days of Jenkins. Built on the descending sixth

and other figures displayed in this natural ' concentus,' this piece conveys a strange impression of past centuries coming to life again, just as to-day the Oxford bells bring back the past in the midst of the present.

There is yet another side of Jenkins' music : his work as the composer of fashionable dance suites. The amazing number of his pieces in this genre suggests that they were in their majority commissioned for the festive gatherings of good society, and not (or not immediately) for pure chamber-music purposes. Quite a lot must have been composed for the aristocracy of Charles I's time ; not so many during the Commonwealth ; but the greater part seem to have been written after the Restoration.[3]

It would be impossible here to go into a detailed account of his astonishingly varied and colourful dance music, just as it would be senseless to try to count or put in order, his hundreds of melodies, shapely and flowing, skilfully invented, always pleasant

[1] Add. 30487.   [2] *Memoirs*, p. 90.
[3] See Hughes Hughes, *Catalogue of Music MSS. in the British Museum*, III.

and interesting. It is a proud, a great period of creative work once again, and it is high time that all this lovely music was revived. It seems incredible that even now it rests in peace on the shelves of the Bodleian and Christ Church libraries.

Of even greater interest are the compositions of the last years of Jenkins' life. They consist mainly of fantasias for small, more modern combinations such as two violins and viola da gamba, or two violé da gamba, or even three violins and basso continuo. All these works are strongly influenced by the new concert style, as well as by the cosmopolitan atmosphere that prevailed at the restored Court.

There is for instance a group of pieces for one to three bass viols, or for one violin with two bass viols, with or without thorough bass. Here are virtuoso compositions which show the progress of the concert mentality. A special feature of all these fantasias and sonatas are the very vivid viola da gamba parts. Demi-semi-quavers are quite normal in such pieces, not only in one viola da gamba, but in all parts of the score.

Jenkins is not the originator of this curious " concertante " and ornamental style. A direct line runs from the viola da gamba duets and trios of Coperario, Ferrabosco, East, Deering and Ives via William Youngh, Richard Cook, Gregory and Hingeston to Jenkins and his fellows.[1] But Jenkins' employment of the style is especially interesting ; illustrating the versatility of the master.

[1] East and Ives and the above-named composers as well as some more masters of slightly later date (including also Rogers, Christopher Simpson, Christopher Gibbons, B. Hely and Matthew Locke) wrote a number of pieces for 2 and 3 bass viols of equal pitch. The use of this combination represented yet another form of compromise between the new and the old attitude. It was an attempt to reconcile the tradition of the contrapuntal fantasia with the growing popularity of the homophonic bass viol virtuoso-solo. Here again the predominance of one instrument over the others is the chief feature. The honours go round from viol to viol. Many pieces in the ' concertante-ornamental style ' are to be found in Add. 31424 and 31430. Rogers appears prominently in these collections, as also in the Bodleian, Oxford, D. 241-4 and E. 431-6, and in the Municipal Library of Hamburg. 12 fantasias for bass viols and organ of Rogers' composition were presented to the Archduke of Austria in 1653 and called " the best musicke that could be made " (see Davey, p. 248). Rogers also presented the Queen of Sweden with a collection of fancies and consorts ; some of these pieces are to-day preserved in the Royal Library in Uppsala. East remarks in his *Seventh Set of Books* which contains the duos for bass viol : " Wherein are Duos for two Base Viols, so composed, though there be but two parts in the eye, yet there is often three or four in the eare " ; meaning that he endeavoured to achieve a full polyphonic and also harmonic effect although only two parts are employed.

Example 72 : from Sonata for two viole da gamba (conclusion),[1] by John Jenkins.

An aria with variations by Jenkins, composed for violin, viola da
gamba and basso continuo, composed in the same highly ornamental style, is especially attractive. The melody might have
been written early in the 18th century :[2]

[1] Durham Cathedral, Mus. MS. D.5, No. 10.
[2] Durham Cathedral, Mus. MS. D.5.

Example 73 : Aria for violin, bass viol and continuo by John Jenkins (circa 1660).

Incidentally in this piece, violin as well as bass viol already displays a considerable range ; we note that the violin climbs up to f-sharp.

Yet not the viola da gamba concertos but the trio fantasias for two violins and bass viol are Jenkins' most modern pieces. They were composed when Jenkins was already over 70.[1] If one expects these works to be the products of a conservative dried-up old gentleman he will be agreeably surprised. These fantasias are much livelier, more optimistic, playful and understandable than the intricate earlier works which were written either for Charles I's court, or during Jenkins' own Babylonian exile in various lonely country manors. A three-part fantasia may illustrate the positive and stimulating effect that both the rising concert life and foreign influences exercised on early Restoration chamber music. The gay fullness of the best days of the ' golden age ' has once more reappeared[2] (see Appendix No. VII).

Some pieces contain episodes which must have appeared very daring to Jenkins' contemporaries. A well-known example occurs in fantasia No. 1 of the series[3] :

Example 74 : from fantasia No. 1 a 3 by John Jenkins (circa 1665).

Much of this music leads directly to Purcell and even to Handel. These fantasias prepare the developments of form and

[1] See Brit. Mus. Catalogue of Music, MSS., III.
[2] Add. 31428. All the composer's trios of this type are in Bodl. Libr. C. 86–87.
[3] Ibid.

style which the later masters carried to such perfection. Several elements of the concerto grosso are found here, and also early essays in cantabile writing. Jenkins' work need fear no comparison with Purcell's in respect of musicianship and technical resourcefulness. No one can deny Purcell's right to be widely celebrated, but surely Jenkins' importance ought to be recognised. For he gathers to himself and displays to the best advantage all that was of practical value in the whole of his period. His vitality is boundless, his variety unfailing, his productivity immense. He may be called the great all-rounder of English chamber music.

The Jenkins of these fantasias should really be given a seat of honour alongside the progressives of the day. Yet a good proportion of his earlier work belongs to the conservative category which properly concerns us now. Some further attention is due to these conservatives.

George Jeffreys (d. 1685) wrote creditable music for viols of which his three-part fantasias for descant, tenor and bass are best.[1] There is here no question of concert ambitions. They are examples of old-style polyphony. The same can be said of a rather more primitive fantasia a 3 by Henry Loosemore (d. 1670),[2] and of Charles Coleman's (d. 1664) works in general. Coleman enjoyed considerable fame in his time as Court musician, after having played a fairly prominent part in certain musical activities during the Commonwealth. His numerous compositions[3] are kept in the conservative style, yet are fresher and less intellectual than those of most of his colleagues. There is a certain drive in a beginning like this :

[1] Add. 10338.
[2] Add. 34800.
[3] Most of them are found in Add. 18940–4, 31423, Christ Church, Oxford, 353–6, 367–70, 379–81, 61–6, 1011, 1022, Bodleian, D.217, 220, c. 64–9, E. 410–4, 431–6.

Example 75 : from fantasia a 5,[1] by Charles Coleman (circa 1660).

Coleman wrote several sets of works for brass band, *Music for His Majestie's Sagbuts and Cornets* which were performed on great occasions at the Court. They are bright and tuneful pieces, worth while reviving. Many tunes were printed in contemporary collections, such as *Musicall Banquet* (1651) and *Court Ayres* (1653).

John Hingeston, Cromwell's house musician, was the first to add violins to the bass viols when using in his duos and trios the concertant-ornamental technique we discussed in reviewing the work of Jenkins. We can recommend Hingeston's compositions for careful study : there are numerous fantasias and suites a 2–6, some named after the months of the year, mostly contained in two old Oxford MSS.[2], all of them original and distinguished in their thematic material :

Example 76 :

from fantasia (a) No. 8 a 2 (introduction to suite), by John Hingeston.

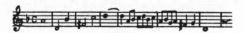

---

[1] Christ Church, Oxford, 423–8.
[2] Bodleian, Oxford, D. 205–11 and E. 382.

(*b*) fantasia-suite No. 1 a 5 :

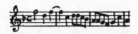

and very competently worked out. Like Coleman, Hingeston
composed some slow polyphonic pieces for brass band, to be
performed at the restored Court (orchestration : cornets, sagbuts
and organ).

Christopher Simpson is the chief representative of a rather
large group of musicians 'who stand between the conservatives
and the ' modernists ' of Restoration chamber music, with a
natural inclination to the more traditional. Simpson and his
fellows composed much solo music with and without accompaniment—that kind of instrumental solo which we found in the
works of the beginning of the century and which managed to keep
fairly independent of foreign influences for a comparatively long
time.

Simpson's own series of fantasias, *Monthes and Seasons*, with
virtuoso violin and bass viol parts, must be mentioned as particularly valuable.[1] Each piece bears the name of a month or a
season (we can discover no relation, however, between the programmatic titles and the music). There are passages of great
technical difficulty. When all the three parts of the score
perform their own ' ornamental concertos ' at the same time,
the result must have appeared neck-breaking to the composer's
contemporaries :

Example 77 : from fantasia " Spring " for violin, two bass
viols and basso continuo by Christopher Simpson.

_____
[1] Bodleian, Oxford, C. 54–8 ; see also Add. 18940–4.

German influences begin to be felt more distinctly in this type of music. Simpson, Hingeston and Jenkins employed elements of technique as used by such composers as Thomas Baltzar and the great Gerhard Diessener,[1] who both lived and worked in England for some time.

Simpson, however, is the uncontested master of the ' Divisions on a Ground,' i.e., the set of variations on a given bass which is repeated again and again. Here he employed a fine art of figuration which is on the whole originally English. This style originated in the consorts of the ' golden age.' It is melodically simple and mostly based on passages and broken chords ; there is nothing speculative or intricately polyphonic in this music. Only the basso continuo reminds the student of this music that the old standards of taste were changing rapidly.

The viola da gamba was Simpson's instrument. His *Division Violist* (1667) constitutes an important landmark in the history of the instrument as well as of the ' tema con variazioni.'[2]

Apart from Simpson, Captain Cooke (1616–72),[3] Henry Butler (dates unknown),[4] Daniel Norcome (1576–1647),[5] and many others wrote viol divisions of this kind, many of which are contained in Playford's *Musick's Recreation on the Violl* (1652). Such divisions were, however, not confined to the viola da gamba. Divisions appeared for the violin in the *Division Violin* (1685, 1688 and 1693) which includes pieces by Simpson, Mell, Becket, Tollet, Solomon Eccles and others ; for trios of strings in Lenton's and Tollett's Consorts (published 1695) ; later also for recorder in the *Division Flute* (1706) which contains works by Banister sen. and others.

Simpson was, however, not entirely preoccupied with the viola da gamba. He wrote suites and other pieces for 2 and 3 viols, 2 trebles and bass and other combinations, rather in the average style of the period.[6]

A considerable number of composers like Simpson worked

---

[1] Compositions by Baltzar in Bodleian, D. 241–4, E. 451 ; for Diessener (Disineer), see *Zeitschrift für Musikwissenschaft*, 1933–34.

[2] Copies in Brit. Mus. and Durham Cathedral.

[3] See below, p. 229.

[4] See above, p. 213 (footnote).

[5] A set of divisions by Norcome was recorded by P. Scholes (played by the Dolmetsches) for Columbia History of Music series.

[6] Add. 18940–4, Christ Church, Oxford, 1021, 1027, 1083 ; Tenbury 296–9. See also above, pp. 221 (footnote).

chiefly outside the Court. Thomas Farmer (d. about 1693) was one of the ' Waits of London,' which is to say, he was in the service of the municipality. His *Consort of Musick in 4 Parts and Second Consort of Music in 4 Parts* (1690) containing lessons, grounds and overtures in the French style, are pleasantly invented though occasionally somewhat amateurishly arranged.[1] The activities of John Banister, sen. (1630–79), as a composer covered works for 1–4 strings and also music for trumpets, chiefly suites and grounds of the familiar type.[2] His works are better than those of Farmer. His melodic gift was recognised by his contemporaries, and much of his work was included in the collections of the time.[3] The already mentioned ' Captain ' Henry Cooke (1616–72) was a well-known figure in the musical life of the Commonwealth and of the Restoration, as a composer as well as in his capacity as a teacher (in which he was very successful). His contributions to instrumental music include pieces for two viols in Jenkins' average dance-music style, and also for trio combinations.[4] The name of Sylvanus (Silas) Taylor occurs in MSS. and collections of the time. He is essentially an amateur and is represented by single airs and suites.[5] William Ellis, friend of Anthony à Wood and organiser of weekly concert meetings in Oxford from the time of the Commonwealth onwards[6] appears also as composer of suites a 1–4.[7]

A substantial amount of light chamber music had been composed during the years of the Commonwealth, and the publication of such music continued unabated after the Restoration. Most of these were in the easy-going style of Jenkins' and Simpson's melodious suites, though they were not always as well invented and worked out. The influence of the popular tunes of the day is easily recognisable in many pieces. At the same time this music revealed the increasing influence of such Italian and French

---

[1] Further compositions for 1–5 parts in Add. 17853, 24889, 29283–5, 31429 and 31466.

[2] See Add. 15118, 18940–4, Harleian, 3187–8 ; Christ Church 361–2, 1125, 1183 ; Bodleian, c. 54–8, e. 410–4. A suite with trumpets includes 7 part books.

[3] *Division Violin* (1685), *Musick's Recreation on the Viol* (1652), *New Ayres & Dialogues* (1678), etc.

[4] Suites in Bodleian, Oxford, D. 220, E. 405–9 and 110–4.

[5] Bodleian, Oxford, E. 429 a–e.

[6] See above, p. 205.

[7] Christ Church MSS. 1022 and 1236. Some notes on S. Taylor in Westrup's *Domestic Music under the Stuarts*, Mus. Ass. Proc. 1941–2, p. 43 f.

composers as Corelli, Vitali, Draghi, Grabu, Lully and Matteis (who all stayed in England at the time), without, however, being progressive in a deeper sense.

Invigorated by the work of the great composers of the time, popular instrumental music of the Restoration in general was a spate of happy, cheerful compositions. Even though it was not very profound art, it profited from the active participation of the leading masters, just as much as in turn these composers derived from the response of the popular masses a degree of inspiration which the Court and its bloodless, sottish nobility was never able to give.

Not only the concert halls and playhouses but also many homes of upper and lower-middle-class citizens were the centres of such light instrumental music. Most of this music is for one or two violins, with or without basso continuo. At the end of the period the editor of *Apollo's Banquet* (1690) goes so far as to say (preface) :

The Treble-Violin is at present the only instrument in fashion, and the delight of most Young Practitioners in musick for its chearful and sprightly sound.

It is not possible to deal in detail with all the composers of light chamber music who thrived between 1660 and 1688. Only a few names and titles of works can be given for the benefit of students who may wish to pursue this line of research.

Among the more important collections of such music not so far mentioned (much was edited by the house of Playford), were *Courtly Masquing Ayres* (1662), which contain suites by many noted composers ; *Choice Ayres and Dialogues* (1676–85) ; *New Ayres and Dialogues* (1678), which contain mainly violin solos and duos ; *Ayres and Dialogues* (1669 and 1685), which give Lawes' "Royal Consort" and other pieces for trio ; *Aires and Symphonys for ye Bass Viol* (1682)[1] ; *The Pleasant Companion* (1682), an instruction book for the flageolet by Thomas Greeting, with many tunes by Banister, Locke, Humphreys, Robert Smith and others ; also the *Genteel Companion* and the *Delightful Companion*, both instruction books for recorder by Humphrey Salter and Carr, with a large number of tunes ; the slightly later *Sprightly Companion* (1695) for the oboe, with pieces a 1–4 instruments[2] ;

[1] All works in the British Museum, except the last one which is in Durham Cathedral Library.
[2] Available only in Brit. Mus. K. 4. b. 22, 3 (not in catalogue).

Youth's Delight on the Flageolet and *A Vade Mecum for Recorder* (about the same time). Further there are publications of works by individual composers, such as James Sherard, 12 *Sonatas for 2 Violins and Bass* (1680),[1] published by Roger in Amsterdam ; and John Banister jun.'s *The compleat Tutor to the Violin, with the newest tunes now in use* (1688). In addition there are countless MS. dances, suites, tunes and other pieces by John Birchenshaw (d. about 1681),[2] John Dowdon,[3] Richard Girdler,[4] George Hudson, the violinist (d. 1678),[5] Robert Smith (d. 1675),[6] Thomas Tollett (d. after 1696),[7] and many others, including old Anthony à Wood himself.[8]

* * * * *

The names of Christopher Gibbons, Locke, Blow and Purcell, the ' progressives ' among Restoration ,composers, occur again and again in the huge repertoire of general-purpose dances, fantasias and divisions. The importance of these few modernists lies, nevertheless, not in the number of pieces which they added to this corpus, however large their share of instrumental airs may have been, but in the fact that they developed some elements of style which were revolutionary in English music.

Christopher Gibbons (1615–76), son of the great Orlando, is the oldest composer of the group and decidedly one of the most fascinating musicians of this interesting period. He introduced a new personal and almost ecstatic note into instrumental music. This originality is best seen in his three- and four-part fantasias, most of which are introductions to suites of dances.[9] These are pieces of a grimly passionate nature, abounding in sudden dissonances and queer passages. Some of his scores are alive with ' false relations.' Suspensions are not resolved but just left ' in the air,' however dissonant they may be. Oddest is the behaviour of the melodic line which show none of the traditional decorum

[1] Copy in Oxford, Bodleian and Amsterdam, University Library.
[2] 12 tunes for violin & bass (Christ Church, Oxford, 1016–7), suites a 3 (Bodleian E. 410–4).
[3] Many pieces a 1–3 (Christ Church, 90–1, 361–2).
[4] 6 pieces a 2 violins & bass (about 1685) (Add. 29283–5).
[5] Suites a 3 (Christ Church, 1006–9).
[6] Many Brawls and other dances as well as chaconnes a 3–4 & basso continuo (Christ Church 90–1, 361–2, 1003, 1025–7).
[7] Tunes for strings a 3 (Add. 39565–7) and a 4 (Christ Church 1183).
[8] 3 pieces for 2 trebles and bass (Add. 31429 and possibly 29283–85).
[9] Chief MSS. : Bodleian, Oxford, C. 102, D. 231 a–g, Christ Church MSS. 8 and 21 ; Brit. Mus. 30487 and 31431.

of the earlier English fantasias. The bass in particular jumps up and down in ninths, twelfths and other unusual intervals.

The reader is referred to Christopher Gibbons' fantasia a 3 (Appendix No. VIII of this book).[1]

Even Lawes' music did not go to such lengths of eccentricity as this angular effort. This is radically expressionistic emotionalism, or as North calls Christopher Gibbons's music " bold solid and strong but Desultory & not without a little of ye Barbaresms."[2]

The life-work of the great ' futurist ' Matthew Locke (1630–77) recalls Christopher's nervous, unstable and often violent art, combined, however, with greater emotional depth.

Locke was one of the few great composers of the Republican period who were very active in the operatic field as well as in that of instrumental music. By 1660 he had established himself as one of the leading musicians of the time. He was made ' composer in ordinary ' to the king, the first to hold this post under the restored monarchy.

Locke's earlier works show clearly enough the generally progressive tendency of the master. Among them are the three- and four-part fantasias, some of which have found their way to the modern printing press.[3] They include also such original and enjoyable musical pictures as this two-part ayr of 1654 :

Example 78 : from fantasia-ayr a 2[4] by Matthew Locke.

[1] Add. 30487.
[2] *Musicall Gramarian*, p. 27.
[3] Ed. by Peter Warlock & André Mangeot.
[4] Add. 17801.

He wrote numerous suites, such as the famous *Little Consort of three parts*, composed " at the request of Mr. William Wake for his schollars in 1651 "[1] and printed by Playford in 1656 ; the *Broken Consort* of six suites for three instruments, all consisting of fancy, corant, aire (or almand or echo) and saraband[2] ; the *Fflat Consort for my Cousin Kimble* of 1656[3] (obviously so called because most of the pieces are in D-minor, C-minor, E-flat-major, etc., which have many ' flats ') ; and many more suites and single movements of all kinds.[4] Locke, following Hingeston and Coleman, wrote movements for " His Majestie's Sagbutts and Cornets " which were actually performed at King Charles II's Coronation during his procession through the town. They are dated April 22, 1661.[5]

In most of these works Locke is an experimentalist and innovator. True, some of his music is sophisticated, and several of his combinations are really far-fetched, as has been pointed out by earlier historians.[6] But on the other hand Locke could invent striking popular melodies such as this [7]:

[1] Add. 17801.

[2] Ibid.

[3] Ibid. and Add. 31426.

[4] Most of these works are in Add. 17801, others in Add. 10445, 31426, 31430–1 and Bodleian, Oxford, D. 233–6.

[5] Add. 17801.

[6] W. Nagel, p. 227, and others.

[7] From *Fancies and ayres of 2 Parts, Basse and Treble* (20 lessons), Add. 31431.

Example 79 : Hornpype by Matthew Locke.

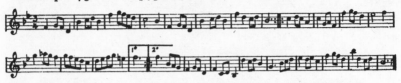

which can only be called the work of a genuine musician.

Locke's music is in several respects the counterpart of Lawes'. It is still essentially polyphonic, but polyphonic in a style which so far we have only found in Lawes' works, where we first met a curious transmutation of polyphony. We noticed a certain contradiction between Lawes' traditional polyphonic language and his readiness to accept certain elements of foreign modernism, while at the same time developing a very personal expression within the polyphonic idiom. Locke goes far beyond either William Lawes or Christopher Gibbons, as far as extravagant polyphony is concerned. The extravagance of his melodic line is sometimes extraordinary. The polyphonic combination of several of these lines often results in open friction. Typical of his procedure is his modification of the technique of imitation on which the whole of the polyphony of the previous period was based. He loosens the strict rules of literal imitation by imitating only the direction of a motif, not its intervals :

Example 80 : from fantasia a 4 by Matthew Locke.[1]

(*a*) Initial subject

(*b*) Imitation (direction kept but intervals reduced) ; bar 13

(*c*) Imitation (intervals augmented) ; bar 16

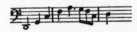

Moreover, into the polyphonic system, especially of the fantasia, he eagerly introduces every modern element which he can get hold of from anywhere in Europe, and everything is

[1] Fantasia a 4, Add. 31435 (ed. P. Warlock).

elaborated with such passionate personal conviction that in the
end the polyphony of the old fantasia changes from top to bottom.
There is often a great eloquence in Locke's polyphonic melodies,
such as is only found elsewhere in contemporary Italian sonatas :
Example 81a : from fantasia a 4 by Locke.[1]

and similarly :
Example 81b : from fantasia a 3 by Locke.[2]

Locke's harmonies are surprising, and quick modulations are
familiar in his works.
Example 82 : from fantasia a 3.[3]

Daring though he was before, the ' new era ' after 1660 seems to
have given a new impulse to Locke's modernism, and his most
interesting works were written during the years immediately
preceding his death, though not exclusively for the Court. By
far the greatest of his later works, and one of the most extraordinary documents of old music of all countries, is Locke's
incidental music to Shadwell's *Tempest* of 1672, written for two
violins, alto and bass viol, either for single instrumental voices, as

[1] Same piece, second section.
[2] Fantasia a 3 ; *ibid.*
[3] Add. 17801.

for chamber performance, or for massed strings as for orchestral representation.

I owe my acquaintance with these eleven instrumental master-pieces to Professor Dent who revived the work in a public performance in Cambridge in 1933. Nobody will fail to recognise the dramatic strength and originality of every one of these musical microcosms. The portentous gravity of the Introduction (strongly influenced by the new French Ouverture) ; the excited dialogue of first violin and tutti in the Galliard, the resolute directness of the Gavot; the strange, tender beauty of the Saraband and its otherworldly dissonances ; the rhythmical finesse of the Lilk (lilt), are obvious even to those who are not used to listening to old music. The ' Curtain Tune ' is the culmination of the whole work. It depicts the storm, its slow and sinister approach, its violent raging, interrupted by sudden lulls, and its final settling-down to calmness and serenity. A miniature *Pastoral Symphony*.

Example 83 : Matthew Locke, Curtain Tune from *The Tempest*[1] :

[1] Copies in Brit. Mus., in Prof. Dent's Library, etc., new edition by G. Whittaker, Oxford University Press, 1935.

MATTHEW LOCKE

CURTAIN TUNE (THE TEMPEST)

MATTHEW LOCKE (2)

MATTHEW LOCKE (3)

This piece not only contains the first orchestral tremolo, expressing the threatening force of the storm, and several musical 'stage directions' such as "soft," "lowd," "violent," but it definitely has the first crescendo, diminuendo and ritardando in the history of music ("lowder by degrees," "soft and slow by degrees").

Much could be said about the remaining items of the suite, the gay Rustick Air, the graceful Minoit (surely one of the first minuets in English music), the Corant, Martial Jigge and concluding canon ; space forbids me to go into details.

It was this kind of music that called forth the bitter and eloquent protests of Thomas Mace.[1] The representatives of the old gentle polyphonic age could not follow Locke's stormy advance.

Locke is an ingenious, courageous and highly intelligent musician. To us he is particularly interesting as his personality reflects very clearly the difficult and complicated social situation of his time, a time of hopes, disappointments, inhibitions, possibilities and new opportunities. He is the real revolutionary in English music. It was in great part owing to his efforts that English music was extricated (at least temporarily) from its conservative position. The great strength of Locke's work lies in the fact that it belongs to two neighbouring ages, and that it benefits from both. The later productions of the early-deceased master belong essentially to the new age which was to culminate so brilliantly in Purcell.

Locke admitted fairly freely elements of foreign style. Especially French features appear in increasing frequency in his music, notwithstanding the fact that Locke himself was a very determined champion of English musical independence, as against Charles' dependence on continental countries.

Both French and Italian elements of style come even more into the foreground in the few works of chamber music of Locke's younger colleague in the Chapel Royal, John Blow (1649–1708).[2] Blow's importance lies, of course, in his songs, anthems and organ compositions. But his instrumental chamber music is also dignified, of ripe scholarship and certainly of considerable musical value.

No harm could come of this 17th-century internationalism in art, as long as it was not carried so far as to produce a national inferiority complex in the minds of the composers and bring

---

[1] See above, pp. 210.

[2] Pieces known to be by Blow are a sonata and a ' ground ' for 2 violins and bass, a symphony for 2 flutes and bass and some shorter items (see Add. 29283–5 and 33236). Blow's ballet music (such as the famous *Venus and Adonis* Masque) is orchestral to a much higher degree than Locke's *Tempest* music.

them into thraldom to the vigorous art of other peoples. After all, the Italian school of the Corellis and Vitalis was of extraordinary eminence at the time.

At the same time the dangers of too faithful an imitation of Italian and French music were fortunately recognised by all thése men. They tried to learn from the great Frenchmen and Italians, but at the same time to preserve the independence of their own art.[1]

The problems which English music had to face towards the end of the 17th century are most clearly seen in the work of Henry Purcell (1658–95), the man who succeeded in overcoming them all.

Purcell, born in the year of Cromwell's death, won a position for English music never equalled before.

His output of chamber music includes 4 fantasias a 3, 9 a 4, 1 a 5, 1 In Nomine a 6, 1 a 7, 1 sonata for violin and bass, 22 trio-sonatas and a number of smaller pieces.[2] Some of the fantasias were written when Purcell was only 22. They were the last chamber-music fantasias ever written—they say farewell to the form in which English chamber music had celebrated its greatest triumphs. The purpose of these pieces is, however, not quite clear ; were they just studies, undertaken to keep Purcell familiar with the old tradition of polyphonic fantasias ; or were they written in order to put new life into an out-dated form ? For though Purcell's forms have much in common with those

[1] As Locke repeatedly came to blows with the advocates of complete surrender to French and Italian music, as Banister sacrificed his position at the Court for the ideal of a national art ; John Blow, too, had to make a stand. Asked by James II shortly before his downfall in 1688 to equal one of the most celebrated Italian anthems, he performed his " I beheld and lo " on the following Sunday. Father Petre who was charged to convey James' approval to Blow yet tried to draw him in with the criticism that the piece was too long. To this Blow replied : " That is the opinion of one fool ! I heed it not," a remark that would have cost him his job had not the Revolution saved him. See J. Pulver, *Biographical Dictionary*, under Blow.

[2] Some of Purcell's instrumental works are easily available, notably twelve trio sonatas (Lyre Bird Press ; ed. G. Whittaker) ; ten trio sonatas (Lyre Bird Press ; G. Whittaker ; the plates of this edition were taken to Paris in 1940 but owing to the German invasion the publication of the prints did not materialise although a future publication now seems likely—there is also an old edition of these ten sonatas which includes the so-called " Golden Sonata " published by Augener, ed. G. Jensen). The sonata for violin and basso continuo was published by Curwen, Langnick and Associated Board ; a handy new edition in an arrangement for viola and piano by W. Forbes and A. Richardson, Ox. Univ. Press, has just been published. The fantasias and sonatas were published by Curwen (P. Warlock and A. Mangeot).

of his great predecessors, the language of these pieces is very new indeed.

If we are really to understand these works we shall have to consider Purcell's position in English music. It is not unlike that of Mozart in German music. Indeed these two personalities have so much in common that we cannot help remarking the similarity of their cultural role. Revolutionary and individualist ideals, inhibited by the influence of a social reaction, yet proclaimed with the greater insistence and intensity, inspired both composers. Mozart's surroundings are known to have been dark and narrow. Purcell similarly grew up in an atmosphere of Court brutality, tyranny and intrigue that could not but repel every decent human being, and most of all a great artist. Ideas of reform, professed by the more radical supporters of the ' glorious revolution,' must have filtered through to the musician at the Court, just as the equalitarian theories of Rousseau, Voltaire and Diderot were later to work in the prisoner of the See of Salzburg. These ideas incited Mozart to side with the progressive and democratic freemasons' movement, to rebel against his tyrannous employer and to expose the whole rottenness and corruption of the nobility, a desire which is so strikingly expressed in *Figaro*. Purcell, too, must have been familiar with ideas which were at least strongly critical of the ruling society and the governing authorities. In 1681 the play *The Sicilian Usurper* (an adaptation by Nahum Tate of *Richard II*, with music by Henry Purcell) was banned after the first performance on political grounds.[1] So Purcell took the risk of setting to music texts of a bitingly satirical character.[2] Yet quite apart from such occasional direct documentation of politically progressive tendencies (Purcell was, of course, not primarily a ' political ' composer), ease and freedom of living, thinking and inventing, coupled with profound personal passion, and a struggle for free, individual expression are common to both masters.

[1] See Vol. XX of Purcell's *Collected Works*, Introduction by Dr. Alan Gray.
[2] The text of a song contained in *The Marriage Hater Matched* (Comedy by Durfey ; Purcell edition, Vol. XX) ends with these words :
  Be moral in thought,
  To be merry's no fault,
  Though an Elder the contrary preaches ;
  For never, my friends,
  Was an age of more vice,
  Than when knaves would seem pious,
  And fools would seem wise.
thus recalling the words of Gibbons' famous *Silver Swan* (see above, p. 159).

This atmosphere of freedom and progress, and the healthy influence of advanced foreign styles in combination with a tremendous technical mastery based on a glorious tradition, produced similar results in both composers : an almost volcanic eruption of production ever intensifying and ever deepening, until each died, exhausted, at an early age.

It has been said that there is a " heroic atmosphere " in Purcell's sonatas.[1] This quality is very similar to the noble and courageous eloquence of Mozart's G-minor symphony or C-minor fantasy.

A new breath of fresh air enlivens every one of Purcell's works. There is a new ' human touch ' in his dramatic compositions. The stiff and official-minded libretti dealing with subjects of classical antiquity (some of which Purcell in his official capacity had to set to music) are outnumbered by stories from the everyday life of the common citizen such as *The Rival Sisters* (Gould), *Rule a Wife and Have a Wife* (Fletcher), *The Old Bachelor* (Congreve), *The Double Dealer* (Congreve), and many others. The heroes of his plays are characterised by their human qualities, their weaknesses, passions, and sufferings. These people really *live* through Purcell's music. Even in *Dido and Æneas* Dido is no more the marble figure from some ancient Greek frieze, but *the* suffering, tragic woman.

Purcell's instrumental works, even his earliest, breathe the new spirit, too. There is nothing left of the awkwardness and violence that sometimes occurred in Locke's works, or of the hyper-contrapuntal intellectualism which we noticed in Thomas Ford's fantasias and in at least some of William Lawes' works. Purcell took over from his predecessors all that was bright, colourful, tuneful, and passionate. There is an intensity of sentiment, a sense of dramatic power, and at the same time a sensual tenderness such as we have never met before. We feel that something new has happened to English music.

The last traces of medieval scholasticism, still apparent in many of the compositions of his immediate forerunners, have vanished. An astonishing freedom of expression prevails. Startling suspensions, insistent accents, chromatic passages with audacious harmonisation abound in Purcell's fantasias and sonatas.

French, German and Italian influences are too obvious to be

[1] A. Einstein, *Greatness in Music*, trans. Cesar Saerchinger, New York, 1941.

explained away by those who would like to proclaim Henry Purcell as the ' exclusively English ' composer. Although Purcell is in many respects the natural heir of Jenkins, Locke and Blow ; although there is much in Purcell's melodies and harmonies (especially their brightness and popular qualities) that is unthinkable without the whole history of both English folk music and art music; he must be called an international as well as a national artist. Purcell himself was quite open about his fondness for foreign styles. He called his son John Baptista (after Lully), and says in the foreword of his Sonatas a 3 of 1683 that they " imitated the Italian way."

The ardour of Purcell's emotions is most convincingly evident, in spite of the archaic *fantasia* form, in his fantasia for 5 viols " upon one note."[1]   If we listen to the change from C-major to a plaintive F-minor, and the sudden and dramatic trumpet-like entry of a new C-major, we feel that a new age is approaching, the age of the Vienna classics.

There are good studies of Purcell. I shall not repeat what has already been pointed out by his biographers,[2] and I shall not expatiate on all the exciting features of the other pieces, the harmonic ventures of the four-part fantasias, the ingenuity of the three-part pieces, the heroic calmness of the six- and seven-part In Nomines, the radiance of the trio-sonatas. I must leave it to individual study to delve into these masterpieces.

Purcell has had at least as much influence on the development of the mind and character of the British people as had many a general, statesman, or philosopher. He belongs to the people. Much of the liveliness in Purcell's rhythms can be traced to the " English Dancing Master," that great collection of popular tunes and dances which is a source of inspiration even to composers to-day. He used melodies of a type known and understood by common men. In his passionate harmonies, which were so new in his time, he expressed their hopes, struggles and desires. Thus in his works he gave back to the people an even greater wealth and beauty than he had drawn from them. Therefore the public to-day 'should know of his work, not only that part which is generally performed.

[1] The note C is kept in the third viol part throughout the piece. It is reprinted in full in the Appendix (No. IX).

[2] J. A. Westrup in his comprehensive study deals particularly with the master's instrumental works.

Our love and admiration for Purcell will not lose but gain, his greatness will increase if we view his work in the context of the social forces surrounding and inspiring him. Life, wonderful, stimulating, radiant life prevails in the creations of this great artist. Like Antæus who was strong so long as his feet touched earth, Purcell was great, because throughout his life he was always able to gather fresh strength from the life of the people.

*   *   *   *   *

The question of the position of the composer in society, suggested by our discussion of Henry Purcell, has been raised more than once in these pages, where we have already indicated disagreement with the theory that the individual genius alone, by virtue of his own personal endowments, " makes," advances or moulds the history of art.

The directions in which an artist develops his function, style and talent is largely conditioned by the social factors of his time, its fashions and conventions (with which the artist may or may not feel himself in harmony) the ascendancy of one set of ideals, the suppression of another, as this or that social group predominates, all play their part in influencing his development. The general state of a society is thus reflected in the art it produces.

However, the example of Purcell shows once again clearly that a creative artist is no mere photographer of conditions, but a living human being in his own right, reacting to *all* important tendencies of his time ; a great work of art often contains elements which are mere undercurrents in contemporary society. The problems which the great artist sets out to solve will be recognised by his fellow-men as their own, and they will be individually enriched by his profounder insight. The composer, in particular, can make the people think and feel with a depth and illumination hitherto unknown to them. Listening to great music, such as a Purcell Sonata or Aria, they perceive " what oft was felt, but n'er so well express'd." 250 years ago man's emotional and intellectual experience was enormously widened, his individual initiative and joy of living powerfully stimulated by such a great artist as Henry Purcell.

The vital creative role which the composer fulfils for the people places on him a heavy responsibility. The more truthfully he faces the realities of life—in all its aspects—the more will be the enduring inspiration he gives to his fellow-men, turning many of them towards the *progressive* undercurrents which the dominant interests of the day may studiously ignore or positively suppress. There is in every classical work of art an element of protest, more, there is in each great artist something of a revolutionary. The relationship between the artist and his society is a mutual one ; he is neither a passive tool nor yet a dictator but a man of his time, open to its influences, a vehicle through which they flow, expressing in an art form the impression his social consciousness has received ; the quality of his awareness will be the measure of his greatness through which his creative power may influence and mould society afresh.

To represent all composers as consciously " political " artists, and their best work as what is often called " propaganda " art would be a gross mistake, equivalent to ignoring the fact that each of the arts has its own distinct medium of imaginative expression.

During the lifetime of many a composer there are occasions when he makes use of his art for an immediately political purpose (although such occasions have been comparatively rare in the career of most recent composers). Mozart the composer of the freemason cantatas is a political composer, but the Mozart of the C-major symphony is not. Chopin's Polish national dances, the mazurkas and polanaises, were written to inspire Polish independence ; but not so his piano preludes. Tallis's harmonisations of the plain-song responses of the Anglican service were composed with an ecclesiastico-political aim ; his string and keyboard music was not. Byrd kept himself aloof from the political and religious changes of his time but his music did much to free the mentality of his age from stiffness and medieval prejudice and helped to humanise those who heard it, to thaw, with its warmth of feeling, their emotional frigidity. Social influences often act in an indirect, roundabout, delayed and even contradictory way, but no great work of art has ever been conceived by the complete negation of social forces. To try to explain the artist's work in isolation from the social life around him would be like first strangling a man in order to demonstrate on his dead body the working of the breathing organism.

CHAPTER VIII

AT the end of the 17th century English chamber music collapsed. It is true that for some years a fair average level of achievement was maintained. Several musicians worked on into the new century : Henry Purcell's brother Daniel (1663–1717), John Eccles (1650–1733), John Banister junr. (d. 1735), Raphael Courtevil (d. after 1700), Robert King (d. after 1711), Richard Goodson (1655–1728), Benjamin Hely (d. after 1700), James Paisible (d. after 1700) and others. But they sacrificed the English idiom, and their art became subservient to Corelli, Vitali and the Scarlattis, Lullys and L'Oeillets, the Fingers, Kellers, Fuxes and Keisers. To an even greater extent this is true of the music of the 18th century. I say this with all the respect due to such composers as Arne, and the able and well-meaning Croft, Boyce and Wesley.

What were the causes of this sudden eclipse ?

It was brought about by a change in the ' cultural climate ' of England. The Revolution of 1689 was the final triumph of those elements in English society whose struggle, during 150 years of history, had been accompanied in the sphere of art by activities fitting to times of struggle and forward drive. Success, however, brought an end to the struggle, and subsequently there came a profound change in the attitude of the successful class.

Instrumental chamber music was the music of the rising merchants and the progressive sections of the aristocracy as they were fighting their way through progress and set-backs, to final victory. The new forces in the days of Elizabeth were advancing vigorously in the economic and political field, always engaged in a struggle against those at home and abroad who wished to re-establish the old order of life. This condition of conflict filled the leaders, as well as the mass of citizens, with a fighting spirit, with hope, vigour and emotional profundity. In its forward march, this new society again and again encountered obstacles which had to be overcome. The Elizabethan was pre-occupied with problems of the mind and soul—as the Athenian was during the era of Pericles. In such societies and at such times men are not only inclined towards music and poetry, they *need* them.   Hence the profoundly personal spirit in Elizabethan music, poetry and drama ; and hence the stupendous progress, especially of chamber music.

The patronage of bourgeois aristocracy under these conditions had led to a state where chamber music was the art of the time. It had become a favourite way of expressing personal emotion. The musical artist had expressed for society what everybody was feeling : from the political to the personal, from black despair to rosiest hope, from all-embracing metaphysical visions and problems to the intimate human considerations of friendship and love.

Through the victory of the merchant-adventurer or producer-classes a new mental attitude gained ascendancy, the attitude of the busy businessman.   The new leaders in their temporary security turned towards external, commercial conquest.   Their philosophy was concerned with work and religion.   They set themselves to instil the spirit of Puritan zeal and sobriety into all parts of society.   The Republican leaders were unable—though perhaps willing—to give musical life new depth and a new impetus.   By nature they faced the other way.

After 1660, when the Puritan straight-jacket was removed, one last wave of creative musical activity arose.   Not that the monarchy then restored was a particularly inspiring factor in itself ; but certain circumstances combined to give some English composers another great chance to develop—in an activity which was chiefly centred round the Court.

This was the time when Locke, Blow, Humphries and Jeremiah Clark chiefly created, and this was alsot he time when many an old music lover seemed to be able to breathe again.   It was in 1668 that Samuel Pepys wrote : (I went) " with my wife and Deb. to the King's House, to see ' The Virgin Martyr.'

. . . that which did please me beyond anything in the whole world was the wind-musique when the angel comes down, which is so sweet that it ravished me, and indeed, in a word, did wrap up my soul so that it made me really sick, just as I have formerly been when in love with my wife ; that neither then, nor all the evening going home, and at home, I was able to think of anything but remained all night transported, so as I could not believe that ever any musicke hath that real command over the soul of a man as this did upon me.[1]

---

[1] *Diary*, 27.ii.1668.   The play is by Massinger.

For Pepys considered that " music is all the pleasure that I live for in the world, and the greatest I can ever expect in the best of my life."[1]

But a new change was on the way.

Charles II's court was soon as isolated as that of his predecessor. The final downfall of the backward and narrow old aristocracy which had been temporarily swept to the surface by the Restoration was only a question of time. The ' Glorious Revolution ' followed ; and forthwith ensued the final establishment of a bourgeois nobility whose ancestors in the middle ages had been rebels ; and in its final hour of triumph this class itself became the main bulwark of conservatism.

The bourgeois nobility which was then finally enthroned controlled the destiny of Britain for many decades, and for many decades it tended to impress its cultural ideals on the people of this country. In the 18th century these ideals were, above all, those of ' practical ' culture, outward looking, taking account of purposes and effects rather than of origin and cause. The triumphant practical achievements of these decades of English history bear witness to the qualities of the men who built up an empire, and with it a colossal agricultural, industrial and commercial machine ; powerful men, calm and confident, thoroughly sure of themselves and their mission, enterprising, highly intelligent and, above all, practical in all things—practical in their philosophy, practical in their sensible outlook on this world and the next, practical especially in their encouragement of applied science, practical in their very humanitarianism, practical even in their liberal patronage of fine arts. For they spent handsomely on those arts which a practical man can understand—upon paintings of their wives and daughters, and later upon landscapes showing the richness of their land, upon architectural magnificence, upon finely wrought furniture and fabrics.

And what of music ?

The attitude of the English gentleman towards music underwent a radical change. We may recall the good old days as they are illustrated in an incident mentioned in Thomas Morley's treatise (1597). Somebody had confessed that he was unable to take part in a homely performance of music, " as is the custom," " and everyone began to wonder," says Morley, " yea some

[1] *Diary*, 12.ii.1667.

whispered to others demanding how he was brought up." The new outlook, so far as participation in musical performances is concerned, is clearly defined 100 years later by John Locke, the philosopher, who wrote in 1693 :

A good hand upon some instruments is by many people mightily valued ; but it wastes so much of a young man's time, to gain but a moderate skill in it, and engages him often in such odd company.[1]

Here is Romain Rolland's description of the sovereign aristocrat at his musical best—

the distinguished English gentleman, statesman and artist, thoroughly sane and well-balanced, with the quiet activity, the serenity of mind, the good humour and the rather child-like optimism which one often meets with north of the Channel, pleasantly gifted as a musician, but superficial and seeking in music a wholesome pleasure, as Milton advised, rather than a passion beyond his control.[2]

The music he favoured was the music proper to an age of realism and empiricism : first of all patriotic songs which were produced in great abundance all through the 18th and 19th centuries ; then for diversion, pleasant airs for the voice, made and sung as pastorals and glees in the 18th, as drawing-room songs and ballads in the 19th century ; and finally, if instrumental music must ' invade ' the home, piano solos by the women folk.

As for opera, he would patronise it, to be sure, as a foreign affair, which indeed, alas, it was, and his patronage and riches in the end brought into being one of the most remarkable musical phenomena of our time—the Covent Garden Opera Season, a great national festival of foreign music. This institution was born of the spirit to which Dr. Burney, the father of musicology, confessed when talking about Italian Opera in England :

Music is a Manufacture in Italy, that feeds and enriches a large portion of the people ; and it is no more disgraceful to a mercantile country to import it, than wine, tea, or any other production of remote parts of the world. . . .

Music, once a " ladder to the intelligence of higher things "[3] became, in the words of Dr. Charles Burney, in the 18th century

---

[1] Quoted by P. A. Scholes, *Oxford Companion*, p. 282.
[2] *A Musical Tour through the Land of the Past*, trans. B. Miall, 1922, p. 43.
[3] Morley.

" an innocent luxury, unnecessary, indeed, to our existence, but a great improvement and gratification of the sense of hearing."[1]

As such, it may properly be bought and paid for, and bought with money rather than with application and study. The public concert, at which music was purveyed as a commodity, developed enormously in the 18th century.

Passive listening to music (at least as far as instrumental music was concerned) became the part that the public had to play in English musical life, and the creative as well as the performing part was left to visitors from other countries.

And for listening to music, this country, rich and yearly growing richer, could pay well. There was a spirit of cosmopolitan toleration and broadmindedness among the comfortable upper-class musical amateurs in the 18th century. Foreign musicians were engaged by the hundred, and these continental masters were attracted by English concert life as by nothing else. Among them were some of the greatest of all, from Corelli via Handel, and the sons of Bach to Haydn, Mozart, Mendelssohn. England could afford to invite them ; she enabled many a great musician from the Continent to live and thrive. Though this patronage is a contribution of England to European musical life which should not be overlooked, the creative supremacy of continental music was absolute for many, many years, again particularly in the field of instrumental chamber music. Throughout the 18th century English chamber music, so far as it existed, was quite unable to withstand the competition of more vital foreign influences.

The healthy influx of foreign styles into English music became an invasion. Symbolic of the fate of English music was the enormous vogue of Handel, by whose internationalism English music and all that was great in it was completely absorbed— English, German, French and Italian elements are about equally matched in his works.

So far as education was concerned, the subject of music " largely dropped out of the British curriculum " ; amateur cultivation, which is of such vital importance as an ' echo ' to professional art, tended to be " left to the female portion of the ' comfortable classes,' and even so to be regarded as a mere ' accomplishment.' "[2]

[1] A General History of Music, 1776, Vol. I, Preface, p. XIII.
[2] P. A. Scholes, Oxford Companion, p. 282.

It is true that the finest folk songs were still sung in the seclusion of the 18th-century countryside. All the emotional depth and liveliness of British music is reflected in many immortal folk melodies. Altogether, singing—and in particular folk-song—continued with surprising vigour, in view of the collapse of the more elaborate types of music.

But all this music of the villages was then chiefly of local significance; it became less and less important for national culture as a whole[1] and after 1800 the centre of gravity, the main force of production, the main source of the country's prosperity, finally shifted from the land to the towns.

It was a new cultural climate in which, as Matthew Arnold said in speaking of the poet Gray, " there was a spiritual east wind blowing." The result was that the creation of speculative, imaginative, inward sorts of music ceased for a long time, and this climate was far more severe upon music than upon any other art. In the case of chamber music especially, it killed education and thus destroyed the means whereby musical appreciation and ability might have been preserved against the time when the climate should change.

For change the climate did, in the course of this century and the next, when a great impulse of humanitarianism and liberal thought energised the culture of this country. In fact, throughout the 18th century something like a spiritual revolt was going on, a revolt against the ' official ' trend in cultural life. From the time of Pope and Hogarth this revolt was a wonderful stimulus to creative thought and impulse in literature, painting and architecture, and in poetry it culminated in the romantic revival about the turn of the century. Throughout this time great artists, carried forward by successive waves of popular movements, expressed in all the arts except in music, the people's desire for life, independence and freedom, and their irrepressible creative genius.

But in the elaborate art of instrumental music, that art in which the greatest triumphs were being celebrated on the Continent, alas, there was no Byron, no Wordsworth, no Shelley; there was no new Purcell, no English Beethoven. Instrumental music could not rise above the reserved romanticism of a John Field.

[1] See A. L. Lloyd, *The Singing Englishman*, Keynote Series Book No. 4, London, 944, pp. 41 ff.

The time came, but the art was forgotten. The tradition had too long been broken.

It does not take very long for a break in continuity to take effect upon an art like chamber music, as indeed upon any music that makes demands on the technical accomplishment of listeners and participants. In all the more highly evolved instrumental music, and thus particularly in chamber music, these demands are high.

We have already seen how near the Commonwealth hiatus came to taking the life out of instrumental music, and how the renaissance of the Restoration was made possible only by the survival from earlier days of a small number of masters who worked round the Court. Moreover the general standard of musical education was quickly debased. We saw for instance that the Chapel Royal was unable to find boys who could read music, and all this after a break of some 20 years ; half a generation. What chance had instrumental music of a revival, however improved the prospects, after a century had elapsed ?

It was in a similar way that about 1600 the victory of Calvinism killed the chamber music of Holland (a beautiful, elaborate art, but vocal, not as in England, instrumental) by closing the church schools which had provided its educational background. The breach was fatal, and the colourful instrumental music imported from Germany into Holland half a century later could not bring back the musical supremacy of that country, even though there were one or two individually great composers such as Carolus Hacquart.

In music a breach of tradition is a particularly serious matter because the *active* participation of a musically educated public is absolutely indispensable to a flourishing and intensive musical life. The great tradition of English chamber music was interrupted by the change in the ' cultural climate ' about the middle of the 17th century. And neither Thomas Mace's raging nor John Hingeston's warnings were able to restore the lost paradise of English music.

It was this change of climate which produced that inferiority feeling in English composers which strikes the continental observer as so very odd in view of the wealth of talent and adventurous spirit manifested in the musical history of this country. Even now, in the 20th century, this feeling persists. It has been one of the main purposes of this book to attack this inferiority feeling by displaying the full glory of one of this country's chief musical achievements of the past.

It is true that interest in old music has sometimes coincided with failure of contemporary creative power. But there is no danger, I feel, of any such failure in England to-day. On the contrary.

Throughout the past hundred years the material foundations were laid for a great and popular musical revival—largely in the choral societies of the industrial areas whose growth has recently been so successfully demonstrated.[1]   Here music—unnoticed yet by the outside world—was soaring high.

And in the last fifty years, especially during the past few years, the creative power of English music has shown itself with new and astonishing force.   Indeed England has once more become one of the world's leading countries in every kind of music.   Is this not because the struggle for social and spiritual progress has entered a new period, a new phase of activity?

A new interest in music has appeared ;   new audiences have arisen ;   orchestras are growing ;   many new composers vie with one another in friendly competition to express the revolutionary changes that are taking place around them and in their minds and souls.

We can look hopefully to the future of English music.

[1] R. Nettel, *Music of the Five Towns*, London, 1944.

APPENDIX

ALFONSO FERRABOSCO JUN.
FANTASIA A 4

FERRABOSCO (2)

FERRABOSCO (3)

FERRABOSCO (4)

FERRABOSCO (5)

COPERARIO
FANTASIA FOR 4 VIOLS

COPERARIO (2)

COPERARIO (3)

W. LAWES
FANTASIA FOR 6 STRINGS

W. LAWES (2)

W. LAWES (3)

W. LAWES (6)

W. LAWES (5)
(30)

W. LAWES (6)

W. LAWES
FANTAZYA [(Not too fast)
Violin I

LAWES (2)
(10)

LAWES (6)

LAWES FANTAZYA (7)

MICHAEL EAST
FANCY FOR 4 PTS. FROM "THE SEVENTH SET OF BOOKS,"
　(Moderate speed)　　　　"NAME RIGHT YOUR NOTES"

EAST (2)   (15)

JOHN JENKINS
FANTASIA A 4

Very moderate speed. (Style of bowing non-legato : between staccato and portamento)

JENKINS (2)

JENKINS (3)

JENKINS (4)

JENKINS (5)

JENKINS (6)

JENKINS (7)

JENKINS (8)

JOHN JENKINS

FANTASIA A 3

JENKINS (2)

JENKINS (3)

JENKINS (4)

(60) (Andante)

(poco rit.)

(poco rit.)

JENKINS (5)

JENKINS (6)

(100)

(poco rit.)

(poco rit.)

CHRISTOPHER GIBBONS
FANTASIA—INTRODUCTION A 3

GIBBONS (2)

GIBBONS (3)

Henry Purcell
Fantasia of 5 parts ("Fantasia upon one note")

(2)

(4)

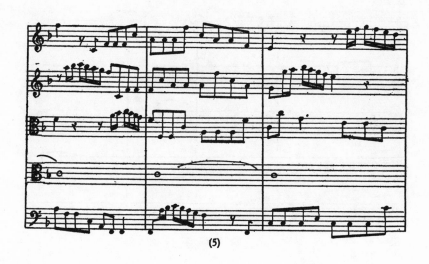

(40)

(6)

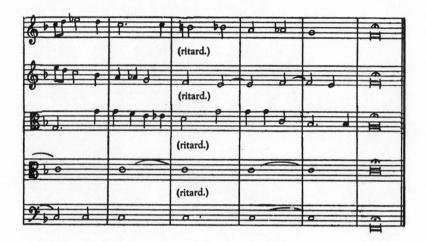

(ritard.)

(ritard.)

(ritard.)

(ritard.)

INDEX

INDEX

ADAM OF ST. VICTOR, 40
Adler, Guido, 42 (4)
Adson, John, 136f., 171, 194
Aeolic harp, 17
Air (ayr), 114 (2), 125 (1), 130, 136ff.,
    168 (4), 177, 180, 183, 186 (1),
    193ff., 210, 217, 225, 229, 232f., 250
Alanus Anglicus, 25
Alcock (16th century composer), 90
Alcuin (Albinus Flaccus), 17
Aldhelm, Bishop of Sherborne, 17, 24
Alfred, King, 16
Allelujah (in Mass), 40
Allemande (almand), 74, 99, 110, 137,
    139, 168 (4), 181, 196 (2), 217
Allison, Richard, 90, 119, 125 (1), 136
Ammianus Marcellinus, 15 (2)
Anderton, O., 99 (1), 133
Andrews, Hilda, 210 (2)
Anglican Reform, 78 (f), 84, 193, 246
Anonymus 4 (in Coussemaker's
    " Scriptores "), 21 (5), 37f., 43 (1)
Anselm of Canterbury, 12
Antaeus, 245
Anthem, 240
Antiphon, 42
Archiviola, see Violin, forerunners of
Archlute (archilute), see Theorbo
Aria (see also Air), 159, 216 (3), 222f.,
    245
Arkwright, G. E. P., 151 (1)
Arne, Thomas Augustine, 247
Arnold, Matthew, 252
Ars nova, 20 (3)
Aston, Hugh, 67, 106
Athens, 247
Atteignant, Pierre, 72
Aulos (ancient Greek flute), 14
Austria, Archduke of, 221 (1)

BACH, Johann Sebastian, 8, 94 (7),
    157, 186, 251
Bacon, Francis, 89, 132, 189f.
Bagpipe (cornamuse, sambuca, sym-
    phony, tympanum), 35ff., 47, 53,
    127
Baldulph, 17 (1)
Baldwyn, John, 90, 93, 109, 112f., 142
Ball, John, 33 (3)
Ballad, 29, 33, 35, 49, 59f., 250
Ballet, 117 (1), 214, 216 (3), 217,
    240 (2)
Baltzar, Thomas, 209, 211 (3), 228
Banastir, Gilbert, 72

Banister, John, sen., 205, 208, 215,
    228ff.
—— —— jun., 231, 241 (1), 246
Bards, 15
Barnard, John, 176
Baroque, 152, 213 (5)
Bartholomeus of Glanville, 30
—— of Padua, 54
Baskervill, Ch. Read, 34 (2)
Bass viol, see Viol
Bass violin, see Violin and Violoncello
Bassano, H., 150
Basse dance, 71, 72 (2)
Basso continuo, see Thorough bass
Bassoon, 128, 134
Bateson, Thomas, 142
Baudri of Bourgeuil, 20
Becket (17th century violinist), 228
Beethoven, L. van, 159, 252
Belcantists, 2
Bells and bell ringing, 29, 36, 44, 46,
    53, 89 (1), 220
Benedictus of Abingdon, 21
Bennet, J., 150
Bennett, H. S., 34 (3), 65 (4)
Berdic, 17
Berkeley, Lord (16th century), 65
Besardus, J. B., 136
Besseler, H., 23 (4)
Beverley (Yorks), 49
Bevin, Elvay, 90, 112, 142
Bicinium (see also Duo), 95f.
Birchenshaw, John, 231
Black, J. B., 100 (2), 115 (2), 116 (1)
Blanke, Edward, 105, 109 (2)
Blom, E., 10, 42 (3)
Blow, John, 205f., 215, 231, 240,
    241 (1), 244, 248
Boeheim, Hans (Pfeifferhans), 33 (2)
Bombylium, 36
Bordune (ostinato, pedal), 46, 153,
    244
—— strings, 133
Boretius, 16 (2, 4), 51 (3)
Boyce, William, 247
Brade, William, 138f.
Bramley (16th century composer),
    83 (3)
Bramston (16th century composer), 72
Bransle (brael, brawl ; the dance), 72,
    138, 210, 231 (6)
Breaking bass (see also variations), 181
Brett, A. C. A., 205 (1)
Brewer, Thomas, 196, 205, 219

'21   307

Brewster (16th century composer), 90
Bridge, J. C., 50 (2), 56 (2)
Bristol, 49
Britton, Thomas, 208
Broken consort, see Consort
Browne, Sir Thomas, 103 (1)
Browning (16th century folksong and
    instrumental form), 112f., 156 (1),
    161
Bruckner, Anton, 89
Buck, John, 90
Bukofzer, M., 23 (2), 38 (2), 59 (1),
    91 (1)
Bull, John, 142, 157f.
Bullroarer (prehistoric instrument), 25
Burney, Dr. Charles, 15 (2), 42 (3),
    53 (3), 96 (2), 135 (1), 250f.
Burns, Robert, 25 (4)
Burton, Robert, 192 (1)
Butler, Charles, 89 (2), 130, 132 (4),
    133, 139, 187 (2), 190f., 208, 213
    (5), 228
Byrd, William, 10 (11), 11, 76, 82 (3),
    93, 95, 97, 105, 109, 112, 114 (1),
    118, 121, 140, 153, 156, 167,
    170 (2), 172, 246
Byron, Lord, 252

CADENCE (harmonic and melodic), 44,
    104
Caedmon, 15
Calvinism, 253
Cambridge, 207, 236
Campion, Thomas, 193
Canon, see Round
——— pavana, see Pavan and Round
Cantabile, 86, 134
Cantata, 246
Canterbury Cathedral, 24f.
Cantus firmus, see Tenor
Canzon (canzona), 128f., 154
Canzonet, 104, 110 (2), 130
Carmina burana, 34 (1)
Carols and carollers, 25, 29, 51, 59f.
Carr, W., 69 (3)
Catch, see Round
Caurroy, Eustache du, 213 (5)
Cavendish, Michael, 137 (1)
Cecil, Sir Robert (16th century), 114
Celts, 15
Chaconne (ciaconna), 231 (6)
Chamber music (see also Instrumental
            music)
——— definition of characteristics
        of, 1ff., 128f., 134f., 208f.
——— in modern life, 134
——— and the listener, 8
——— possibility of revival of
        early English, 8, 134
——— early forerunners of, 46ff.,
        70f.

Chamber music festivals and perfor-
    mances of, 9
——— gramophone recordings of
        early English, 9, 228 (5)
——— modern publications of
        early English, 10 (11),
        47 (3), 57 (1), 58 (1),
        60 (1), 71 (3), 110 (4),
        122 (1, 2), 127 (3),
        153 (2, 3), 167 (1),
        170 (2), 177 (1), 241 (2)
Chambers, E. K., 16 (4), 23 (3),
    28 (6), 32 (1)
Chansons, 57, 60
Chappell, W., 17 (1), 26 (4), 60 (1),
    66 (1), 69 (2), 100 (1), 112 (3)
Charles I, King, 173ff., 187ff., 202,
    205, 210 (1)
——— II, King, 200, 204ff., 213ff., 233,
    240
Chaucer, Geoffrey, 22, 25 (5), 35, 69
Chester, 49
Chichester Cathedral, 199 (1)
Child, William, 199, 212
Chimes (see also Bells), 53
Chopin, Frederic, 246
Choral music (in Middle Ages), 13f.,
    67ff., 78, 80ff., 85, 125
Chorus (medieval instrument), see
    Crowd
Chromatic music (musica ficta or
    falsa), 38, 143, 169ff., 223, 243
Chrotta, see Crowd
Church (Catholic) and music, 12ff.,
    30, 78ff., 101, 106, 175f.,
    193
——— and instruments, 12, 14ff.,
        21f., 24-34
Church (High), 78f., 173ff., 187, 193,
    198, 200f., 206
Church music, medieval, character of,
    13f., 43f., 48, 61, 77,
    80ff., 97, 106
——— 17th century, character of,
    128
Churchyard, Thomas, 72, 73 (1)
Cithara (ancient Greek instrument),
    14. See also Cither
Cither (cittern, cytele, cythol), 26, 36,
    37, 47, 53, 128, 130f., 133, 135f.
Clark, Jeremiah, 248
Clarsech, 36
Clarinet, 134
Clarion (medieval wind instrument),
    47, 51
Clavichord (see Pianoforte, fore-
    runners of)
Clavicymbal (see Pianoforte, fore-
    runners of)
Clubs for music-making, 126
Cobb, Daniel, 179

Cobbold (Cobold), William, 90, 150
Cobham, Thomas de (Bishop of Salisbury), 32 (1)
Coleman, Charles, 199, 205, 215, 224ff., 233
Coloratura, 78
Commonwealth, music during, Chapter VI (passim), 213, 220, 224, 229, 232, 253
Concert, public, 207f., 221, 229, 251
Concertante, 164, 181, 221
Concerto, 86, 226
—— ecclesiastico, 165
—— grosso, 165, 224
—— for solo instruments, 166
Congreve, William, 243
Consonances, 38, 43, 47, 59 (1), 187 (2)
Consort (sometimes called symphony), 46, 130–140, 180ff., 210, 217, 228ff., 233
Cook, Richard, 221
Cooke, Captain Henry, 205, 228
Cooper, R., 72
Coperario, Giovanni (John Cooper), 148f., 157, 167, 172, 179, 221
Corelli, Arcangelo, 220, 241, 247, 251
Corke, A., 90
Corkine, William, 138, 140
Cormack (16th century composer), 172 (1)
Cornamuse, see Bagpipe
Cornet (wind instrument) 25f., 36, 53, 127f., 132f., 136, 225f., 233
Cornyshe, William, 72
Cosmo I, Pope, 128
Cosyn, John, 114
Cotton, John, 17, 36 (1), 44, 45 (2)
Coulton, G. G., 16 (1), 21 (6), 27 (2), 28 (3–5), 30 (3), 33 (3)
Counter-Reformation, 78, 98, 128
Country dances, 69, 100
Courante (coranto), 72, 74, 110 (4), 181, 186 (1), 210, 212, 217, 233, 240
Court music (also development of Chapel Royal), 9, 22, 31, 36, 51ff., 57, 62, 66, 68ff., 103, 114, 126ff., 138, 149 (2), 161, 173–187, 193, 197ff., 204ff., 214ff., 223ff., 235, 240, 243ff., 248ff., 253
Courtevil (Corteville), Raphael, 247
Coussemaker, C. E. H. de, 21 (5), 29 (2), 37, 38 (1, 3), 41 (1)
Covent Garden, 250
Coventry, 49, 56
Cranford, William, 114 (1), 168, 172
Cranmer's Reform (see also Anglican Reform), 79
Croft, William, 247
Cromwell, Oliver, 188, 199f., 202, 225, 241

Crowd (crwth, cruit, chrotta, chorus, crowder), 31 (4), 36f., 47
—— players, 53
Crowest, see Duncan
Cummings, W. H., 199 (1, 2)
Curtain Tune, 236
Cutting(s), Thomas, 139
Cymbal (see also Psaltry), 26, 53, 133

Daman, William, 94f.
Damett, Thomas, 31 (3)
Dance music in England (see also the various dance forms), 10 (11), 26, 38, 43 (2), 47ff., 60, 69–74, 98ff., 108, 110ff., 137f., 161, 168 (4), 172, 177 (1), 179 (1), 181ff., 196 (1–5, 7), 197f., 201 (1), 214, 217, 229, 231, 244
—— popular and folk, 69, 99f., 154, 244, 246
Dancing, 26, 28, 30, 51, 97ff., 112, 192
—— in churches, 19, 25, 30
Danza della muerte, 71
Dauney, W., 29 (1)
Davenant, William, 208
Davey, Henry, 20 (1), 73 (3), 77 (1), 82 (3), 91 (1), 96 (2), 109 (5), 110 (1), 113 (2), 139 (5), 190 (5), 200 (1), 216 (3)
Deering, Richard, 168f., 202, 213, 221
Dent, E. J., 23 (2), 175 (1), 236
Dialogues (see also Duos), 229ff.
Dickinson, E., 15 (1), 18 (1), 28 (2)
Diderot, Denis, 242
Diessener (Disineer), Gerhard, 211 (3), 228
Differencias (16th century Spanish form), 113
Diggers, 188
Diomede (16th century composer), 172 (1)
Dissenters, 18 (2)
Dissonances, 38, 43, 47, 84 (2), 128, 185, 187, 231, 234, 236
Dividing bass, 181
Divisions, see Variations
—— on a ground, see Ground
Dixon, Clement, 139
—— John, 139
Dolmetsch, A., 9f.
Dolmetsch family, 9, 228 (5)
Dominant, 43
—— seventh, 185
Domps (dumps), 69ff.
Donington, R., 10
Donne, John, 8
Double bass, see Violone
Double stoppings, 83 (1), 138
Dowdon, John, 231
Dowland, John, 87 (1), 99, 110 (4), 114 (1), 119, 121ff., 130f., 136ff., 169, 213

Draghi, Giovanni Battista, 230
Drum, 14, 36, 127, 139
—— kettle, 127, 208 (2)
Drummers, 31, 127f.
Drummond, W., 118
Ductia (medieval form), 22, 47
Dulcimer, 19, 21, 31, 35f., 47, 53, 133
Duncan and Crowest (Story of the Minstrelsy), 46 (3), 114 (3), 128 (1)
Dunstable, John, 45, 61, 62 (1), 91 (1)
Dunstan, Bishop, 17, 20 (1)
Duo, instrumental (see also Dialogue), 95, 103ff., 108, 221, 229
Dutch music, see Netherlands
Dygon, John, 72
Dynamics, development of, 128, 213
—— indications for, 236ff.

EAST, Michael, 114 (2), 140, 195f., 219, 221
Eccles, John, 247
—— Solomon, 201, 228
Echo, instrumental, 181, 233
Edward I, King, 52
—— II, King, 32, 56
—— IV, King, 56
—— VI, King, 65, 83 (2), 127
Eglestone, John, 90
Eitner, R., 94 (2–3), 216 (3)
Elizabeth, Queen, 74, 96, 98, 100, 101–103, 113–116, 125ff., 134, 173, 176, 247f.
Ellis, William, 205 (4), 229
English Dancing Master (see also Dance music in England), 197f., 244
Ethelred, Abbot of Rivaulx, 26, 28, 46
Evans, W. McClung, 119 (1)
Expressivo, 134

FALSA musica, see Chromatic music
Fanfares, 52
Fanshaw, Mr., 162 (3)
Fantasia (instrumental form), 10 (11), 94–97, 100, 103ff., 130, 137ff., 140–171 (passim), 177, 179 (1), 183ff., 193ff., 206, 213 (5), 217ff., 223ff., 231, 233ff., 241f., 244f.
Farmer, John, 119
—— Thomas, 229
Farnaby, Giles, 161 (1)
Farthing (Fardying), Thomas, 72
Fauxbourdon (falso bordone), 38 (2), 44, 59, 61
Fayrfax, Robert, 72
Fellowes, E. H., 10, 11, 109 (5), 112 (10), 153 (2), 156 (1), 168 (1), 170 (2), 177 (1–2)
Feltham, Owen, 209
Ferrabosco, Alfonso, sen., 85f., 93f., 114 (1)

Ferrabosco, Alfonso, jun., 10 (11), 71 (1), 93, 121, 137ff., 151ff., 155, 157ff., 165, 168, 172, 184, 186 (1), 196, 211, 221
Feudalism, 12, 19, 27, 44, 61, 63ff., 97, 106
Fiddle (Fiedel ; see also forerunners of the violin), 36, 47, 131
Field, John, 252
Finalis, 42
Finger, Godfrey, 211 (3), 247
Fitzwilliam Virginal Book, 70, 103, 161 (1)
Flageolet, 230f.
Fletcher, John, 2, 122, 126, 243
Flood, Valentine, 139
Florence, 78, 167
Floyd (Flude), 72
Flute (see also Recorder), 14, 18, 35f., 128, 130ff., 139
—— players, 31, 127
—— music for, 240
—— traverse, 131, 133
Folia (16th and 17th century instrumental form), 113
Folkdances, see Dances
Folksongs, see Songs
Forbes, Watson, 241 (2)
Ford, Thomas, 138, 176–179, 243
Foreign influences in English music, 23, 24, 36, 54, 72, 113, 154f., 166f., 180, 181, 212ff., 228ff., 234, 236, 240ff., 242, Chapter VIII (passim)
—— musicians in England, 52, 127, 206, 211ff., 228, 230
—— music, influenced by English music, 138f.
Form, development of, 80ff., 97, 105ff., 135, 137, 140ff., 208f., 217f.
Foster, Edmund, 179
Franck, César, 135
Freemasons, 242, 246
French music, 23, 24, 34, 40, 54, 58, 72, 88, 89, 212ff., 229f., 236, 240f., 243ff., 247, 251
—— Revolution, 78, 207, 242
Frescobaldi, Girolamo, 186
Fuellsack, Zacharias, 110 (3), 138
Fugato, 88, 154
Fugue, 84 (2), 142, 152, 156, 158
Fux, J. J., 247
Fyfe, see Pipe

GABRIELI, Giovanni, 129, 155
Gaelic harp, see Harp
Galliard(a) (the dance), 10 (11), 72 (2), 73, 87, 88, 98f., 104, 110, 112 (2), 123, 130, 136ff., 154, 157, 236

Galpin, Canon F. W., 10, 14 (1), 15 (2), 16 (6), 17 (4, 5), 20 (1), 25 (1, 3), 29 (4), 31 (4), 36 (2), 46 (3, 4), 47 (1, 2), 52 (2), 53 (4), 69 (1), 128 (2), 131 (3), 132 (3, 4), 134
Garlandia, John de, 38
Gastoldi, G. G., 130
Gavot, 110, 236
Gerbert, M., 17 (2), 42 (1), 44 (3), 45 (2)
German music, 33 (2), 35, 89, 95, 125, 154, 211, 213ff., 216 (3), 228, 242ff., 247f., 251, 253
Gevaert, A., 83 (4), 84 (1), 92 (1)
Gibbons, Christopher, 199, 205, 215, 221 (1), 231ff., 234
—— Edward, 90, 172
—— Orlando, 2ff., 8, 10 (11), 11, 123 (1), 125 (1), 140, 153–164 (passim), 167ff., 172, 184, 195f., 231, 242 (2)
Gibbs, John, 90, 150
Gifford, Humphrey, 70 (2)
Gigue (jig, the dance), 34, 72, 217, 240
—— (Geige ; medieval instrument), 36
—— players, 53
Giles, Nathaniel, 83 (3), 150
Giraldus Cambrensis, 19, 33 (2), 37, 45, 46
Girdler, Richard, 231
Gittern, 31, 35, 47, 133
Glareanus, 43 (2)
Glee, 250
Glorious Revolution, 242, 247, 249
Goldar (16th century composer), 90
Gombert, Nicolas, 106
Goodson, Richard, 247
Gosson, Stephen, 119
Gould, B., 243
Gower, John, 61
Grabu, Louis, 214, 230
Gray, Dr. Alan, 242
Gray, Thomas, 252
Gregorian chant (plain song), 13, 42, 43, 45, 79, 80–84, 91f., 246
Gregory, 221
Greek music, ancient, 14, 45
Green, Mrs. A., 50 (3), 63 (1)
—— Dr. S., 19 (footnote)
Greeting, Thomas, 230
Griffith ap Cynan, 29 (1)
Grillo, A., 155
Grocheo, Johannes de, 22, 36, 47
Groh, Johannes, 154
Groteste, Bishop, 29
Ground (basso ostinato), 111f., 137f., 228f., 240 (2)
Grove's Dictionary, 10, 133
Guilds in medieval towns, 30, 49, 75

Guilelmus Monachus, 43 (1)
Guitar (see also Gittern), 53, 133
Guy, Michael, 106 (1), 107

Hacquart, Carolus, 253
Hake (16th century composer), 90
Hampton Court, 202
Handel, G. F., 157, 223, 251
Harmony, development of, 42ff., 47, 59, 61, 134, 164 (1), 167–171, 183ff., 221 (1), 235f., 244
Harp, 16, 17, 19, 29, 35, 36, 46, 47, 51, 121, 131ff., 164 (1), 217
—— music for, 37, 186f.
—— players, 31, 52, 53, 83 (2), 127
Harpsichord, 36, 131, 133, 164 (1)
—— music for, 130, 217
Harrison, W., 65
Hartlib, Samuel, 192 (2)
Hatton, Sir Christopher and Lady, 114
Hawkins, 29 (3), 30 (1), 36 (1)
Haydn, Jos, 251
Hayes, G. R., 9, 10, 36 (2), 44, 52, 66, 83 (2), 86 (1), 103 (2), 114 (2), 127 (3), 128 (1), 132 (4), 133, 186 (3)
Hely, Benjamin, 221 (1), 247
Hengrave Hall (Sussex), 128
Henry III, King, 52
—— IV, King, 61
—— VI, King, 31, 52
—— VII, King, 61, 63, 64, 66, 72, 101, 127
—— VIII, King, 10 (11), 63, 66, 68f., 72ff., 90, 97, 101, 127, 131, 134, 161
Hentzner, R., 127 (2)
Herrick, Robert, 191
Heywood (early 16th century), 72
Hildebrand, Christian, 110 (3), 138
Hill, Chr., 63 (1), 173 (1), 204 (1)
Hilton, John, 179, 196, 213
Hingeston, John, 199f., 202, 221, 225ff., 233, 253
Histriones (see also Minstrels), 28
Hogarth, William, 252
Holborne, Anthony, 99, 110ff., 122–4, 130f., 135, 172, 186 (3)
Holborne, William, 130
Holland, see Netherlands
Holmes, John, 157, 180
Holmes, Thomas, 157, 163
Hood, Robin, 33
Horn, 35, 36, 43 (2)
—— players, 51
Hornpype, 71f.
Howes, F., 11
—— W., 199
Hubatsch, O., 34 (1)
Hudson, George, 231

Hughes, Dom Anselm, 29 (3)
—— Hughes, 220
Hume, Tobias, 110, 121, 136, 138, 139
Humphreys, Pelham, 205, 230, 248
Hunt, E. H., 10
Hurdy-gurdy, 21 (1), 36, 53
Hymns, 23, 30, 45

IMITATION (contrapuntal technique),
    59, 81f., 92, 122 (2), 148, 164
Independents, 188
In Nomine (16th century instru-
    mental form), 83–91, 97, 100, 103,
    108ff., 119, 121, 135, 137, 148 (1),
    150, 156 (1), 157, 162, 168 (2), 183,
    196, 216 (3), 217, 219, 241, 244
Instrumental music :
    keyboard, 74, 246
    percussion, 36, 52, 127, 128, 133
    strings (see also the various instru-
        ments, Viol, Lute, etc.), 21,
        26, 29, 31, 36, 37, 38, 46,
        47, 127ff., 132, 140
    —— bowed, 133, 136
    —— compass of, 164, 223
    —— for a not clearly defined com-
        bination of, 94, 131
    —— plucked, 136
    wind (see also the various instru-
        ments, Organ, Flute, etc.), 21,
        26, 31, 36, 43, 46, 47, 127f., 133,
        139, 248
    brass, 21, 36, 47, 127f., 133, 225f.
    wood, 35, 36, 47, 127f., 133
    and bourgeoisie (merchants), 63ff.,
        102, 108, 113–16, 126, 128, 176,
        247, 249ff.
    at Court, see Court music
    experiments in, 89 (1), 170f., 180,
        185
    early ensemble playing of, 45ff.
    fought by the Church, 15ff., 24–34,
        201 (1)
    makers of instruments, 127, 133
    notation of, 38, 136, 164 (1), 213
    and nobility, 18ff., 50f., 58f., 66f.,
        102f., 114, 126, 128, 205, 230,
        247, 249ff.
    popular forms of, 34ff., 37, 54, 102,
        197ff., 229ff.
    style of, 39f., 57ff., 71–74, 85–94,
        103–112, 129f., 134, 136, 140–71,
        218ff.
    in pageants (see also Mystery Plays),
        50, 127, 131
    in pantomimes, 139
    in early Middle Ages, pagan
        element in, 12ff., 18f., 27, 201 (1)
    pictured in medieval churches or
        MSS., 16, 19, 20, 21 (4), 46

Instrumental music :
    social function of, 75ff., 113–116,
        143, 187ff., 220f., 245f.
    social background of, 75ff., 101ff.,
        113–116, 123ff., 143, 159–
        60, 173–76, 187–94, 198–203,
        204ff., 240, 242–46, Chapter VIII
        (passim)
    vocal music performed by instru-
        ments, 20 (3), 57, 68 (1), 82f., 125
    and witchcraft, 25f.
    in Ireland, 37
    in Scotland, 28, 37
    in Wales, 32, 37
Interludes, 117
Irish harp, see Harp
Italian music, 22, 47 (4), 54, 72, 95,
    125, 128ff., 149 (1), 153ff., 164,
    166, 169ff., 175, 180, 186, 212ff.,
    216 (2), 229f., 235, 240f., 243f.,
    Chapter VIII (passim)
Ives, Simon, 179, 196f., 199, 221

JAMES I, King, 115 (3), 116, 125ff.,
    132, 134, 174, 211
—— II, King, 241 (1)
Jannequin, 88, 89
Jaw's harp (jew's harp), 25
Jeffreys, George, 205, 213, 215, 224
Jenkins, John, 158, 186 (2), 199, 205,
    213f., 216–224, 228f., 244
Jesuits, 78
Jig, see Gigue
Joculatores, 28
John of Salisbury, 26
John XXII, Pope, 28
Johnson, Robert, 90, 172 (1)
Johnston (early 16th century), 72
Jones, Robert, 137
Jonson, Ben, 118, 122, 175
Jordan, Jack, 139
Jugglers, see Minstrels
Jusserand, J. J., 21 (6), 32 (2), 33 (2),
    50 (3), 51 (1, 2)

KEITH, Sir William, 114 (2)
Keller, Godfrey, 211 (3), 247
Ker, W. P., 23 (1), 52 (1)
Keymis, Laurence, 115 (2)
Keyser (Keiser), Reinhard, 247
Kimble, Mr., 233
King, Hugh, 98
—— Robert, 247
King's Lynn, 49
Kippis, Dr., 19 (footnote)
Knights, L. C., 64 (1), 65 (1–3)

LAFONTAINE, H. C. de, 10, 211 (2)
Landino, Francesco, 54
Láng, P. H., 10, 16 (3)
Langland, William, 61
Laniere, Nicholas, 194, 214

Laudes (of the Jesuits), 78
Lawes, Henry, 179, 199
—— William, 10 (11), 132 (4), 176, 179–187, 196, 210, 213, 217f., 230, 232, 234, 243
Lay (French), 41
Leading note, 42f.
Lederer, V., 45 (2)
Leicester, 49
Lejeune, Claude, 213 (5)
Lenton, John, 228
Lessons for consort, 126, 130, 135ff., 229
Lestrange, Sir Hamon, 219
Levellers, 188
Lilt (lilk), 236
Lindsay, J., 20 (2)
Lloyd, A. L., 33 (4), 252 (1)
Locke, John, 201, 250
—— Matthew, 10 (11), 186 (2), 200, 205ff., 212f., 215, 221 (1), 232–40, 243f., 248
Lollards, 32, 63
London, 49, 53, 65, 75, 114, 143, 153, 193, 201, 207, 214, 229, 250
Longchamps, Bishop William de, 24
Loosemore, Henry, 196, 224
Louis the Pious, 51
—— XIV, King of France, 214
Lucas, Jonet, 26
Ludford (16th century composer), 72
Lully, Jean Baptiste, 210, 214, 230, 244, 247
Lupo, Joseph, 172 (1)
—— Thomas, 83 (3), 143–149, 157f., 165ff.
Lute, 35f., 114, 118, 120, 125, 127f., 130ff., 136, 138f., 192
—— in literature, 2, 10, 118, 120
—— music for, 72 (1, 2), 109, 137, 169 (1)
—— players (lutenists, lutists), 31, 53, 127, 132, 139, 194, 211
Luzzaschi, Luzzasco, 130
Lynn, see King's Lynn
Lyra (lyre ; see also Rubebe), 15, 18, 36, 42, 53, 131, 133
—— viol, see Viol
—— da braccio, see Violin, fore-runners of

MACE, Thomas, 140, 190, 207, 210, 240, 253
Machaut, Guillaume de, 54
Madrigal, 104f., 117, 125 (1), 130, 143, 148, 156, 159, 170, 177 (1), 195, 213
Major key and scale, 41ff., 48, 93, 168f.
Major, John, 44
Mallorie (16th century composer), 83 (3)
Mandora, 132

Mangeot, André, 232 (3), 241 (2)
Manning, B. L., 24
—— R., 29
Marches, 127 (3)
Marenzio, Luca, 170
Mary, Queen of Scotland, 114 (2)
Masks (in the 17th century), 127, 175, 210f.
Masquing airs, courtly, 171
Mass, 40, 67, 93 (1), 180
Massaini, Tiburtio, 155
Massinger, Philip, 248 (1)
Matteis, Nicola, 211 (3), 230
Matthysz, Paulus, 138, 153 (3)
Maynard, John, 137, 139f.
Mazurka, 246
Mell, Davis, 194, 199, 211 (3), 228
Mendelssohn, Felix, 251
Mensural (measured) music, 40f., 68
Merbecke, John, 106
Mericocke, Thomas, 90
Metres (in verse), 40f., 73
Metru, Nicolas, 213 (5)
Meyer, P., 51 (2)
Miall, B., 250 (2)
Michelet, Jules, 25
Mico, Richard, 196
Middleton, Thomas, 122
Milan, Luis, 94
Milton, John, sen., 150, 201
—— —— jun. (the poet), 192, 200ff., 250
Minor key, 41ff., 168f.
Minot, Laurence, 52 (4)
Minstrels (jugglers, histriones, mimi, ministeriales, joculatores), 16, 21, 23–35, 46–56
—— in Scotland, 28
—— in Wales, 29 (1), 32
—— and Church, see Church (Cath-olic) and Instrumental music
—— persecution of, 28f., 32, 51, 55f.
—— as political rebels, 32ff.
—— punishment for illegal activities of, 28f.
—— social organisation of, 48ff., 54ff.
Minuet, 157, 159, 240
Miserere (16th century instrumental form), 83, 150 (4)
Modes (medieval scales), 33, 41ff., 94
—— (medieval rhythmic patterns), 40f.
Modulations, 169ff.
Monochord, 53
Monody, 164
Monteverdi, Claudio, 129
More, Wyllyam, 83 (2)
Morley, Thomas, 10 (11), 73f., 83 (3), 87 (2), 94ff., 103–106, 108–110, 114 (1), 117, 126, 130, 135, 137f., 141f., 161, 169, 171f., 187, 195, 212, 249f.

Morris dances, 100, 154
Motet in England, 29 (3), 31, 57ff.,
    67f., 79–83, 91–93, 96f., 101,
    103, 106, 108, 137, 140, 143,
    155, 195, 202
—— on the Continent, 67, 106, 129,
    180
—— isorhythmic, 23
—— instrumental, 82f., 91ff., 103,
    140f.
—— Latin texts in, 23, 39f., 81ff.
Motif, 87f., 168, 177ff.
Mouton, Jean, 106
Mozart, W. A., 8, 242f., 246, 251
Mudd, Thomas, 90, 194, 213
Mulliner, Thomas, 94
Munday, William, 90, 94 (4), 109
Mundie, John, 150
Murray, Margaret A., 25 (7), 26 (1–2)
Music as free-lance profession, 119ff.
—— and poetry, 8, 15 (2), 22, 40f.,
    75, 78f., 117ff., 126
—— and other arts, 75, 116 (2), 129,
    152
—— national character in, 4
Musica reservata, 78
Mystery plays, 30f.

NABULUM (medieval instrument), 36,
    53
Nagel, W., 114 (3), 233 (6)
Nakers, 36, 52f.
Nationalism in English music, 44, 63,
    206, 212, 253f.
Natural scale, 43 (2)
Naylor, E. W., 70 (2, 5, 6)
Nef, C., 43 (2)
Netherlands, music of the, 2, 13, 67,
    72, 85 (1), 90, 106, 162 (1), 164,
    180, 253
Nettel, R., 254 (1)
Newton, Isaac, 201, 207
Newman, Mr., 94
Nigellus of Canterbury, 24
Noordt, Sybrandus van, 85
Norcome, Daniel, 137, 139, 228
North, Roger, 84, 195 (1), 205f.,
    207 (1), 211f., 216, 232
Norwich, 49f.
Notker Balbulus, 42 (1)

OBERNDOERFFER, David, 138
Oboe (hautbois), 25, 36, 128, 133, 139,
    211, 230
Odington, Walter, 43 (1)
L'Œillet, Jean Baptiste, 247
Okeover, John, 196, 219
Old Hall MS., 29 (3), 31, 91 (1)
Opera, 78, 85, 214, 232, 250
Orchestra, 128, 210ff.

Orchestral music, 125, 127ff., 136,
    211ff., 239, 240 (2)
Orchestration, beginnings of, 131f.
Organ, 20, 26, 29, 31, 38, 47, 71, 120,
    128, 132f., 164 (1), 199 (1)
—— music for, 20 (3), 68 (1), 94, 113,
    186, 192, 212, 216 (3), 240
—— players, 53, 199
—— as accompaniment and basso
    continuo, 82, 133
Organistrum, 21, 46
Oriental music, 36, 45
Ornaments, 78, 136, 176
Orpharion (see also Cittern), 133, 136
Osborne, H., 89 (1), 190 (6)
Otto, Valerius, 154
Ouverture, 214, 229, 236
Oxford, 193, 202, 205, 207, 209, 229
—— Earl of, 119

PAN-PIPES, 46
Pandora (bandora), 128, 130f., 133,
    137 (1)
Paris, 214
Parsley, Osbert, 10 (11), 89 (2)
Parsons, Robert, 10 (11), 85, 89f., 93,
    98, 108, 112, 114 (1)
Part-singing, 13, 41, 45f., 58
Pastoral (song), 250
—— (symphony), 236
Paul, V., Pope, 128
Pavan(a) (pavin, the dance), 10 (11),
    72 (2, 3), 73, 87f., 90, 104, 110f.,
    112 (1), 114 (2), 122, 130, 136ff.,
    154, 168f., 172, 177, 181, 183,
    186 (1), 196 (1), 217, 219f.
Peacham, Henry, 113, 114 (4), 187,
    190, 212 (3)
Peasant Wars, songs of the, 33
Peasantry and music, 49, 102, 252
Peasible (Paisible), James, 249
Pecock, Bishop, 32
Peerson (Pierson), Martin, 126 (1), 196
Pennola, 36
Penorcon, 131
Pentatonicism, 45
Pepys, Samuel, 200, 207, 248ff.
Peri, Jacopo, 84
Pericles, 247
Perkins, W., 190
Petri, Father, 241 (1)
Petty, 188 (2)
Peuerl, 154
Philips, John, 207
—— Peter, 138f.
Pianoforte, 134
—— forerunners of, 36, 53, 133
—— music for, 85, 246, 250
Pickering's lutebook, 109, 139
Pickforth (16th century composer), 90
Pier's Plowman, 33

Pilkington, Francis, 118, 126, 137
Pipe (fyfe, tibia), 35f., 46f., 50, 53, 120, 127, 132ff.
Pipers, 26, 31, 52, 127
Pirenne, H., 12
Piva, 72
Plainsong, *see* Gregorian Chant
Playford, John, 127 (1), 197, 207, 233
Polish music, 246
Polonaise, 246
Polyphant, 127 (1)
Polyphonic music, 13, 41, 47ff., 58, 67, 74, 79ff., 85, 92ff., 106, 108ff., 134f., 137, 139f., 148, 164, 167, 176–187, 193, 195, 206, 208, 217ff., 221 (1), 228, 233, 241f.
Pommer, 36
Poole, E. H., 17 (1), 31 (1), 56 (1, 3)
Pope, Alexander, 252
Porter, Walter, 130, 194, 199
Powys, Ll., 194 (2)
Poynt, Thomas (?), 90
Praetorius, Michael, 112 (1), 130
Prelude, 74, 130, 196 (6), 246
Près, Josquin des, 106
Presbyterians, 188
Preston (16th century composer), 90, 162
Price (17th century violinist), 138
Proctor, W., 205 (4)
Programme music, 109, 123f., 236
Prose, 30, 40
Protestantism and music, 12
Prynne, William, 26 (3), 201
Psalms, 118 (1), 212
Psaltry (Psalterium, sautre, cymbalum), 14, 21, 29, 36, 42, 46f., 53, 133
—— players, 53
Public, general, 75, 127, 173, 193, 208ff.
Pulver, J., 10, 70 (2), 114 (2), 119 (5, 6), 121 (1), 216 (3), 241 (1)
Purcell, Daniel, 247
—— Henry, 10 (11), 11, 84, 155, 205f., 215, 223f., 231, 240–45, 247, 252
Puritans and music, 18off., Chapter VI (*passim*), 248
Pyttins, Richard, 72, 74 (2)

QUARTERTONES, 89 (1)
Quodlibet, 162 (1)

RACKET (medieval wind instrument), 36, 131
Radcliffe, P. F. H., 68 (3)
Raleigh, Sir Walter, 115 (2)
Ramsbotham, A., 29 (3)
Randall of Chester, 33
Randall, William, 90

Rant (17th century instrumental piece), 217
Ravenscroft, Thomas, 149ff., 162 (1), 170, 172
Rebec. 36, 46, 127, 131
Recercar, *see* Ricercar
Recitativo, 164 (1)
Recorder (*see also* Flute), 10, 25, 27, 36, 47, 53, 128, 131ff., 209, 230f.
Reese, G., 10
Reformation, 63ff., 76, 78f., 103, 117
Regnart, Jacob, 89
Rembrandt, 152
Repercussio, 42
Restoration, Chapter VII (*passim*), 249, 253
Rhythm, development of, 20 (3), 39ff., 47f., 59f., 67ff., 105ff., 137, 183, 218, 236, 244
—— triple, 41, 47, 68, 73
Ricercar (recercar), 94
Richard II, King, 52, 58
Richardson, A., 241 (2)
Riemann, H., 28 (1), 68 (4)
Rimbault, E. F., 205 (3), 216 (3)
Ritornello, 58, 130
Ritson, J., 33 (5)
Robertsbridge Abbey, 20 (3)
Robinson, Thomas, 135ff.
Rolland, Romain, 250
Roman de Fauvel, 20 (3)
Roger, Etienne, 231
Rogers, Benjamin, 199, 205, 221 (1)
Romances, medieval, 60
Romans, the, 14f., 27
Rondeau, 41
Rosseter, Philip, 130f., 135, 137
Rossi, Salomone, 155
Rota (rote, medieval instrument), 36, 46f.
—— (form), *see* Round
Rotta (*see also* Rota), 16
Round (rota, canon, catch), 24, 73, 110, 162 (1), 240
Roundella (roundelay), 29, 35
Rousseau, Jean Jaques, 242
Rowe (17th century violinist), 139
Royal Society, 207
Rubato, 134
Rubebe (rebube, rybyb ; sometimes identical with lyra), 35f., 47, 53
Rue, Pierre de la, 106

SACHS, C., 71 (2)
Sachsenspiegel, 28
Sackbut (sagbut), *see* Trombone
Sadler (16th century composer), 90
St. Augustine, 12, 14f.
St. Chrysostom, 14
St. Clement of Alexandria, 14
St. Gallen, 42 (4)

St. George, H., 10
St. Gerome, 18
St. Paul's Cathedral, 94 (4), 114 (1)
Salaries and fees, minstrels' and musicians', 21, 31 (4), 50 (3), 200, 211
Salmon, Thomas, 207
Saltarello, 72
Salter, Humphrey, 230
Sambuca, see Bagpipe
Saraband (serabrand), 181, 186 (1), 210, 216 (3), 233, 236
Scarlatti, Alessandro, 247
Schaeffer, Paul, 138
Scheiffler (17th century German composer), 211 (3)
Schein, Johann Hermann, 154
Schering, A., 17 (2)
Scherzo, 89, 159
Schlesinger, Kathleen, 36 (2), 133
Schmeller, 34 (1)
Schneider, M., 21 (footnote)
Scholares vagantes, 22, 29, 32ff.
Scholes, P. A., 10, 126 (1), 186 (3), 201 (2), 202 (1), 208 (1), 216 (3), 228 (5), 250 (1)
Schrade, L., 38 (4)
Scriabine, A., 119
Section (in motet), see Form, development of
Sequence (in liturgy), 30, 40
—— (in melody building), 110f.
Serpent, 128
Sforzato, 134
Shadwell, Thomas, 235
Shakespeare, William, 25, 70 (2), 74, 98f., 117, 155
Shalm (schalmei, calamus reed), 25, 27, 35f., 47, 53, 133
—— players, 52
Shelley, Percy B., 252
Sherard, James, 231
Short scores, 136, 186 (2), 213
Sidgwick, F., 23 (3), 70 (2)
Sidney, Robert, 114
Simmes, William, 179
Simpson, Christopher, 142, 194, 205, 207, 215, 221 (1), 226ff.
—— Thomas, 138f., 169f.
—— W. S., 28 (7)
Singers, 117
Singing voice, 133, 137 (1), 200
Sixtus V, Pope, 128
Smith, Robert, 230
—— Thomas, 231
Solos, instrumental, 103, 126, 136, 138, 226, 241 (1), 250
Sonata, 85, 128f., 186, 213, 216 (3), 235, 241ff.
—— for pianoforte, 85
—— form, 156f., 159

Sonata in England, 222, 231, 240 (2), 241ff., 245
Songs, artistic (composed ; see also Airs), 95, 118, 120, 170 (2), 211
—— popular and folk, 33, 40, 43ff., 48, 54, 60, 67f., 99f., 102, 137 (1), 148, 161f., 175 (2), 177 (1), 197, 219, 229, 240, 242 (2), 250, 252
Sonnets, 118 (1)
Sordine (medieval wind instrument), 36
Spanish music, 71, 127
Spenser, Edmund, 121
Spinet, 131
Springa, 29
Stainer, John, 38 (4), 45 (1), 57 (1), 58 (1), 60 (2)
Stanley (17th century composer), 139
Stanner (16th century composer), 90
Stantipes, 22, 47
Stoninges, Henry, 83 (3), 90, 112
Strode, William, 194
Strogers, Nicolas, 85, 90, 94 (4)
Stylo (stilo) rappresentativo, 128, 164
Suite, 73, 154, 181, 186 (1), 217, 220, 225ff., 229, 231, 233
Sumer is icumen in (the " Summer Canon "), 23, 44, 54
Sweden, Queen of, 221 (1)
Swinfield, de, Bishop of Hereford, 21
Syddael, W., 89 (2)
Symphony (sinfonia ; instrumental form), 58 (1), 129f., 195, 240 (2), 243, 246
—— (musical practice), see Consort
—— (medieval stringed instrument ; see also Hurdy-gurdy), 21 (1), 29, 35, 47
—— (medieval wind instrument), see Bagpipe

TABOR, 29, 36, 46
—— players, 53, 127, 132f., 134
Tabulatura (tablature), 20 (3)
Tallis, Thomas, 85, 114 (1), 246
Tate, Nahum, 242
Taverner, John, 81, 83 (1), 84f., 94 (7), 106
Tawney, R. H., 13 (1), 19 (1), 173 (1)
Taylor, R., 139
—— Silas (Sylvanus), 172 (1), 229
Tchaikovsky, P. I., 86
Telyn, 36
Tempo indications, 213, 236ff.
Tenor (cantus firmus), 31, 80–92 (passim), 106
—— —— —— definition, 80
Terry, Richard R., 10, 89 (2), 168 (4), 175

Theorbo (see also Lute and Archlute), 130f., 133, 164 (1), 181, 186, 212, 216 (3)
Thorne, John, 90
Thorough bass (basso continuo), 134, 164, 181, 186, 213, 216 (3), 228ff., 231 (2, 4, 6, 8), 240f.
Tibia, see Pipe
Tiburtino, Giuliano, 94
Tintinnabulum (medieval percussion instrument), 36
Toccata, 130
Tollet, Thomas, 228, 231
Tomkins, Thomas, 10 (11), 93, 170ff., 180, 196
Tonus lascivus, 43, 44 (1)
Toys (16th century instrumental pieces), 139
Tremolo, 239
Trevelyan, G. M., 27 (1, 3)
Triangles, 36
Trio, 167, 221, 223ff., 228ff., 233
—— sonata (see also Sonata), 167, 231, 241, 244
Trombone (sackbut), 21 (4), 36, 52f., 128, 131ff.
—— players, 127f., 211
—— music for, 225f., 233
Troubadours, 40
Trouvères, 40
Trumpet, 14, 21, 24, 29, 36f., 43 (2), 47, 52f., 127ff., 132ff.
—— players, 51f., 127f.
—— music for, 208 (2), 229
Tunstede, Simon, 29
Tye, Christopher, 83 (3), 85, 87ff., 104, 157
Tympan, see Psaltry
Tympanum (medieval wind instrument), see Bagpipe

Unton, Sir Henry, 128, 130 (1)
Ut-re-mi (16th century instrumental form), 93, 95
Utrecht Psalter, 20 (1)

Van der Straeten, E., 10
Variation suite, 73
Variations on a theme (see also Ground), 113, 137f., 157, 222, 228
Venice, 167
Verney, F. P., 64 (2)
Viadana, Ludovico Grosso da, 165
Vibrato, 86, 134
Vielle, 32, 35f., 53
—— players, 52
Vienna classics, 155, 160, 244
Viol (viola da gamba), 36, 46, 86, 114, 125, 127f., 130, 133f., 136, 139, 186, 206, 209
—— literature, 9f.

Viol, music for, 86ff., 130f., 135, 142–172 (passim), 183, 195, 218ff., 244
—— bass (common viola da gamba), 86, 113, 128, 130, 132f., 136ff., 166, 177 (1), 187, 195, 217, 221ff., 226
—— duos and trios, 221 (1), 222, 228, 235
—— alto, 235
—— tenor, 86
—— treble, 86, 130, 136f., 181, 214
—— lyra, 133, 136ff., 217
—— chest of, 140, 166, 210
—— players, 53, 127f., 132, 139, 216 (3)
Viola (see also Violin family), 134
—— da gamba, see Viol
Violenca, 211
Violin, 86, 128, 130, 133ff., 186f., 195, 206, 209ff., 214, 216 (3), 217, 221ff., 226, 228ff., 235, 240 (2), 241ff.
—— family, 209
—— literature on, 10
—— players, 128, 209ff.
—— predecessors of (see also Fiddle), 21 (1), 36, 131, 133
Violoncello (see also Violin family), 86, 134, 210
—— literature on, 10
—— forerunners of (bass violin, etc.), 132, 210
Violone (forerunners of double bass), 153, 162f.
Virelay, 35
Virginal, 70f., 125, 128, 131ff.
—— music for, 113, 119, 137f.
—— players, 127
Virtuoso, 195 (1), 209f., 211ff., 216, 221f., 226
Vitali, Giovanni Battista, 241, 247
Vitry, Philip de, 54
Vogelsang (unknown violinist of the 17th century), 211 (3)
Volta, 74 (3)
Voltaire, F. M. de, 242
Voluntary (instrumental form), 127 (3)

Waddell, Helen, 29 (1)
Wagner, Richard, 87 (3)
Wait (instrument), 36, 50, 128, 130, 133
—— (player), 49ff., 62, 127, 229
Wake, William, 233
Walker, E., 96 (2), 113 (2)
Ward, John, 162f., 172, 180
Warlock, P., 10 (11), 110 (4), 122 (2), 232 (3), 234 (1), 241 (2)
Wayser, William, 90

Webster, John, 122
—— Maurice, 195, 213
Weelkes, Thomas, 114 (1), 122 (2),172
Welch, Chr., 10 (4)
Welsh harp, *see* Harp
Wesley, Samuel, 247
Westminster Feast (1306), 53, 131
Westrup, J. A., 11, 114 (3), 115 (3), 128 (3), 200 (1), 229 (7), 244 (2)
Whistle-flute, 133
Whitbroke, William, 90
White, Robert, 85, 92
—— William, 160, 165, 172
Whitmore, Sister, 35 (3)
Whittaker, G., 10 (11), 236 (1), 241 (2)
Whythorne, Thomas, 82 (2), 95f., 131
Wilbye, John, 172
Willaert, Adrian, 94
Wilson, John, 199, 202, 205 (4)
—— Thomas, 94
Winchester Cathedral, 20 (3)
Wither, George, 120f.

Withy, John, 179
Wolf, J., 20 (3), 22 (1), 23 (5), 28 (1), 35 (1), 38 (2), 40 (1), 45 (3), 47 (3), 71 (3)
Wood, Anthony à, 21 (2), 194, 205, 207, 209, 211, 229, 231
Woodcocke, Clement, 90, 112
Woodhouse, Sir P., 219
Woodson, Leonhard, 90
—— Thomas, 93
Wooldridge, H. E., 20 (3)
Worcester Church, 20
Wordsworth, William, 252
Work, Thomas, 90
Wright, Thomas, 24 (2-4), 33 (1), 35 (2), 52 (4)
Wyclif(fe), John, 47

YASSER, J., 45 (2)
Yonge, Nicholas, 102 (1)
York, 49
Young, William, 10 (11), 199, 213 (5)